FDR and the Spanish Civil War

AMERICAN ENCOUNTERS / GLOBAL INTERACTIONS

A SERIES EDITED BY GILBERT M. JOSEPH AND EMILY S. ROSENBERG

This series aims to stimulate critical perspectives and fresh interpretive frameworks for scholarship on the history of the imposing global presence of the United States. Its primary concerns include the deployment and contestation of power, the construction and deconstruction of cultural and political borders, the fluid meanings of intercultural encounters, and the complex interplay between the global and the local. American Encounters seeks to strengthen dialogue and collaboration between historians of U.S. international relations and area studies specialists.

The series encourages scholarship based on multiarchival historical research. At the same time, it supports a recognition of the representational character of all stories about the past and promotes critical inquiry into issues of subjectivity and narrative. In the process, American Encounters strives to understand the context in which meanings related to nations, cultures, and political economy are continually produced, challenged, and reshaped.

FDR AND THE SPANISH CIVIL WAR

NEUTRALITY AND COMMITMENT
IN THE STRUGGLE THAT DIVIDED AMERICA

Dominic Tierney

Duke University Press   *Durham and London*

2007

© 2007 Duke University Press
Duke University Press gratefully acknowledges the support
of the Program for Cultural Cooperation between Spain's
Ministry of Culture and United States Universities.

Printed in the United States of America
on acid-free paper ∞

Typeset in Charter by Tseng Information Systems, Inc.

Library of Congress Cataloging-in-Publication Data
appear on the last printed page of this book.

To my parents, John and Angela

Contents

Acknowledgments

Over the course of almost a decade this project began as a master's thesis, evolved into a doctoral thesis, and finally became a book manuscript. The first person I would like to thank is Steve Casey, who offered truly invaluable guidance at an early stage that pushed me in the right direction. Avi Shlaim and Yuen Foong Khong provided wise and thoughtful comments as my thesis advisors. Warren Kimball, Melvyn Leffler, Peter Carroll, Martin Ceadel, Michael Fullilove, and an anonymous reviewer read the entire manuscript and made excellent suggestions that improved the book considerably. Tom Buchanan, Barbara Farnham, Richard Traina, Allen Guttmann, Paul Preston, and Andrew Hurrell also gave extremely useful advice on aspects of the book.

I would also like to thank Valerie Millholland, my editor at Duke University Press, for ably guiding the project through the publishing process, and Fred Kameny for his accomplished copy editing. I am grateful to Natalie Hanemann for drawing the maps of Spain. The librarians and other staff at the libraries and archives I visited were uniformly helpful. I thank Sage Publications for permission to include material from my journal article "Franklin D. Roosevelt and Covert Aid to the Loyalists in the Spanish Civil War, 1936–1939," *Journal of Contemporary History*, vol. 39, no. 3 (2004). I express my gratitude to the Economic and Social Research Council, the Franklin and Eleanor Roosevelt Institute, the Frank Knox Memorial Trust, the Mershon Center at Ohio State University, and the Olin Institute for Strategic Studies at Harvard University for providing financial support. I thank Amy Oakes for her constant love, guidance, and encouragement, and for her willingness to offer superb comments on the entire manuscript. Needless to say, all mistakes remain my own.

CHAPTER 1

The American Sphinx and the Spanish War

In early 1939 the American ambassador to Spain, Claude G. Bowers, walked into the White House to brief President Franklin D. Roosevelt on the outcome of the Spanish Civil War, which had just been decisively won by the rebel general Francisco Franco. As Bowers was shown into the president's office, he was surprised to find a somber figure. Usually FDR would throw back his head and make a joke before discussing any serious issues. But Roosevelt hardly smiled, and before Bowers had even sat down, the president offered this summary of American policy in the Spanish Civil War: "We have made a mistake. You have been right all along."[1]

The story of how Roosevelt reached this conclusion is a fascinating and important one, and it is a story that is untold. What was the relationship between FDR, described recently as the most important figure of the twentieth century, and the Spanish Civil War, often viewed as the "last great cause," a vortex of passion, sacrifice, idealism, cynicism, and tragedy, and an event that shaped the road to the Second World War?[2] How did Roosevelt perceive the Spanish Civil War? In what ways did the conflict in Spain change the president's thinking about the fascist threat to Europe and the United States? Did Roosevelt shape the U.S. government's response to the Spanish Civil War? What does the case tell us about FDR's impact on policy making more generally?

The evidence shows that the president played an increasingly central role in his country's decision making in the Spanish Civil War. Over time Roosevelt's beliefs about Spain were transformed. His initial disinterest in which side won gave way to a position of partisanship for the leftist government, and he tried both legal and illegal means to aid the Spanish Republic. These changing perceptions of Spain influenced Roosevelt's views about the nature of wider fascist aggression, with consequences for the coming world war, and they created an enduring guilt over the failure of a cause in which Roosevelt had come to believe.

The story of American diplomacy and the Spanish Civil War is rich in dramatic detail. The cast included the great leaders of the age—men like Hitler, Mussolini, Chamberlain, and Stalin—together with figures such as Ernest Hemingway and Eleanor Roosevelt. The episodes were often striking. Thousands of Americans traveled to Spain to fight as volunteers for the Spanish Republic. At the same time, Texaco Oil Company provided Franco with all the oil he needed, on credit, for the duration of the war. Congress engaged in a "race with a freighter" to introduce an arms embargo before a ship packed with weapons could sail from New York harbor to Spain. America's leading isolationist senator, Gerald P. Nye, became the major voice arguing *in favor* of selling arms to the Spanish Republic. And in an intriguing incident, President Roosevelt sent his alcoholic brother-in-law to Paris as a secret emissary to arrange the illegal shipment of aircraft to the Spanish Republic.

Roosevelt has long provoked fascination. Enigmatic and mercurial, he has been described by many writers as a sphinx. Roosevelt's early political success and easy confidence, his battle against debilitating polio, his continued drive in the face of adversity, and then his ultimate triumph seem to be almost a metaphor for the country he helped to rescue from the Great Depression. Born in 1882 into a genteel and affluent family, this optimistic patrician leader sought from an early age to emulate his cousin Theodore Roosevelt. But in the end FDR would far surpass TR in achievements, inaugurating the New Deal age of government activism, and guiding the United States as it made the transition from isolationism to globalism through the defeat of Germany, Italy, and Japan.

ON THE NIGHT of 17 July 1936 a group of rebel Spanish generals initiated a coup d'état. The generals planned to overthrow the Spanish Republic—then enjoying its five-year anniversary—and replace it with an authoritarian regime. The "Nationalist" rebels, soon under the leadership of General Francisco Franco, were defeated by "Loyalist" Republican forces in the key cities of Madrid and Barcelona, and a war of attrition resulted. The major European states formally agreed not to sell weapons to either side in Spain, but two parties to the agreement—Germany and Italy—nevertheless sent large quantities of men and arms to the Nationalists, while a third—the USSR—sent substantially less aid to the Spanish Republic. With influxes of foreign support arriving at critical moments, the Nationalists steadily overran Loyalist territory until Barcelona and Madrid were captured in the spring of 1939 and the war ended.

By any standards the Spanish Civil War was an enormously important conflict. It altered the course of European and therefore world politics. It gripped the attention of people who knew nothing of Spain but felt in their hearts that the Spanish Civil War was their struggle. It aroused passion and butchery, and spurred great art and mendacious propaganda. And today it probably captures the imagination of people more than any other event between the two world wars. Quite simply, the issues at stake in the Spanish Civil War—democracy against fascism, Christianity against communism, the future of Spain and Europe—were vast in scale and significance.

The Spanish Civil War was the first major conflict in Western Europe since 1918. As well as costing the lives of over 500,000 Spaniards, the war strengthened the relationship between Germany and Italy, and provided the fascist dictators with an apparent new ally in General Franco. The Germans used the conflict to test weapons and tactics that later proved highly effective against Poland in 1939 and the western democracies in 1940. Even though the United States was physically removed from the conflict, the Spanish Civil War affected most of the key strands of American diplomacy. Events in Spain seemed likely to spark a full-scale European war in which the United States might ultimately become entangled. The conflict offered further evidence of aggressive fascist intent, and for some American officials it demonstrated Moscow's revolutionary threat. The Spanish Civil War deeply divided the Latin American countries that the United States was attempting to court in the 1930s with its "good neighbor" policy. Crucially, the conflict occurred during Roosevelt's period of awakening to foreign affairs, 1936–39. No longer were domestic recovery and the New Deal the priority. Instead FDR pronounced that events in Europe were his greatest concern.

The Spanish Civil War has often been called "the last great cause." For people around the world the conflict in Spain represented a fundamental clash of values and ideals. "There was something pure about the Spanish war. The enthusiasm it engendered was a springtime that briefly loosened the wintry grip of a world grown old and weary and cynical. As did no other event of our time, it caught the conscience of a generation."[3] The "crusade" mentality toward Spain was especially pronounced among intellectuals and artists. Ernest Hemingway, Pablo Picasso, and George Orwell all drew creative inspiration from events on the Iberian Peninsula.

The "last great cause" slogan is associated with the left's interpretation of the Spanish Civil War as a fight between fascism and democracy. Many on the left believed that if Hitler and Mussolini were not stopped in Spain, Paris and London would be next, followed by Washington. The Nationalists and their fascist patrons had demonstrated their barbarity by carrying out repeated atrocities, including the bombing of undefended cities such as Guernica. The Loyalists, in sharp contrast, had issued a rallying cry to the global progressive community, and tens of thousands answered the call. Volunteers traveled from around the world to fight for the Spanish Republic in the international brigades, motivated mainly by ideology and idealism rather than material gain. Viewed from this perspective, liberals, socialists, and communists idealized the Loyalist war effort as a just and true cause around which to rally.

But for other observers, the great cause in Spain was General Franco's fight for Christianity and against Bolshevism. The truth is that the left in Spain did not have a monopoly on idealism, and the right did not have a monopoly on cynicism and brutality. Many who fought for the Spanish Republic did not believe in liberalism or even democracy, and the thousands of priests and other religious figures who died in the Republican zone attest to the excesses of revolutionary justice. The Loyalists' main ally, the Soviet Union, often manipulated the conflict for narrow self-interest.

The Spanish Civil War became widely viewed as a war of opposites, whether it was religion against atheism, the rich against the poor, or fascism against democracy: a war in which people tried purposefully to ignore the gray areas and maintain a black-and-white image of *la causa*. The belief that the Spanish Civil War was a titanic struggle quickly crossed the Atlantic and took root in the western hemisphere. The United States is usually described as having been "isolationist" in the 1930s, but the Spanish Civil War had an intense impact on thousands, perhaps millions, of Americans. It created a bitter domestic controversy over American foreign policy on a scale not witnessed since the rejection of the Versailles Treaty in 1920. Herbert Matthews, who covered the Spanish Civil War for the *New York Times*, wrote: "No event in the outside world, before or since, aroused Americans in time to such religious controversy and such burning emotions."[4]

In 1936 the United States introduced an embargo on arms sales to both sides in the Spanish Civil War and announced strict nonintervention in the conflict. This policy was initially uncontroversial, but by 1939 the embargo issue had produced a political storm. Franco could do without American weapons because the Nationalists received massive military assistance from Germany and Italy. In contrast, the Spanish Republic did need arms;

thus its war effort was disproportionately impaired by the American embargo. The United States was one of the world's major suppliers of aircraft, the weapon which the Spanish Republic needed most of all. In battles
where the Nationalists lacked air supremacy, the Republic could hold its
own. But in 1938 the Nationalist air ace Joaquin Garcia-Morato declared,
"the sky was ours," and as a result, the Republican front collapsed.[5]

American liberals, socialists, communists, the Protestant clergy, and a
large number of intellectuals could see before their eyes that their government's policy was contributing to the slow strangulation of the Spanish Republic and the victory of fascism. They campaigned for the lifting
of the arms embargo, holding hundreds of rallies and sending petitions
with thousands of names to Washington. In contrast, the American Catholic hierarchy saw in Spain a very different war, fought between Christianity
and communism, and they strongly opposed lifting the embargo. As the
Spanish controversy intensified, for every anti-embargo petition there was
a pro-embargo petition. In 1939 "Lift the Embargo Week" was followed by
"Keep the Embargo Week." The divide between liberals and Catholics over
Spain was especially significant because these two groups were the pillars
of Roosevelt's New Deal coalition. Thus the Spanish Civil War debate in
the United States was also an ideational civil war within the Democratic
Party. Americans did not just campaign politically; they also campaigned
militarily. Over 2,600 Americans traveled to Spain to fight in the Loyalist international brigades, of whom 900 were killed. A few U.S. citizens
also fought for Franco. It would be hard to imagine this happening today:
thousands of Americans risking the censure of their own government, and
putting their lives at risk, to fight in a country with which they have no
ethnic or nationalist ties, but instead feel a powerful idealistic or ideological
motivation to act.

Despite the efforts of American liberals, the arms embargo remained in
place throughout the war. President Harry Truman, the U.S. secretary of the
interior Harold Ickes, and the journalist Herbert Matthews all eventually
concluded that the embargo had played a major role in the Loyalist defeat.[6]
Many politicians in the United States came to perceive Roosevelt's nonintervention policy as a disastrous mistake, one that aided the fascist powers,
undermined the cause of democracy in Europe, and encouraged the wider
conflict in the Second World War. The assistant secretary of state Sumner
Welles believed in 1944 that "the position adopted by [the U.S.] government with regard to the Civil War in Spain . . . constitutes the greatest error
in the foreign policy of this country during the past twelve years."[7] Histo-

rians have tended to concur, arguing that the Spanish embargo was one of FDR's cardinal blunders. Robert Dallek, for example, has stated that FDR's policies in Spain encouraged the aggression that he wished to prevent. In common with Roosevelt's treatment of Jewish refugees, and Japanese-Americans in the Second World War, the Spanish embargo was one of the president's "unnecessary and destructive compromises of legal and moral principle."[8] Allen Guttmann has argued that if the president had lifted the Spanish embargo, then "World War II might well have been avoided."[9]

It is difficult to assess this counterfactual, but the Spanish Civil War certainly helped set the stage for the larger struggle to come. To paraphrase Mark Twain, history did not repeat itself, but the Spanish Civil War and the Second World War rhymed. The conflict in Spain ended in April 1939, only five months before Hitler invaded Poland. Germany and Italy first fought together in Spain, against a coalition of antifascists ranging from liberal democrats to communists—similar alliances, in fact, to those at the height of the Second World War in 1942. The new brutal methods of warfare in Spain, especially the orchestrated bombing of civilians, foreshadowed the slaughter of 1939–45. Furthermore, Roosevelt's first active challenge to fascist aggression in Europe came in 1938, when he tried and failed to block General Franco's victory in Spain.

Since 1939 the conflict in Spain has remained in the collective memory of both Europe and the United States. In 1984 Ronald Reagan remarked that Americans who fought for the contra rebels in Nicaragua were in a long tradition of foreign volunteers stretching back to the "Communist brigade of Americans in the Spanish Civil War." Reagan added—incorrectly—that the American volunteers in Spain had been "in the opinion of most Americans, fighting on the wrong side."[10] From a different perspective, Alfred Kazin, the American literary critic, called the Spanish Civil War "the wound that will not heal," and declared: "the destroyers of the Spanish Republic would always be my enemies."[11] In 2001 a proposal to erect a memorial to the New Hampshire citizens who had joined the Loyalist international brigades produced a heated controversy over the nature of the struggle in Spain. The question of whether the American volunteers had been antifascists fighting for democracy or rather Stalin's communist stooges was still alive sixty years after the event.

The Spanish Civil War ought to be remembered because there are instructive comparisons to be made between the 1930s and the post–cold war world. The Roosevelt era represents the most recent historical period in which the ambiguity displayed in the 1990s about the American world role and the location of its enemies was historically evident. Seyom Brown has commented that "it is striking to realize the extent to which the foreign policies of FDR, the last pre–cold war president, prefigured the foreign policies of Bill Clinton, the first post–cold war president."[12] One lesson from American policy in the Spanish Civil War is that arms embargoes are not neutral in their effects on civil war participants and therefore represent a form of intervention. This lesson has not been fully understood. In the early 1990s a UN arms embargo applied to all the sides fighting in Yugoslavia represented an unintended but highly effective intervention against one side—the Bosnian Muslims. Since the Croats and the Serbs had better access to weapons already present in Yugoslavia, the embargo meant that the Bosnian Muslims were unable to purchase arms to defend themselves.[13]

Despite the importance of the case, there are few studies of American diplomacy in the Spanish Civil War. The "road to the Second World War" is such a dominant paradigm among diplomatic historians of the United States during the 1930s that Spanish policy is often summarily added to a long laundry list of isolationist or appeasement episodes stretching back to the Japanese intervention in Manchuria in 1931. Herbert Feis, an advisor to FDR, noted in 1967: "How baffling all historians have found the task of giving a clear, full and reliable historical report and explanation of presidential policy during the civil war in Spain (1936–39)."[14]

Decades later we still lack a detailed study, and this neglect has produced repeated errors of interpretation. Historians have suggested that FDR was personally uninterested in the Spanish Civil War, or even that Roosevelt favored Franco.[15] Historians have also argued that Roosevelt's beliefs were basically unimportant, because Washington's nonintervention policy was the product of environmental constraints. Leo Kanawada stresses the role of Catholic pressure in favor of the Spanish embargo, while Foster Jay Taylor focuses on wider isolationist sentiment.[16] For Wayne Cole, the State Department played a critical role in the making of American policy in the Spanish Civil War.[17] Richard Traina argues that nonintervention was driven by concerns for British and French policy.[18] To Douglas Little, the Spanish embargo resulted from the salience of anticommunist ideology in the United States.[19] Indeed, almost every conceivable factor has been championed as the key to unlocking the puzzle of American decision making in the Spanish Civil War—apart, that is, from the president himself, who is typically depicted as a passive spectator to events in Spain.[20]

On the basis of newly discovered documents, this book challenges existing historical interpretations and offers an extensive reexamination of

American foreign policy in the Spanish Civil War. The documents reveal that Roosevelt played an increasingly active and important personal role in the conflict. FDR's perceptions of Spain changed dramatically between 1936 and 1939. When the conflict in Spain broke out in 1936, the president's overwhelming fear was that it would spark a second world war. Roosevelt displayed a strong preference from the start for international nonintervention—a desire in effect to quarantine Spain—and he subsequently helped lead the administration's efforts to introduce an American embargo on arms sales to both the Nationalists and the Republicans. In 1937 Roosevelt became more concerned about the extent of fascist intervention in Spain, and considered extending the arms embargo to Germany and Italy for being effectively at war with the Spanish Republic. During 1938 Roosevelt's beliefs were transformed, and he reevaluated Franco's likely triumph in Spain as being clearly harmful for American interests.

Why did FDR alter his views so dramatically? First, German and Italian intervention in Spain looked more threatening in the context of wider fascist aggression in 1938, notably the Anschluss between Germany and Austria and the Munich Crisis. Second, FDR increasingly feared that a triumph by Franco in Spain could worsen Latin American security. The president saw the Spanish Civil War as a potential model for German intervention in future civil wars in the western hemisphere. A Nationalist victory could thus start a domino effect of fascist successes closer to home. Third, Roosevelt displayed an aversion to the brutality of Franco's war effort. For all these reasons, the importance of the Spanish Civil War in the president's mind became greatly magnified, with FDR suggesting in 1939 that the war in Spain could be the first round of an impending European civil war. By this stage Roosevelt had moved much closer to—although without fully accepting—the left's interpretation that defense of the Spanish Republic was the last great cause.

In 1938 the president's support for nonintervention gradually gave way to a desire to challenge fascist aggression in Spain. FDR developed an illegal scheme to send covert aid to the Spanish Republic, encouraged the purchase of Loyalist silver for American cash, conjured up a plan for pan-American mediation, tried to ship large quantities of humanitarian supplies to Spain, and attempted to lift the arms embargo. The nature of Roosevelt's changing beliefs was unique: most of his foreign policy advisors wanted to avoid any risky intervention in Spain. Neither was the president simply following a domestic lead: the Catholics, a key part of FDR's New Deal coalition, vocally backed Franco. Because of Catholic pressure, most Congressional politicians were extremely cautious on the Spanish embargo issue.

Roosevelt's policies ultimately did little to shape the course of the Spanish Civil War. His record was one of failure, with most of his initiatives collapsing. At the very moment when FDR most clearly saw the cause of the Loyalists as being America's cause, the Republic was in its death throes. However, viewed in a wider perspective, Roosevelt's initiatives in 1938 were highly important. The Spanish Civil War represented a crucial stage in the development of Roosevelt's overall foreign policy strategy from 1935 to 1941: aiding the democracies and the victims of aggression with methods short of war. Spain marked the first occasion when Roosevelt did not just *talk* about opposing Hitler and Mussolini but actually introduced a range of policies to halt the march of the fascist states. Partly as a result of the Spanish Civil War, Roosevelt questioned his attachment to neutrality legislation, and searched instead for innovative ways of challenging Germany and Italy without sacrificing domestic support. After 1939 the president repeatedly expressed his guilt and remorse for the Spanish embargo, and he maintained an enduring hostility toward General Franco and the Nationalists. In the weeks before his death in 1945, Roosevelt signaled a postwar aim of regime change in Spain. But the cold war ultimately brought the United States into an alliance with Franco.

The major purpose of this book is to investigate the nature of Roosevelt's beliefs about the Spanish Civil War and to establish the extent to which his personal views influenced American policy. One of the book's wider aims is to use this case study to offer insights into the controversial question of FDR's personal role in foreign policy making in the crucial years before the Second World War. This leads us neatly to the question: Why study Roosevelt's beliefs?

An individual's personality refers to the totality of his or her qualities and traits relating to character and behavior. A belief is the mental acceptance of, and conviction in, the truth, actuality, or validity of something. A belief therefore represents one element of personality, and it is Roosevelt's beliefs about Spain with which we are primarily concerned. But is there actually any need to study individual beliefs? Can foreign policy decisions in general—and specifically American foreign policy decisions in the 1930s—be sufficiently explained by alternative factors, such as the international system, domestic politics, or bureaucratic influence?

Political scientists known as realists have argued that a country's foreign policy is driven mainly by pressures derived from the international system, for example the need to ally or rearm against a threatening and powerful rival.[21] Domestic politics and individual leaders tend not to matter, because international pressures often force the hand of policy makers.

Proponents of this type of argument have great difficulty explaining the isolationist period in the United States during the 1920s and 1930s, when domestic factors played a critical role in ensuring that interwar America punched below its weight on the international stage. If American policy had indeed been driven by international security threats as the realists suggest, then one might expect Washington to have allied against Germany, Italy, and Japan much sooner and more decisively than it actually did. In the 1930s the question of what America's national interest *was*, and whether the fascist states seriously challenged this national interest, was hotly debated. Senator William Borah wrote in January 1939 that nothing troubled him "so much as what to do with reference to the Spanish embargo." He claimed to be guided only by national interests, but these he thought "most difficult to determine." Any action (or inaction) over the embargo would favor either the communists or the fascists, whom he considered equally anti-American.[22] That American élites interpreted international constraints in the Spanish Civil War in a variety of ways suggests that these constraints did not simply force FDR's hand.

Neither do domestic factors, even in combination with an international systemic approach, provide a sufficient explanation for American policy toward Spain. The period of the Spanish Civil War, 1936–39, was one in which Roosevelt failed to simply follow isolationist opinion down the path to a "Fortress America." Instead he attempted to lead the United States into a policy of aiding the European democracies. Rather than be immobilized by domestic factors, FDR sought to circumvent them. In his desire to lead America toward a new global perspective on international relations, Roosevelt discredited and crushed isolationist critics, often by covert and underhand means. During the Spanish Civil War there is considerable evidence that FDR sought to bypass or co-opt domestic opponents to achieve his political goals.

To show that FDR was important in the decision-making process, we also need to demonstrate that he controlled his administration and that his preferences were not distorted by Secretary of State Cordell Hull and the foreign policy bureaucracy. Several political scientists have argued that what government does can be understood largely as a result of bargaining among elements of the bureaucracy, with each bureaucratic group trying to protect its own organizational turf.[23] There is certainly evidence of this type of behavior in the late 1930s. The various geographical division chiefs in the State Department, for example, fiercely defended their autonomy.

We should be skeptical of claims that a bureaucratic approach can explain American policy making during the Spanish Civil War. This approach

holds that an actor's preferences are based on the interests of the bureaucratic organization that he represents: in other words, *where you stand de-
pends on where you sit*. However, organizational interests were unclear in
relation to the Spanish Civil War. The State Department, for example, was
internally split over Spain, and these divisions changed over time. Furthermore, FDR often involved outside departments such as Treasury and Interior in foreign policy decision making, and these departments lacked any
obvious "interest" to defend in Spanish policy.

Crucially, the bureaucratic politics approach underestimates the power
of the president, especially one with an active personality such as Roosevelt. The very bureaucratic decision-making structure that is said to determine policy is itself often shaped by the personality of the leader. Roosevelt created a competitive decision-making structure, in which conflict was
deliberately encouraged among his advisors and cabinet heads, all of whom
were forced to bring important policy problems to FDR for him to resolve.
Owing to his personal beliefs, Roosevelt also tended to distrust the professional diplomats of the State Department and often sought alternative,
sometimes unusual, avenues to create foreign policy. Sending his brother-
in-law to Paris as an emissary to investigate the secret shipment of arms to
Spain is a good example.

Roosevelt's competitive decision-making model has sometimes been
criticized as inefficient. There was no clear chain of command; instead
FDR tended to divide the same task among several groups and individuals.
David Reynolds argues that this practice exacerbated bureaucratic politics:
FDR divided without ruling.[24] Yet for all the confusion that this system
created, it did succeed in generating new sources of information. Warren
Kimball and Waldo Heinrichs argued that Roosevelt may have been "disin-
genuous, deceptive and devious," but FDR held all the threads of decision
making in his hand.[25]

Roosevelt was an extremely adept politician who played a critical role
in foreign policy decision making in the 1930s. David Reynolds writes that
"the ambiguities of F.D.R.'s foreign policy grew as much out of his own character and attitudes as they did out of his celebrated deference to the dictates
of public opinion."[26] Robert Dallek concludes: "No modern president has
wielded his personal influence more effectively than FDR," noting in particular Roosevelt's communication skills, his optimism and confidence, and
his personal popularity, even with many groups who steadfastly opposed
the New Deal.[27]

If Roosevelt's beliefs were an important factor in the foreign policy
making process, did the president in fact hold consistent views? Roosevelt

has been portrayed by some historians as an isolationist, by others as an ambitious and pragmatic internationalist, constrained by domestic isolationism.[28] Alternatively Roosevelt has been depicted as a "drifter," lacking policies or opportunistically following domestic currents.[29] This book qualifies all of these approaches. Although Roosevelt was rarely a systematic thinker, he did hold coherent beliefs about international affairs and the Spanish Civil War. After 1936 FDR appreciated the threat posed to national security and the international order by Germany, Japan, and to a lesser extent Italy. He consistently sought means to reduce international aggression and improve cooperation with Britain. Roosevelt's uncertainty about the motives of international actors, especially during 1936–38, led him to pursue schemes for co-opting the dictators into the international system, as well as, simultaneously, strategies of deterrence and sanction. In 1938 Roosevelt clarified the fascist threat, shifted gears, and moved more assertively to aid the European democracies. Therefore, for a full understanding of American foreign policy and the Spanish Civil War, we will have to wrestle with the beliefs of the American sphinx.

It is very difficult to be sure what Roosevelt thought about international affairs. Partly this is due to the inherent problems with ascertaining any individual's beliefs from the documentary evidence. Such sources are usually written to convey information, to persuade, or to justify, rather than to reveal "inner" motivations. Certain influences on policy rarely feature fully in the documents. For example, presidents can be reluctant to acknowledge the role of domestic politics in foreign policy decisions, because they swore to uphold and defend national security, not follow popular whims.

In this regard Roosevelt's beliefs are especially challenging to dissect. FDR was incredibly secretive, his thinking veiled by a "chameleon-like," "elusive and dissembling," or "multifaceted, mercurial, enigmatic" personality.[30] Tugwell wrote that Roosevelt "deliberately concealed the processes of his mind. He would rather have posterity believe that for him everything was always plain and easy . . . than ever to admit to any agony of indecision."[31] Henry Stimson described the president's mind as one that did "not easily follow a consecutive chain of thought but he is full of stories and incidents. It is very much like chasing a vagrant beam of moonshine around a vacant room."[32] Searching in the archives for documents that reveal the inner Roosevelt can be a frustrating business. FDR very rarely even tried to set out on paper his real motivations. His letters are generally short, and either jovial or business-like, a style in part designed to shield his personal beliefs so that he could deal more effectively with isolationist pressures.

Instead, the president engaged in telephone conversations that were not systematically recorded. Even the historical sources that do exist are sometimes incomplete. Roosevelt told the French, for example, never to divulge the American position on the Brussels Conference of 1937 on Far Eastern affairs.[33]

Problems in understanding Roosevelt are compounded when we consider the case of the Spanish Civil War. François Furet has written that "the history of the Spanish Civil War was covered with a blanket of silence and lies that would remain in place throughout the twentieth century."[34] Truth was an early casualty of the fighting in Spain, with the Spanish Nationalists and Loyalists engaging in a fierce international propaganda battle to win sympathy in Europe and the Americas. Franco presented the war as a crusade against a Jewish-communist-Masonic conspiracy. For Republican supporters the conflict was a struggle for democratic freedom against privilege and oppression, or an opportunity to forge a brave new revolutionary world. George Orwell wrote in 1943 about the dishonesty and propaganda of the war, concluding that "history stopped in 1936":

> In Spain, for the first time, I saw newspaper reports which did not bear any relation to the facts, not even the relationship which is implied in an ordinary lie. I saw great battles reported where there had been no fighting, and complete silence where hundreds of men had been killed. I saw troops who had fought bravely denounced as cowards and traitors, and others who had never seen a shot fired hailed as the heroes of imaginary victories; and I saw newspapers in London retelling these lies and eager intellectuals building emotional superstructures over events that had never happened. I saw, in fact, history being written not in terms of what happened but of what ought to have happened according to various "party lines."[35]

Until recently many historians found that the ideals and passions of the Spanish Civil War made objective analysis impossible. Dante Puzzo wrote: "In treating matters so emotionally evocative it would be fatuous, or worse, to pretend to an Olympian detachment."[36] But many of the above problems can be ameliorated or overcome by careful historical study. We can compare policy statements, letters, diaries, and memoirs to see whether the evidence is consistent and corroborative. Although the president personally gave little away, the writings of those close to Roosevelt contain a large amount of material about his views and their relationship to policy decisions. The work of Waldo Heinrichs and Warren Kimball presents a model in this regard. Based on meticulous research, Heinrichs and Kimball conclude that Roosevelt had fixed assumptions and that he controlled his bureaucracy. Kimball writes that "Roosevelt's consistency, shrouded as it was in rhetoric and tactical maneuverings, is striking."[37] We can analyze how the president's beliefs influenced his receptiveness to, and assessment of, incoming information, his evaluation of options, as well as his choice of a course of action. We can also test these findings by examining the consistency between policy outcomes in reality, and the outcomes that would have been predicted if international, domestic, bureaucratic, or individual factors had in fact shaped American decision making.[38]

Focusing on personality does not mean that other factors were unimportant or irrelevant. International pressures and domestic politics certainly played a role in Washington's response to the Spanish Civil War. To see individual decision makers as autonomous is a fundamental error. Therefore, this book analyzes the nature of the constraints in 1936–39 and attempts to comprehend how FDR interpreted the political environment, and reacted to and manipulated external forces. To understand why British opinion helped to shape American policy, we have to understand Roosevelt's view of Anglo-American relations: there is no a priori reason why British opinion should have mattered so much. Similarly, bureaucratic pressures did influence the president, but mainly this pressure came from individual bureaucrats whom Roosevelt trusted and chose to listen to. American Catholic opinion mattered to FDR because of the president's understanding of the crucial Catholic role in the Democratic New Deal coalition—a coalition that FDR himself had constructed. In all these cases, actors other than Roosevelt interpreted each constraint in substantially different ways.

The example of FDR and the Spanish Civil War is particularly useful for understanding the president's role in foreign policy making in this period because it represented a worst-case scenario for effective decision making. The disastrous court-packing plan of 1937, the failed Democratic Party purge, and the "Roosevelt recession" left the president's prestige at an all-time low between 1937 and 1939. "No calamity," Frank Freidel has argued, "more clearly illustrated Roosevelt's lack of power than the Spanish Civil War . . . He stood on the sidelines, largely as an inactive spectator to the Spanish tragedy."[39] If Roosevelt mattered in Spanish policy, when constraints were apparently so overwhelming, he must have played a major personal role in decision making more generally.[40]

CHAPTER 2

International Intervention and Nonintervention

In the weeks before Spain erupted into civil war in the summer of 1936, deepening international tensions reminded many people of the final days before the First World War. Roosevelt, for example, wrote to his ambassador in Berlin. "All the experts here, there, and the other places say 'there will be no war.' They said the same thing all through July 1914."[1] The U.S. ambassador to the Soviet Union, William C. Bullitt, felt similarly: "We are back where we were before 1914, when the familiar and true remark was, 'Peace is at the mercy of an incident.'"[2]

This historical analogy seemed prescient in 1936 because of the rapidly worsening international security environment. The ideals outlined by President Woodrow Wilson during and after the First World War—national self-determination, territorial integrity, disarmament, free trade, and collective security—were undermined in the subsequent years by economic crisis and weakening political structures. The Wall Street crash of 1929 led governments to abandon the tenets of economic liberalism and attempt to ward off the Great Depression through closed markets. America fought in 1917 to make the world safe for democracy, but twenty years later democracy was a waning force, not just in the fascist states but also in Spain and across most of Eastern Europe. Above all, the disintegration of the postwar international system was caused by the aggressive and imperialistic foreign policies of Italy, Germany, and Japan. In 1935–36 Mussolini's fascist Italy invaded and conquered Ethiopia. In 1935 Hitler defied the Versailles Treaty of 1919 by announcing German rearmament, and in 1936 he remilitarized the Rhineland. In the Pacific, Japan appeared to be set on Asian dominance when it invaded Manchuria in 1931. Six years later, in July 1937, the war restarted between Japan and the Chinese Nationalist government. Fascist unity was evident with the creation in 1936 of the Rome-Berlin Axis and the German-Japanese Anti-Comintern Pact.

In this increasingly threatening security environment, Spain suddenly erupted into civil war. After the commander of Allied forces Ferdinand Foch viewed the Versailles Treaty, he declared that it was not a peace settlement, merely "a twenty year truce." The question was: Would the Spanish Civil War engender the fulfillment of Foch's prophecy by sparking all-out conflict on the continent? In 1936 Spain was an unlikely candidate for the fulcrum of Europe. For Spain was on the fringes of the continent, both geographically and economically. In the daily way of life, parts of the country appeared to have changed little since medieval times. It was a land of extremes, with huge economic inequality and a large landless peasantry in the South who lived as virtual slaves. In 1931 75 percent of the Spanish people owned less than 5 percent of the land, while 2 percent of the people owned 65 percent of the land.[3] The privileged Spanish church tended toward reaction, viewing liberalism as a fundamental threat to the established order. Rapid industrialization in Catalonia and the Basque region created a working class radicalized by the lack of political and economic reform, and attracted to anarchism and revolutionary socialism. Both regions also witnessed a rise in separatist movements.

The revolt of the generals in July 1936 was the thirteenth such revolt since 1809. In this intervening period, the once mighty Spanish empire had declined and then disintegrated, with almost all the final remnants lost in the disastrous war against the United States in 1898. In 1923, after a period of economic and political dislocation, King Alfonso XIII supported General Primo de Rivera as dictator of Spain. In the wake of further internal problems, the de Rivera regime collapsed, Alfonso went into exile in 1931, and the Spanish Republic was born. The Republic would last until 1939, its eight years of life encompassing mass politicization, deepening social and political division, weakening democratic structures, and ultimately civil war.[4]

Between 1931 and 1933 the moderate left governed Spain. The new administration sought to modernize the country, provide regional autonomy, introduce land reform, and limit the power of the church and the army. Such reforms raised but did not meet the expectations of the Spanish working classes. Yet many privileged Spaniards regarded the leftist government as an illegitimate Bolshevist or Jacobin regime. Spanish conservatives tended to divide into those willing to use constitutional methods to block reform, and those who never accepted the Republic's right to exist and plotted to destroy it from the first. The more pragmatic conservatives governed Spain from 1933 until 1936. In a foretaste of the future, a left-wing revolt in Asturias held out for three weeks in 1934 until General Franco used artillery to bomb the insurgents into submission. Massive repression followed the rising, which further polarized opinion. As a result, the leftist parties united in a Popular Front and won the watershed elections of February 1936.[5]

The ensuing months saw rising social conflict, a breakdown in law and order, and small-scale land seizures. These events were exaggerated by the rightist press, which portrayed Spain as descending into anarchy. The Spanish officer corps held the firm belief that the army had the right, and even the duty, to intervene and defend the country from radical threats to its social order. On 11 July a Dragon Rapide biplane left Croydon in Britain and flew to the Canary Islands. To hide its true function, the plane carried several British holidaymakers (the plan had specified platinum blonde girls). After dropping off the girls the plane picked up General Franco and transported him to Africa in preparation for the coup.[6]

On 17 July 1936 large elements from the Spanish army rose in North Africa and the mainland in a coordinated seizure of power. The rebel generals anticipated that a military rising across Spain would encounter minimal resistance as in 1923, but the coup failed in key cities and the Spanish Civil War ensued. What mattered most in determining the local fate of the *pronunciamiento* was the unity of the military, popular support, and the actions of the security forces. The Catholic heartlands of Old Castile, Seville, Valladolid, Zamora, and Salamanca all fell to the rebels. In Pamplona the fiercely monarchist population transformed the coup into a street festival. Trickery sufficed to win the town of Oviedo. Colonel Antonio Aranda feigned loyalty to the Republic long enough for local miners to set out to defend Madrid, and then promptly declared for the rebels. In Cadiz the generals won by savagely repressing workers who had launched a general strike.

But Madrid, Barcelona, and Valencia, together with the great estates of southern Spain, remained Loyalist. The conservative Basques also favored the Republic, desiring to protect their autonomy against the ultra-centralist generals. The first Americans involved in the Spanish Civil War were amateur athletes attending the People's Olympics in Barcelona: games organized to protest against the official Olympics in Berlin. When shots rang out, at least one of the American athletes ran outside to help the Loyalists build a barricade. The coach of the team would later return to Spain to fight in the international brigades.[7]

When the dust settled on the initial rising, the Spanish Republic was left in control of much of industrial Spain as well as the gold reserves. It also

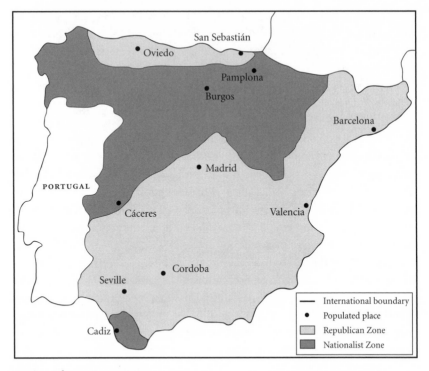

San Sebastián
Oviedo
Pamplona
Burgos
Barcelona
Madrid
PORTUGAL
Cáceres
Valencia
Cordoba
Seville
Cadiz

— International boundary
• Populated place
☐ Republican Zone
■ Nationalist Zone

Spain, July 1936

maintained the loyalty of perhaps half the mainland army and air force and a larger proportion of the navy. The Nationalists held the best agricultural land, the support of a majority of the Spanish army's field officers, and crucially, the effective but brutal Army of Africa, composed of the professional Foreign Legion and Moroccan mercenaries. Franco came to dominate the Nationalist coalition partly because several of his rivals died. In July 1936 one of the key plotters, General José Sanjurjo, was killed in mysterious circumstances in an air crash in Portugal. In November the leader of the Spanish fascist Falange movement, José Antonio Primo de Rivera, was shot in a Republican prison. General Emilio Mola, another core conspirator, died in a plane crash in June 1937.

In the summer of 1936 the war could have taken many different courses. What substantially determined its evolution was the nature and extent of foreign intervention. Paul Preston writes that "the Spanish Civil War, in its origins, was a Spanish social war and, in its course, and outcome, an episode in a greater European civil war that ended in 1945."[8] Both sides in

Spain recognized the crucial significance of foreign intervention and immediately requested external aid, with the Nationalists turning to Germany and Italy, and the Spanish government to France. Spain's strategic position and valuable raw materials ensured that the outcome of the Spanish Civil War would be highly significant for the wider balance of power. In the European capitals, democrats and dictators fashioned their response to events in the Iberian Peninsula.

On 20 July 1936 a telegram arrived in Paris from the Spanish Republican leader José Giral: "Have been surprised by dangerous military coup. Request you to help us at once with arms and aircraft. Fraternally yours, Giral."[9] The civil war was of immediate importance for French interests, given Spain's geographic position and the extensive French foreign capital invested in Spanish industry. The Popular Front government in Paris sympathized with its sister regime in Madrid. France was certainly permitted under international law to sell arms to a recognized government facing a rebellion, and Prime Minister Léon Blum quickly decided to authorize the sale of war materials to the Spanish Republic. With French weapons the Loyalists might well have crushed the rising in its infancy. But within a few days Blum changed his mind, and instead appealed on 27 July for international nonintervention in Spain.[10]

Blum's decision partly reflected French domestic pressures. France in the 1930s was enduring the "hollow years," split by stark political division between left and right. There were genuine fears that if France intervened to aid the Loyalists in the Spanish Civil War, its involvement could spark a French civil war. Meanwhile the British were pressing the French to be cautious. With a revisionist Germany growing in power, French security relied above all on the entente with Britain. London suggested that it might stand aside if wider hostilities arose because of French support for the Spanish Republic. Blum saw international nonintervention as a way out of his dilemma: if the French could not support the Republic, no country would support either side. A nonintervention agreement would thus prevent others from doing what the French were incapable of doing.[11]

Britain backed the French initiative partly because of concerns about the possibility of a left-wing revolution in Spain. Prime Minister Stanley Baldwin feared Stalin more than he feared Hitler, and with British investments in Spain amounting to £40 million, London was worried that Spain was about to be Bolshevized. The greatest British concern, however, was strategic: to prevent the Spanish Civil War from transforming into a wider European war, creating an alignment between Germany and Italy, or undermining the broader policy of appeasement. The declining international security situation during the 1930s, and British financial difficulties, starkly illustrated the gap between London's imperial commitments and its capabilities. The British response was a policy aimed at satisfying the reasonable grievances of Germany and Italy, and thereby transforming them into status quo powers as part of a general European settlement. International nonintervention in Spain was precisely the kind of negotiated multilateral solution that the British government wished to apply more broadly to European affairs.[12]

In the end, twenty-seven countries agreed not to intervene in Spain by sending troops or selling arms to the combatants. Their decisions did not amount to a formal treaty but rather a series of unilateral declarations of government policy, accepting the French proposals of August 1936.[13] The League of Nations, which by 1936 had proved incapable of preventing Italian aggression against Ethiopia, played little role in the Spanish Civil War. Instead, the League Council voted to leave supervision of the French initiative to a specially formed Non-Intervention Committee.[14] As Hugh Thomas wrote, this committee "was to graduate from equivocation to hypocrisy and humiliation."[15] Germany, Italy, and the Soviet Union announced a policy of nonintervention in Spain in 1936, but all three countries broke their word within a few weeks.

Hitler's involvement in the Spanish Civil War was opportunistic and his motives complex. Nazi Germany played almost no role in the origins of the pronunciamiento. Indeed, Spain held little interest for Hitler until 1936. Soon after the revolt, Franco contacted Hitler through German expatriates in Spanish Morocco. The Spanish Nationalists needed German aircraft to transport the rebel Army of Africa to Spain, because it was stranded when much of the Spanish navy remained loyal to Madrid. Within twenty-four hours after Franco's emissaries arrived in Germany, arrangements were under way to save the rebellion. Hitler sought to defeat communism, gain a new Spanish ally, and forge a closer alliance with Italy. Transport aircraft were quickly sent to Africa along with accompanying fighter support and anti-aircraft guns. Within ten days, fifteen thousand crack Nationalist troops had been flown over the Straits of Gibraltar to the mainland. Additional German forces were dispatched in September and October 1936, including over a hundred modern aircraft which formed the Condor Legion. In all, Berlin sent 840 aircraft and fourteen to sixteen thousand German troops and advisors, along with two hundred tanks.[16]

Yet it was Mussolini rather than Hitler who demonstrated the greatest commitment to a Nationalist victory in Spain. Although Italy had provided subsidies for fascist groups in Spain before 1936, Rome was not directly involved in the rising. Acting independently but in parallel with Berlin, Italy decided in July to send bomber and transport aircraft to aid Franco. Mussolini saw an opportunity to gain strategic bases and prevent the emergence of a communist Spain. As the Nationalist advance faltered in late 1936, the Italians injected massive military support. In all, around seventy to eighty thousand Italian troops served in Spain, together with 759 aircraft. In the context of ongoing Italian warfare in Ethiopia, this represented a huge investment in the Nationalist cause at substantial economic cost. From 1936 to 1939 Italy was engaged in an undeclared war against the Spanish Republic.[17]

The Russian archives indicate that Spain was a pawn in Stalin's wider strategy, and that Soviet aid to the Spanish government was largely a reaction to fascist intervention. The Soviet Union aimed to maintain the Spanish Republican war effort, to suck in the fascists and keep them occupied. Intervention would assist the wider cause of the international left and channel the Spanish revolution along pro-Soviet lines. In the mid-1930s Stalin, threatened by Germany and Japan, deemphasized world revolution and sought an alliance with Britain and France. In this context Stalin feared that a victory by Franco would decisively weaken the French strategic position. But Stalin ultimately wanted Britain and France rather than the Russians to stand up to Hitler. With the Soviet economy and society in painful transition, European war was to be avoided unless Moscow could remain aloof. During September 1936 the decision was made to send a substantial number of modern tanks and aircraft to Spain, as well as about two thousand advisors (in all, about three thousand Soviet personnel served in Spain). The first shipment of aid arrived in October, in time for the critical defense of Madrid. Soviet aid totaled about eight hundred to a thousand planes and four hundred tanks. In addition, Soviet agents helped to organize the Spanish Loyalist international brigades, which numbered about 42,000–51,000 men, drawn from around the world.[18]

Moscow provided arms on Soviet terms and for Soviet ends. The material aid was accompanied by growing influence over the Spanish administration and a ruthless purging of leftist opponents. Soviet agents in Spain hunted for supporters of the exiled Russian communist Leon Trotsky, and set up show trials much like those occurring in Moscow. The thousands of passports handed over by members of the international brigades provided a bounty for Soviet intelligence, which it used to penetrate western societies, especially the United States. The Republic sent over five hundred tons of gold to Moscow in October 1936 for the purchase of weapons. Stalin subsequently defrauded the Loyalists by manipulating exchange rates and thereby charging 30–40 percent above the market rate for weapons. Stalin remarked that the Spanish would never see their gold again "any more than they can see their own ears."[19] However, if Moscow "betrayed" Spain through cynical manipulation, the USSR remained the one state that offered any significant aid. From a Loyalist viewpoint, Soviet "betrayal" might well have been considered preferable to British and French "betrayal."[20]

The Spanish Civil War had a significant impact beyond the great powers. Czechoslovakia sold a few weapons to the Spanish Republic. Antonio Oliveira Salazar in Portugal provided medical equipment and sanctuaries for the Nationalists as well as several thousand troops.[21] In the face of Spanish Republican anticlericalism, the pope gave qualified support for the Nationalists in September 1936 and de facto recognition on 19 December. The pope's attitude was cautious in part because of Nationalist atrocities. In the spring of 1937 the Spanish bishops sent a collective letter justifying Franco's "crusade." The Vatican accepted it with silence. Full diplomatic relations between the Vatican and the Nationalists were established in 1938.[22] In Latin America, Mexico supported the Spanish Loyalists, and shipped $2.2 million worth of arms to the Republic by 1937. Costa Rica and Colombia were neutral. El Salvador, Guatemala, Nicaragua, Argentina, Brazil, and Paraguay were all pro-Franco.[23]

During the first few weeks of the Spanish Civil War the full extent and repercussions of foreign intervention were unclear. By the end of 1936, with Soviet aid arriving in Loyalist Spain, and Germany and Italy having massively increased support for Franco, the international alignments had been established that would last until the end of the war. Yet even at this stage, when thousands of troops and hundreds of tanks and aircraft from "nonintervening" countries were in Spain, Britain and France believed that because wider war had been avoided, their policy remained viable. The Non-Intervention Committee represented, in theory at least, an agreed framework for limiting the Spanish Civil War, covering virtually every major supplier of arms in the world.

The exception was the United States. Washington was reluctant to involve itself directly in European political arrangements. There was therefore no question that the United States might join the Non-Intervention Committee. Even so, any attempt to prevent or limit arms sales to Spain would require the cooperation of Washington. Indeed, the Non-Intervention Committee could hardly proceed without a parallel American embargo. From August 1936 London and Paris repeatedly impressed upon the U.S. government the critical nature of events, the delicacy with which the Spanish Civil War was being handled, and the importance of American collaboration in limiting the war to Spain. It remained to be seen how Washington would respond to the Spanish tragedy.

CHAPTER 3

Roosevelt's Perceptions of the Spanish Civil War, 1936–1937

How did Roosevelt view international affairs in 1936? Given the widely differing interpretations of the Spanish Civil War, what did FDR believe was at stake in Spain? Many contemporaries and historians, peering into the complex and apparently contradictory mind of the president, declared him to be an enigma. Roosevelt rarely revealed his innermost thoughts, particularly on paper. FDR's administrative style was also famously chaotic. Yet to the careful observer, there is method in the apparent madness, a consistency of belief and governing style underlying the confusion. The president was, as he once told his treasury secretary, a "juggler," someone who never let his "right hand know" what his left hand did.[1] To understand Roosevelt's perceptions of the Spanish Civil War in 1936–37, we must first comprehend his wider beliefs about international affairs in this period. These wider beliefs represented the lenses through which FDR perceived the opening acts of the conflict in Spain.

Roosevelt shared many values with his fellow Americans and maintained a strong belief in the broad, perhaps universal, applicability of these values. FDR discussed his commitment to certain political ideas, for example "democracy," although in very vague terms. When asked by a journalist to define his philosophy Roosevelt replied: "Philosophy? Philosophy? I am a Christian and a Democrat—that's all."[2] Accused by many contemporaries of being a radical, even a communist sympathizer, Roosevelt remarked that his greatest success was saving American capitalism. As an individual, the president was optimistic and confident, combining a Progressive mentality with a very practical view of politics. James MacGregor Burns has argued that Roosevelt's character was based on the relationship between the do-good morality of his aristocratic roots and his political emergence in a troubled twentieth century.[3] Even Roosevelt's friends

25

did not describe him as an intellectual, but they did comment on his other qualities: his first-class temperament, his adept and seemingly intuitive political skills, his charm, his courage, his resourcefulness, and his vision.

What were Roosevelt's basic assumptions about international relations? FDR was deadly serious about preventing the United States from becoming involved in another world war. His comments during a speech in Chautauqua in August 1936—"I've seen war . . . I hate war"—reflected sincerely held beliefs.[4] But the president saw an important international role for the United States: as a model global citizen, as a promoter of free trade and disarmament, and, much more cautiously, as a defender of international order. In his first inaugural address Roosevelt set out as a guide for state behavior the notion of the "good neighbor" that respected treaties and the rights of other states, ideas later developed in the Atlantic Charter and the Four Freedoms. The existence of empires clashed with Roosevelt's vision of a world of good neighbors, and FDR sought the eventual dismantling of the European colonial system.[5] For Roosevelt peace and prosperity were necessarily linked, and therefore he believed in the central importance of restoring world trade. The president sought to reduce barriers to trade with the Reciprocal Trade Agreements Act of 1934 and particularly the Bretton Woods system of 1944. Disarmament was seen as an ideal goal in international affairs. Arms races produced bankruptcy or war, and FDR tended to distrust governments engaged in military buildups.[6] In the president's eyes, progress toward all these goals was possible. Roosevelt's optimism and confidence in his own charisma and political skills meant that at least until 1938, he believed most international issues to be negotiable, even with dictators.

When Roosevelt was inaugurated president in 1933, he was already a well-traveled man with an aristocratic pedigree. He had married President Theodore Roosevelt's niece, Eleanor. But more than just marriage connected the Democratic Roosevelt and the Republican Roosevelt. From an early age FDR sought to emulate TR's career by contributing to society in a meaningful fashion. As assistant secretary of the navy during the First World War, FDR supported American entry into the war. He identified himself strongly with Wilsonian Progressivism and campaigned unsuccessfully for American membership of the League of Nations. FDR became the Democratic vice-presidential candidate in 1920, but the Republican Warren Harding won by a landslide. Despite suffering from crippling polio in 1921, Roosevelt continued to be heavily involved in politics and argued for a more engaged and internationalist American foreign policy during the 1920s. He urged the United States to join the League of Nations or a reformed successor organization, and pushed for greater American involvement in efforts at international disarmament.

Yet as the Democratic presidential candidate in 1932, Roosevelt rejected American membership in the League of Nations, partly to win the backing of the isolationist newspaper publisher William Randolph Hearst. Roosevelt was also highly attuned to a domestic environment dominated by the politics of the Depression and wary of foreign involvement. Learning from the failure of Wilson to gain American membership of the League, Roosevelt believed that a president needed to carefully nurture domestic support for international policies.[7] As a result, during FDR's first term there was no sharp break with the economic and political nationalism of the 1920s. Instead, Roosevelt's priority in this period lay in rescuing the United States from its disastrous economic crisis. At the London Economic Conference in 1933, Roosevelt was willing to undermine international efforts to stabilize currencies because of what he perceived as domestic economic necessity. He also supported the Johnson Act of 1934, which prevented American loans from being raised by countries that defaulted on debts incurred during the First World War, including Britain and France. FDR told Senator Tom Connally of Texas in 1935: "We have to get our own economic house in order before we can do anything in the foreign field."[8]

Roosevelt made clear his opposition to American involvement in another European conflict. After the collapse of the Geneva Disarmament Conference in 1934, he stated that the United States should avoid matters of European peace and war. Accepting the need for neutrality legislation to prevent entanglement in foreign conflicts, he signed the Neutrality Act of 1935, which prohibited Americans from selling arms to belligerents in international wars. Although Roosevelt sought greater executive discretion over the enactment of arms embargoes, he saw advantages in being able to quickly act to keep America free from becoming embroiled in war. Five weeks after the Neutrality Act was passed, Roosevelt enforced it against Italy and Ethiopia.[9]

Despite his apparent retreat from internationalism, the president recognized the threat posed by Germany and Italy to world peace and sought means of slowing down the drift to war. While American isolationists wanted to distance the United States from a corrupt and perpetually conflicting Europe, Roosevelt believed that his country could influence European and world affairs through moral example and the promotion of disarmament and free trade. The president endorsed the Hoover-Stimson

Doctrine of 1932, whereby the United States refused to recognize international territorial changes brought about by force, notably Japan's conquest of Manchuria. In addition, Roosevelt appointed the internationalist Cordell Hull as secretary of state.[10]

By 1931 the President was deeply concerned at warlike trends. Three years before he had privately labeled Hitler a "madman."[11] Now he stated for the first time that world affairs worried him more than domestic matters. Roosevelt felt that democracy was "verily on trial" globally, but he told the Pan-American Conference in Buenos Aires in December 1936: "Democracy is still the hope of the world."[12] During 1936–40, as David Haglund has persuasively argued, Roosevelt's administration displayed increasing fears about the fascist threat to Latin American security. In his first term the president was primarily concerned with improving economic relations and safeguarding American investments in the region, which amounted to $3 billion. The "good neighbor" policy emphasized reciprocal trade agreements and the principle of nonintervention in the affairs of other American states. However, this policy quickly became strategic as well as economic in its aims and scope. During his second term Roosevelt saw improved relations with the American republics as a principal means of containing fascist influence in the region. Germany was by 1936 the second-biggest exporter to Latin America. Cordell Hull was also worried by the political activities of over one million Germans living in Latin America, especially in Brazil. These concerns were widespread in the United States and transcended the divide between isolationists and internationalists. Many isolationists considered the "fortress America" model of national security to encompass Latin America, and they supported efforts to develop hemispheric economic and political cooperation.[13]

In response to these threatening European and Latin American developments, Roosevelt was limited in his capacity to act by the ambiguous nature of international affairs and his personal doubts about the best strategy to follow. The period 1931–37 was not the neat "road to war" that hindsight can suggest. In 1936–37 it was uncertain whether another world war would even occur. Hitler talked constantly of his desire for peace, and although German rearmament and the remilitarization of the Rhineland violated the terms of the Versailles Treaty, these infringements were limited so far to issues of German national sovereignty. Furthermore, it was unclear whether Hitler would be able to wage aggressive war. Roosevelt privately suggested that the German people were more peacefully inclined than their leaders. In 1933 Roosevelt sought a return to "that German sanity that existed in the Bismarck days." The president also hoped that the negative economic effects of German rearmament might limit Hitler's options or even provoke a revolution.[14]

It was especially debatable in 1936–37 whether a clear and present danger existed to the western hemisphere. France was aligned with Poland, Czechoslovakia, Britain, and the Soviet Union. The United States operated a large Pacific fleet, and substantial Soviet forces checked Japan in the Far East. Friction between Germany and Italy over the control of Austria suggested latent tensions between the dictators. Furthermore, while Roosevelt was concerned from the start by Nazi Germany, he was much more sanguine about co-opting Mussolini into an ordered international settlement. Particularly before 1935, Roosevelt saw "the admirable Italian gentleman" as a moderate nationalist who wanted to restore social order in Italy.[15] Japan's aims were also unclear, and it was a year into the Spanish Civil War before Tokyo engaged in full-scale conflict with China. These doubts about the international situation are evident in a letter from Roosevelt to his ambassador to Italy William Phillips on 6 February 1937: "What a confusion it all is. Every week changes the picture and the basis for it all lies, I think, not in communism, or the fear of communism, but in Germany and the fear of what the present German leaders are meeting for or being drawn toward . . . I am 'watchfully waiting' even though the phrase carries us back to the difficult days from 1914–17. I would not dare to say this out loud because sometimes it is better to appear much wiser than one really is."[16]

Given the ambiguous nature of international affairs, Roosevelt was unsure about which strategies would reinforce global order. He experimented with schemes requiring the cooperation of the European dictators, supporting, for example, the basic goals of British and French appeasement. On a number of occasions Roosevelt suggested an international conference to settle existing disputes, and he was sympathetic to the notion of offering economic concessions to Germany and Italy. When Roosevelt was asked by the British whether he would cooperate with the League of Nations regarding oil sanctions against Italy after the invasion of Ethiopia, his response was negative, a factor in the British and French decision to offer Mussolini much of Ethiopia in the Hoare-Laval Pact. Roosevelt would only threaten to publicize the names of oil companies trading with Italy. The president called upon businesses to avoid trade with either side, but oil exports to Italy subsequently rose sharply.[17]

Roosevelt's commitment to appeasement waned markedly by 1938, and the president considered parallel, sometimes contradictory, schemes of international deterrence and sanction. He displayed incredulity at the failure of the British to enforce the terms of the Versailles Treaty and was doubtful about the morality and likely effectiveness of British concessions. On the cover of a State Department report from 1937 calling for strong presidential backing for European appeasement efforts, Roosevelt scrawled the line: "half-baked and certainly *not* our current policy."[18] The president repeatedly considered plans to use American economic power to prevent war. In March 1935, for example, he contemplated a collective blockade of Germany if it failed to agree to international disarmament. In October 1937 Roosevelt proposed a vague scheme to "quarantine" international aggressors.[19] These ideas were the first elements of a broader strategy that would emerge from 1935 to 1941: aiding the democracies and the victims of aggression with methods short of war. Roosevelt searched for effective action to promote international order without risking that the United States might directly enter the conflict. This balancing act was complicated by his own uncertainty about how events would play out, as well as by domestic constraints. At this stage the president mainly considered negative schemes involving the selective denial of American resources to aggressors.

Roosevelt's response to Japanese expansion in the Far East was incoherent, reflecting several fundamental dilemmas: the need to contain but not provoke Japan; the fear that the British would not cooperate in a firm stance, leaving the United States acting alone; and domestic isolationist sentiment. The United States began a naval building program in 1933, but to avoid initiating a crisis with Japan, this was accompanied by, in Robert Dallek's words, "a Far Eastern policy of inaction and nonprovocation."[20] In July 1937, in response to the Sino-Japanese War, the United States failed to impose neutrality legislation. Without a formal declaration of war, which was not forthcoming, Roosevelt had discretion over embargoing arms sales to the combatants. Believing that China relied more heavily than Japan on arms imports from the United States, and taking advantage of a public that was strongly pro-Chinese, FDR deferred action on neutrality restrictions, and trade in munitions to China subsequently flourished, as did trade in strategic materials with Japan.[21] This stance can be contrasted with Roosevelt's decision in 1935 not to wait for a formal declaration of war by Italy against Ethiopia before imposing an embargo on arms sales: "they are dropping bombs on Ethiopia—and that is war. Why wait for Mussolini to say so."[22] After the Japanese sank an American gunboat in 1937, Roosevelt privately stated that he wanted to contain Japan with an economic blockade. But he refused to take the lead, in part because of public opposition, and the Brussels Conference, designed to resolve the Far Eastern issue, collapsed.[23] There were clear limits beyond which Roosevelt would not go. The president encouraged British and French resolution, and began secret Anglo-American naval conversations in January 1938 to coordinate fleet movements in the Far East. But FDR shied away from guarantees or alliances.

Despite his growing doubts about appeasement, Roosevelt consistently desired to improve cooperation with Britain. He wanted to establish a condominium of interests with the British—evident, for example, from the Anglo-American naval talks. Roosevelt's views of Britain were ambiguous. Perceptions of a cultural, linguistic, and liberal affinity coexisted with notions of the British state as imperialistic, undemocratic, and class-based. In foreign affairs FDR refused to make American policy "a tail to the British kite," especially on colonial issues. He also tended to view British claims of financial weakness as a rhetorical veneer concealing opulent wealth.[24]

From the British perspective during the 1930s, the United States was as much a competitor as an ally, over such issues as trade, raw materials, air routes, and Venezuelan and Middle Eastern oil. The First World War had clearly demonstrated the importance of American finance, arms, and troops to British success in any major European conflict. Yet the British also learned from the interwar period that in matters of international security the United States offered talk but no action, with Washington constrained by narrow-minded isolationism.[25] Chamberlain remarked in December 1937: "It is always best & safest to count on *nothing* from the Americans but words."[26] Chamberlain's sister simply thought the Americans were "hardly a people to go tiger shooting with."[27] London feared that aid from Washington could easily become a liability because of American hostility toward British trade policy, which gave preference to imperial goods.[28] Despite these ambiguities and concerns on both sides, Roosevelt firmly believed that global order required a cooperative Anglo-American relationship. Thus although founded in part upon "doubt, hope and fear," the period 1937–41 witnessed "the creation of the Anglo-American alliance."[29]

While several of Roosevelt's advisors perceived a Manichean division with Bolshevik Russia, FDR displayed considerable equanimity toward Moscow, illustrated by his extension of diplomatic recognition in 1933. Roosevelt sometimes saw Stalin as devious, even sinister, but he did not believe that Russian communism, in contrast with fascism, relied on force to achieve its international goals. He also thought that the United States and the Soviet Union had much in common, as non-European, noncolonial, and forward-looking states. Roosevelt sent Joseph Davies to Moscow in January 1937 to "win the confidence of Stalin" and abolished the anti-Soviet Division of Eastern European Affairs in the State Department.[30] He also counted on Soviet participation in the suggested blockade of Japan. FDR hoped that recognition by Washington would lead to a close commercial and political relationship between the United States and the Soviet Union, but this never materialized, and considerable disillusionment followed the purge trials, the Nazi-Soviet Pact, and Stalin's invasion of Finland in 1939. However, during the Second World War Roosevelt stepped up his efforts to court Stalin, hoping to draw Moscow into a postwar international system based on great power cooperation.[31]

Given these broader beliefs, how did FDR perceive the first months of the Spanish Civil War? As with Hitler, Mussolini, and Stalin, Roosevelt paid little attention to Spain before 1936. In 1898 a young Franklin Roosevelt had endorsed the Spanish-American war and followed the success of his relative Theodore Roosevelt as a "Rough Rider" and American hero. FDR would later take great pleasure in recounting, and probably inventing, the story that he had run away from school to join the war, only to become ill with scarlet fever. The events of 1898 did reinforce Roosevelt's view that "the Old World is behind the New in everything."[32]

Relations between Spain and the United States were generally poor under Ambassador Irwin B. Laughlin (1931–33), who was personally antagonistic toward the Spanish Republic. Particularly troubling was the question of tariffs, which appeared likely to spark a full-scale trade war between Spain and the United States, as well as the threatened confiscation by Madrid of the International Telephone and Telegraph Company, American-owned and worth $80 million. Roosevelt sympathized with these concerns. Amid demands from left-wing Spaniards to revoke the monopoly given to ITT to run the Spanish telephone system, the president wrote to the new ambassador, Claude Bowers: "We expect of course that the terms . . . will be observed." The president apparently felt easier after the Spanish right won the elections in 1933. "I am glad to see that Spain seems to be going along all right with the change of government." Several State Department officials were hostile toward the Spanish Republic, which they saw as dangerously leftist, similar to Kerensky's government in Russia just before the Bolshevik revolution. But FDR did not share their antipathy. Although he too had some concerns about leftist radicals, Roosevelt broadly sympathized with Madrid. FDR told Bowers that he was "anxious to have Spain" on America's "side of the table," and asked him to undertake a study of the status of democracy in the country.[33] In January 1934 Bowers pressed the president over the State Department's handling of trade relations with Spain. FDR's intervention seems to have won considerable concessions for Madrid.[34] Under Claude Bowers, who strongly sympathized with the Spanish Republic, relations between the United States and Spain generally improved, but in a wider perspective they were of little consequence. Indeed, for all the great powers in the months before July 1936, Spain was quite low on the list of international priorities.

Once the revolt began and Spain suddenly moved to the center stage of European politics, Roosevelt drew on a range of official and unofficial sources of information. The State Department provided detailed briefings on the Spanish conflict. In addition, Roosevelt's European ambassadors communicated directly with the president. Claude Bowers wrote on 23 September 1936 with information about fascist aid, and on 29 October he commented on the arrival of Russian planes and tanks. The ambassador to Italy, William Phillips, provided information in January 1937 on the dispatch of thousands of Italian troops. The ambassador to France, William Bullitt, told FDR in April 1937 that there were sixty thousand Italians in Spain. In addition, Roosevelt employed domestic intelligence. In January 1937 the Military Intelligence Division of the War Department estimated that there were forty to fifty thousand Italian troops in Spain and ten thousand Germans.[35] FDR also followed American press coverage of the Spanish Civil War. In a letter to Claude Bowers, the president noted: "Over here the Hearst papers and most of the conservative editors are playing up all kinds of atrocities on the part of what they call the Communist government in Madrid—nothing about atrocities on the part of the rebels."[36] In 1937 Roosevelt paid growing attention to events in Spain and searched for new sources of information. For example, Bowers wrote on 31 March that an American journalist had sent questionnaires to the leaders of both sides in Spain, and that another American journalist had been making speeches for the Nationalists. FDR quickly ordered his assistant secretary to get hold of the questionnaires and find out what this pro-Nationalist journalist had been doing. In typical fashion, neither request should mention the president's name.[37]

Still, much about the war remained unclear and different sources contradicted each other. Reports in 1937 stated that the Republic would win, and then that the Nationalists would win, with the latter predominating as the year progressed.[38] In addition, the president was not always well informed. On 20 April 1938 he publicly asserted as "probably true" reports that American bombs had reached Franco's forces via Germany, Holland, Belgium, or

England. However, as Joseph Green, head of the Office of Arms and Munitions Control, later commented, from July 1936 to April 1938 the United States did not export any bombs to any of these countries.[39]

From its outbreak, FDR realized that the Spanish Civil War was not merely an Iberian tragedy; it was also a major international crisis. In the weeks before the Spanish generals rose, Roosevelt was already deeply worried about the prospects for European peace. Given these fears, he believed that the Spanish Civil War could easily spark a wider European conflagration. By the end of August 1936 he said that Spain was his "greatest worry." The president's concern that European war could break out prevented him from traveling to the West Coast on a campaign trip for the November presidential election. The journalist Arthur Krock, who spent an evening with Roosevelt in August 1936, noted: "It may be that by October [FDR] will have to abandon the campaign, so far as travel is concerned, because of the crisis that appears to be heading up in Europe."[40]

In the summer of 1936 Roosevelt's pro-Loyalism was immediately evident in a conversation with Tom Connally, when the president revealed that his sympathies were with the Spanish government.[41] This support was also demonstrated a year later, on 8 July 1937, when Roosevelt saw the world première of the pro-Loyalist film *Spanish Earth* at the White House. Ernest Hemingway had written and recorded the commentary, and was present at the screening along with the filmmaker Joris Ivens, the journalist Martha Gellhorn, Eleanor Roosevelt, the president's son James Roosevelt, and several military advisors. First the guests had dinner, which Hemingway described as "rainwater soup followed by rubber squab, a nice wilted salad and a cake some admirer had sent in." FDR sat next to Ivens during the screening and asked a series of questions about the military events in Spain, the French and Russian tanks shown in the film, and whether they had been effective in battle. Afterward FDR told Ivens he liked the film very much and suggested emphasizing that "the Spaniards are fighting, not merely for the right to their own government," but also for the right to cultivate land that the old order had forcibly left barren. Gellhorn later wrote to Eleanor, conveying her friends' satisfaction that Eleanor "and Mr. Roosevelt said to make it stronger . . . by underlining the causes of the conflict." "Spain is a vicarious sacrifice for all of us," FDR told Gellhorn, who recalled that overall "Mrs. Roosevelt was *completely* sympathetic, and so was *he*."[42]

According to the secretary of the interior, Harold Ickes, in the fall of 1937 Roosevelt had thought that "it was only a question of time . . . until Franco would win in Spain." But the president's confidence was restored by the

Republican offensive in Teruel in December.[43] FDR's political ideals were radically different from those of the conservative military dictator General Franco, who boasted of eliminating the legacy of the Enlightenment, and believed that democracy and liberalism would inevitably lead to communism. The president never once suggested common ground with Franco, as he did, for example, with Mussolini.[44] As we saw, FDR was also critical of the tendency of the Hearst press to magnify Loyalist atrocities. Roosevelt profoundly disliked William Hearst, who broke with him in 1935 and attacked the New Deal. That Hearst would back Franco was a further reason for Roosevelt to favor the Loyalists.[45]

However, Roosevelt's sympathies for the Spanish Republic coexisted with perceptions that the Loyalists were radical leftists. In his conversation with Tom Connally in 1936, Roosevelt suggested that the Spanish government was "far from 'democratic' as we understood the term." Similarly, in January 1937 he distanced himself from both sides fighting in Spain by telling the publisher of the newspaper *La Prensa*, José Camprubi: "I am not a Fascist, but I am not a Communist either." Camprubi interpreted this statement as signaling Roosevelt's belief that the struggle in Spain was between these two doctrines.[46]

During 1937 a clear development is evident in Roosevelt's thinking about the Spanish Civil War. Initially perceiving Spain in terms of its potential for sparking a wider European war, Roosevelt in 1937 became more concerned about the extent of fascist intervention. On 13 February 1937 Arthur Krock again visited FDR, and the two men discussed the Spanish Civil War. The president claimed that "there probably wasn't going to be a war over Spain; it would have come already if there was to be a war." However, in the same conversation, "the President talked a bit about Europe. He is concerned over the number of Italians in Spain—20,000 fighting men at least, he has heard." Roosevelt told Ickes in February 1937 that forty thousand Italian troops were fighting for Franco. In March Roosevelt heard that Germany would not permit the Republican regime to continue in Spain. In the fall of 1937 the undersecretary of state Sumner Welles thought that FDR was "far more preoccupied with the trend in world affairs than he had been before." There was not even "the slightest possibility that either England or France would take a firm stand" against aggression. In particular, Welles recalled, he and the president "discussed the pusillanimous role that both had so far played in the Spanish Civil War . . . The President was especially incensed over the official farce that the submarines in the Mediterranean attacking ships carrying supplies to the Spanish Republic were 'of unknown nationality' when every man and woman in Western Europe was well aware that they were Italian."[47] Fascist intervention in Spain contributed to the rise of international lawlessness and aggression, which Roosevelt described in October 1937 as "a state of international anarchy and instability."[48] Pledges from Berlin and Rome not to intervene in Spain proved meaningless, ships were torpedoed in the Mediterranean by Italian submarines, and civilians in Spain were killed by German and Italian bombers.

Despite Roosevelt's increasing concerns about German and Italian intervention in the Spanish Civil War, the president at this stage did not identify the Republicans and the Nationalists with a broader European confrontation between fixed international coalitions. It was questionable whether fascist cooperation in Spain foreshadowed a general alliance given the ambiguous nature of international events. In 1937, even after Mussolini's intervention in Spain, Roosevelt still saw him as a potential force for peace. The president suggested in a letter to Mussolini in July that from a personal meeting between the two men, "great good might come."[49]

Roosevelt's perceptions of the British and Soviet role in the Spanish Civil War in 1936–37 reflected his wider beliefs. FDR initially saw nonintervention in Spain as an admirable opportunity to collaborate with Britain. Anthony Eden noted on 6 July 1937 that with regard to Spanish policy, "Roosevelt desired to do nothing without first consulting us."[50] In contrast with several of his advisors, as well as with the British government, Roosevelt does not appear to have shown any concern at all about Soviet intervention in Spain. Eden told the House of Commons in November 1936 that in terms of breaching nonintervention, there were governments (namely the USSR) more to blame than either Germany or Italy. In stark contrast, Roosevelt was relieved to hear about stiffening Loyalist resistance in November 1936, after the arrival of Soviet arms and the formation of the international brigades. Ickes wrote: "I know that after this talk the president felt that the situation of the Spanish Government was not as desperate as he thought it was."[51] It is noticeable that when Roosevelt considered embargoing arms sales to the aggressor states in 1937 because of their intervention in Spain, he had no intention of including the USSR in this category.

In 1936–37 Roosevelt held a coherent series of beliefs about the Spanish Civil War and wider international politics. In 1936 he was primarily concerned with the disastrous possibility that Spain would spark a general European war. As this outcome became less probable in 1937, Roosevelt began focusing on the extent of fascist intervention. The president was sympathetic to the Loyalists from the start but unsure of their democratic credentials. Roosevelt's views of the Spanish Civil War also reflected his wider desire to cooperate with Britain and his tendency to downplay the Soviet threat to international peace and security. This set of beliefs would consistently shape Roosevelt's policy preferences during the first eighteen months of the war.

CHAPTER 4

The Arms Embargo

President Roosevelt behaved in the manner of a true gentleman. His neutrality legislation, stopping export of war materials to either side—the quick manner in which it was passed and carried into effect—is a gesture we Nationalists shall never forget.—General Franco, February 1937.[1]

Once sustained warfare had broken out in Spain, the United States was faced with policy decisions that would have major repercussions for the outcome of the Spanish Civil War and broader European security. Given existing American foreign policy and isolationist sentiment in 1936, there was no question that the United States might send troops to Spain, or even naval vessels, except to rescue U.S. citizens from the war.[2] The key issue was whether Washington would allow either the Nationalist rebels or the Spanish Republic to purchase American weapons on the open market.

During the first weeks of the Spanish Civil War, the president was away from Washington on tour, and as a result the State Department and the American ambassadors in Europe took an active role in fashioning the "moral" embargo on arms sales to both sides in Spain. While the domestic federal bureaucracy had increased substantially during the 1930s as a result of the New Deal, the foreign policy bureaucracy remained small and was dominated by the State Department and the U.S. Navy. Toward the end of the 1930s, in part because of Roosevelt's style and decision-making predilections, other departments such as the Treasury played an important role in diplomacy. The influence of bureaucrats varied markedly, with the key to an official's power being his access to and relationship with FDR rather than his formal position alone.

Cautious, studious, and humble, Secretary of State Cordell Hull appeared to be above politics, despite his twenty-three years in Congress. Hull was a committed Wilsonian with a moralistic approach to international relations, who believed that the path to peace and security lay in reducing tariff barriers and promoting disarmament. The secretary sought a cooperative relationship with Britain and France. He also viewed the noninterventionist "good neighbor" policy in Latin America as both a strategy for building hemispheric solidarity and an exemplary model for other nations to copy.[3]

American nonintervention in Spain appeared to promote several of Hull's core foreign policy beliefs, and the secretary became one of the strongest advocates of the American embargo both during and after the Spanish Civil War. Hull explained in his memoirs that "the initiative in dealing with the Spanish problem lay with the European nations." It would have been "unthinkable" to oppose British and French efforts to restrict arms sales to Spain given their greater proximity to the war.[4] On 4 August 1936 the French discussed with Hull their proposals for a European nonintervention agreement, and clearly signaled the importance of a parallel American embargo to limit the war to Spain.[5] Hull believed, in addition, that selling arms to either side in Spain would quickly entangle the United States in the civil war, because Washington would have to guarantee the delivery of the weapons.[6] Hull also became deeply concerned that any American initiatives in Spain might interfere with efforts to develop hemispheric solidarity through the "good neighbor" policy. He recognized the profound nature of the divisions in Latin America over the Spanish Civil War, which could easily be exacerbated by any attempt on the part of Washington to intervene in Spain.[7]

President Roosevelt valued Hull's place in the administration because of his attention to detail, and his popularity with the press and Congress. In a speech at Chautauqua in August 1936, the president praised Hull as "that wise and experienced man whose statesmanship has met with such wide approval."[8] But despite FDR's sympathies with many of Hull's views, the two men never enjoyed close relations. The lack of intimate conversations about the Spanish Civil War between the president and his secretary of state is noticeable and reflected wider personal issues between Roosevelt and Hull.[9]

By 1936 senior government officials had become loosely divided into "realists" and "idealists" (labels chosen, unsurprisingly, by the realists). Although these groups were never firmly delineated, realists tended to be suspicious of Britain and the Soviet Union, and perceived American interests as being essentially hemispheric. They included men such as Sumner Welles, who became undersecretary of state in 1937 after a stint as ambassador to Cuba. Like FDR, Welles grew up in a privileged family and went to Harvard. He retained a rather aristocratic and aloof air toward many people, but was close to the president. He opposed fascism but wanted America to "ride on no crusades." Welles played a significant role in developing the "good neighbor" policy and tended to see events in Spain through the Latin American lens. Supporting the Spanish Loyalists would complicate his long-term aim of fostering closer ties between the American republics.[10] Like Welles, the assistant secretary R. Walton Moore firmly backed an embargo on arms sales to Spain. Moore was an old friend of Hull and in many respects an isolationist, desiring that the United States remain detached from European politics. According to Moore, the key to European security lay in satisfying Germany's demands for raw materials. Completing this realist triumvirate was William Phillips, who was undersecretary of state from 1933 to 1936, before becoming ambassador to Italy. Phillips supported European efforts at appeasement and strongly favored the Spanish embargo.[11]

William Phillips was one of several American officials who expressed concern at the radical leftist nature of the Spanish Republic. Their perceptions undermined sympathy for Madrid and provided an additional reason to deny arms sales to a recognized government. The American ambassador to Spain, Irwin B. Laughlin, was skeptical from the first, writing in 1931 that the monarchy had collapsed due to "widespread Bolshevistic influences."[12] American diplomats tended to be doubtful about the likelihood of democracy in Spain, based in part on their belief that the Spanish national character was wholly unsuited to representative government.[13]

Fears of imminent Bolshevik revolution increased after the Spanish Civil War broke out. What the generals rose to avoid, their *pronunciamiento* precipitated. In Loyalist Spain there was a massive collectivization of land and industry: 70 percent of businesses in Barcelona were collectivized, including plants owned by Ford and General Motors. Revolutionary justice produced twenty thousand dead in a few months, including thousands of priests and nuns. Republican killings tended to be the work of outraged groups beyond government control, while those by Nationalists were official policy and greater in scale. Republican killings also lessened dramatically as the war progressed. But the damage had already been done to the image of the Loyalists. The *New York Times* described a leftist "reign of terror" in Barcelona.[14] Washington was concerned about attacks on American citizens, who were mostly in government-held territory, and about the confiscation of American-owned businesses. On 3 August 1936 Phillips referred to the "so-called rebels" and noted that "if the Government wins, as now seems likely, communism throughout Europe will be immensely stimulated."[15] American officials in Spain regularly described the Spanish Loyalists as "Reds."[16]

By contrast, "idealists" tended toward a broader conception of American interests, were more positive about cooperation with Britain, and focused on Germany as a security threat. The secretary of the interior, Harold Ickes, was energetic, self-confident, and an ardent interventionist. He sought a tough stand against the fascist states and almost single-handedly prevented the sale of helium to Germany in 1938, fearing that it would be used for military purposes. The secretary of the treasury, Henry Morgenthau, was close to the president and, like Ickes, highlighted the danger of German aggression. As the only Jewish member of Roosevelt's cabinet, Morgenthau pushed for a more generous policy toward Jewish refugees. By the end of 1937 the idealists displayed considerable sympathy for the Spanish Republic, and began to question the wisdom of the embargo policy. However, in the summer of 1936 they joined realists in supporting a policy of nonintervention in Spain as a means of limiting the conflict to the Iberian Peninsula.

Roosevelt did not always trust career diplomats, believing that mediocrity could rise to the top of the profession simply by not offending anyone.[17] In part because of this, the president listened closely to the European ambassadors he had appointed. In 1936 these ambassadors, to a man, supported American nonintervention in the Spanish Civil War. The ambassador to Spain, Claude Bowers, was a partisan for the Spanish Republic but initially urged strict American neutrality.[18] Bowers had received the ambassadorship as a reward for his service in Roosevelt's presidential campaign in 1932. Away from Madrid when the war began, Bowers spent the conflict in St. Jean de Luz in southern France. The ambassador was a historian of the Founding Fathers and perceived the Spanish Nationalists and Loyalists as modern-day Hamiltonians and Jeffersonians. Franco was, after all, aligned with the richest and most powerful elements of Spanish society. Summing up the situation after a year of the war, Bowers concluded: "This is a war against the Republic. It is frankly a war to destroy democracy in Spain. It is a war of Italy and Germany against the Spanish Government."[19]

Despite these strong sentiments, Bowers at first thought that the United States should keep out of the conflict. If Spain were left alone by the great powers the Loyalists would win, and an American embargo would serve as an example to other states. By the middle of 1937, Bowers privately determined that the embargo was preventing the recognized government of Spain from defending itself, although he was as yet unwilling to lobby Washington for a change of policy.

Many State Department officials had little time for Bowers, the popular historian. The dramatic and colorful style of his reports represented the opposite of Hull's meticulous, detailed, and careful approach. Frankly, many thought that Bowers was amateurish.[20] The ambassador was well liked by the president, however, who came to increasingly sympathize with Bowers's views about the Spanish Civil War. In 1925 FDR reviewed Bowers's book on Jefferson and Hamilton: "I felt like saying 'At last' as I read Mr. Claude G. Bowers' thrilling 'Hamilton and Jefferson,'" Roosevelt wrote. "Jefferson managed a mobilization of the masses against the autocracy of the few . . . I wonder if, a century and a quarter later, the same contending forces are not again mobilizing. Hamiltons we have today. Is a Jefferson on the horizon?"[21] For many Americans, of course, the Jefferson on the horizon would soon be the reviewer himself.

After Bowers had been appointed ambassador to Spain, FDR asked him to directly contact the White House whenever he found "anything" that he thought the president "should know."[22] In early 1937 the president told Bowers: "We are all following closely your scene and, as you know, I am very much aware of the great difficulties which are yours. The job has been an upstanding one and as a Historian you should get some comfort from the knowledge that history, if not the Chicago Tribune, will record it so."[23] In 1937 there was apparently some consideration in the State Department to removing Bowers from his post. The president resisted this notion. On 15 June 1937 Roosevelt wrote to Hull with a list of new ambassadorial appointments, including the line "Claude Bowers (to remain)."[24]

William C. Bullitt, who was ambassador to the USSR before becoming ambassador to France in October 1936, enjoyed a close relationship with both President Roosevelt and foreign diplomats and tended toward a dramatic view of international politics as a world of secrecy and intrigue. Bullitt argued that European war could be avoided through Franco-German reconciliation, and that any American intervention in Spain would only serve to complicate this objective. Bullitt's disinclination to aid the Spanish Republic was heightened by his marked distrust for the Soviet Union. Bullitt's years in Moscow had turned him into a staunch anticommunist. In November 1936 he argued that the European states needed to submerge their hatreds or hand "Europe over to the Bolsheviks."[25]

Stanley Hornbeck, head of the Far Eastern Division in the State Department, was one of very few American foreign policy officials to dissent in 1936 from the policy of nonintervention in Spain. He used arguments that would later gain wide currency as the controversy over Spanish policy deepened: "Would not the placing of a prohibition by the American government upon sale of arms by American nationals to the Spanish Government or to both of the contending groups in Spain, insofar as it interfered with the right of the Spanish Government to purchase arms amount to an action of intervention by the American Government?" Nonintervention in Spain might set a dangerous precedent for American foreign policy in future civil wars: would the United States always want to treat equally a recognized government and a group of rebels?[26] In 1936, however, Hornbeck stood virtually alone in this position. In the foreign policy bureaucracy, men who disagreed on many points of foreign affairs agreed on this one issue: the United States should not get embroiled in the Spanish Civil War.

Roosevelt's foreign policy officials primarily considered the impact of the Spanish Civil War on international politics, but for FDR there was a crucial second dimension—the effect of the war on the upcoming presidential election of November 1936. Roosevelt went on to win by a landslide (27.7 million votes to 16.7 million votes). But the scale of this impending victory was not obvious in the summer of 1936, and the election provided clear incentives to avoid risky international policies given the isolationist mood of the American public.

By 1936 isolationism was a widespread sentiment in the United States, one shared by socialists as well as conservative businessmen. Isolationists did not pursue substantive economic and political insulation. The United States, after all, traded extensively, sought a protective role over the western hemisphere as well as over territories in the Far East, and signed numerous treaties. Its financial power had been deployed to win the First World War, and then to underwrite European economic stabilization in the 1920s. Instead, isolationists sought above all to distance the United States from the contagion of European diplomacy and war. They embodied a traditional antipathy toward "Old World" intrigues evident in George Washington's farewell address, sharpened by the desire to avoid a repetition of the American entry into war in 1917. By the 1930s many Americans believed that the decision to go to war had been orchestrated by a shadowy cabal of arms manufacturers and financiers. One isolationist Republican, Senator Gerald Nye, attempted to prove this theory by leading a well-publicized Senate investigation into the nefarious activities of the munitions industry. Most isolationists favored appeasement to avoid war and saw European relations in the 1930s as merely the latest chapter in a traditional jockeying for power. Isolationists tended to think that European war was inevitable, while internationalists believed that it could be avoided with appropriate American diplomacy.[27]

Differences existed among isolationists, for example over the need for defensive preparations in the western hemisphere, but the drift toward

European conflict in the 1930s consolidated and strengthened this hetero-geneous coalition. The desire to avoid repeating the experience of 1917–18 led to the congressional neutrality acts (1935–39), which prevented the sell-ing of arms or the lending of money to countries at war, and stopped Ameri-cans from sailing on belligerent ships. Isolationists also defeated Roose-velt's attempt to join the World Court in 1935.[28]

As expected, the first reaction of prominent American isolationists to the Spanish Civil War was to recommend strict nonintervention by the United States. On 14 August 1936, ten senators, including Nye, urged the president to make a statement of American neutrality. Nye hinted that he might en-dorse Roosevelt's reelection campaign. Roosevelt subsequently stressed his peace record in a speech at Chautauqua, without specifically mentioning the Spanish Civil War. "We shun political commitments," said the presi-dent, who promised to do everything in his power to keep the United States out of foreign wars.[29]

It might appear that international and domestic constraints forced Roosevelt into adopting an arms embargo on Spain. But these pressures were unnecessary, because Roosevelt personally supported noninterven-tion from the start. Indeed, the enactment of the moral embargo correlates closely with his individual perceptions of the Spanish Civil War.

Although Roosevelt was a Loyalist sympathizer in 1936, he did not see a victory by Franco in itself as a serious defeat for American interests. In-stead, he perceived the Spanish Civil War as a major threat to European peace, and wanted the conflict to be left to the Spaniards. FDR strongly supported an embargo on arms sales as the best means of cooperating with European efforts to limit the war to Spain. After American arms dealers openly challenged the moral embargo, the president pushed for a legal em-bargo, which Congress quickly introduced.

The president's son, Elliott Roosevelt, recalled that in the summer of 1936 his father considered leading a campaign to promote international nonintervention in the Spanish Civil War, before significant foreign or do-mestic pressures had yet arisen: "On this trip, foreign affairs and the dic-tator's march to conquest occupied him more than the impending political contest. He turned over in his mind a plan for calling a conference of the seven great powers—the United States, Britain, France, the USSR, Japan, Germany, and Italy—as a step towards preventing the spread of war be-yond the frontiers of Spain."[30] In August 1936 the *New York Times* reported that Roosevelt was hoping to assemble world leaders in a conference to encourage disarmament and free trade, and avert a general war. FDR's secretary would not repudiate the story.[31] Elliott Roosevelt wrote that fears of domestic opposition prevented the conference idea from being developed: "Any whisper of the plan would be explosive with the United States blinkered by isolationism."[32]

Yet there was an obvious reason why Roosevelt did not pursue a peace conference to quarantine the Spanish Civil War: the European states were themselves drawing up a nonintervention agreement. Twenty-six countries accepted the French government's proposals, and the first meeting of the International Nonintervention Committee took place on 9 September 1936. Unsurprisingly, given Roosevelt's desire to enact a similar plan, the president looked very favorably upon the nonintervention proposal. Senator Tom Connally recalled that FDR was optimistic about its likely success. "So far, a total of twenty-seven European countries . . . had agreed to the non-intervention policy and [Roosevelt] saw no reason why we shouldn't amend the Neutrality Act to cover the Spanish Civil War, too."[33]

With knowledge of European efforts at collective neutrality, and with Roosevelt's full backing, a meeting in the State Department on 5 August decided to base Washington's policy toward the Spanish Civil War on the "clearly defined" principles of nonintervention embodied in the Montevideo Treaty of 1933 with the Latin American states. The Roosevelt administration had repeatedly committed itself to nonintervention as a guiding foreign policy standard. Four months later, in December 1936, the United States signed the Declaration of Buenos Aires, again promising not to intervene in the affairs of the other American nations.[34]

The Spanish embargo was portrayed by the administration as a natural and predictable choice, in line with the established policy of nonintervention. After all, in the Monroe Doctrine of 1823 the United States had promised "not to interfere in the internal concerns of [the European] powers." But the embargo also represented a sharp deviation from customary international law and traditional American foreign policy, both of which countenanced the sale of arms to recognized governments facing a rebellion. The Monroe Doctrine also declared that the United States would "consider the [foreign] government de facto as the legitimate government for us [and] cultivate friendly relations with it." Since 1912 only Mexico had been denied arms to quell a revolt, and American secretaries of state had produced voluminous correspondence over the years upholding the right of U.S. citizens to trade as permitted under international law.

Existing neutrality legislation did not cover civil wars, so the resulting policy was a "moral" rather than a legal embargo. The government hoped that patriotism would prevent Americans from selling arms to Spain. William Phillips's letter of 7 August to American diplomatic offices explained that in regard to nonintervention in Spain, "American citizens, both at home and abroad, are patriotically observing this well-recognized American policy."[35] A moral embargo had similarly been enacted in the Italian-Ethiopian War of 1935 against raw material exports, but with mixed results.[36] Despite the lack of legal enforcement, the embargo was an important factor in getting Berlin and Rome to announce a policy of nonintervention in Spain. Indeed, without an American embargo the French scheme might never have got off the ground.[37]

On 10 August the administration was forced to publicly outline its policy toward the Spanish Civil War, when the Glenn L. Martin Company requested the State Department's position on the sale of bombers to the Spanish government. William Phillips recognized that any answer had to be carefully considered, since it would represent "a far reaching precedent." One option was simply to reiterate the administration's general policy of nonintervention. Phillips's draft reply to the Glenn L. Martin Company was read to the president, who approved in general but added: "Make it stronger! Make it stronger!" Roosevelt "wished to go further and to intimate that any such sale would not be in line with the policy of the government." The president approved the final draft, then "had considerable doubts" (we do not know why) before finally agreeing to release the letter. The statement concluded that the proposed sale of bombers would contravene "the spirit of the Government's policy."[38] On 21 August Roosevelt told assembled journalists to ask the State Department for the text of the letter. "I can't tell you the language and it is one of those things where you have to follow the language, word for word. But it is damn good and it went out two weeks ago."[39]

According to the U.S. government, the moral embargo was an act of international cooperation in the cause of peace. But given the widespread American wish to remain aloof from European high politics, the embargo was introduced as an independent parallel measure. This ambiguity about relations with Europe was evident when Norman Thomas, the American socialist leader, visited Cordell Hull. Thomas pointedly asked: "Why does our government follow a policy which so clearly helps the fascists?" "Well Mr. Thomas," replied Hull, "you see the French and British do it that way and they are much nearer than we are." Noting Thomas's reaction, Hull quickly qualified his statement: "Not, of course, that our Spanish policy is a mere copy of theirs."[40]

Despite the moral embargo, the Spanish Republic sought to buy large quantities of arms in the United States. The Loyalist ambassador to Mexico thought that America was "a prospect of unlimited opportunities," and set about collecting a variety of American aircraft in Mexico, in order to ship them to Spain. There were occasional Loyalist successes: for example, a handful of American planes reached Spain via France. But the State Department reacted swiftly and effectively against a range of schemes to trans-ship arms through Mexico, Canada, and elsewhere, eventually gaining the cooperation of the pro-Loyalist Mexican government.[41]

American officials were hopeful that the moral embargo would help to create a *cordon sanitaire* around the Spanish Civil War, thereby leaving the war to the Spaniards. But significant problems arose. In the first place, the United States was aware by 20 August that the British sought to limit breaches of nonintervention, rather than enforce an embargo.[42] The Non-Intervention Committee subsequently did little to prevent or even restrain intervention in Spain. German and Italian infusions of aid to the Nationalists enabled rapid progress in the march on Madrid in August and September 1936. General Mola's northern army captured Irún in September and cut off the Basque region from the rest of Loyalist Spain, before turning toward the capital. Franco's African forces headed north from Seville, taking village after village and spreading terror in their wake. The Nationalists employed systematic torture and massacres to cure Spain of its infection by liberalism and communism. In Badajoz nearly two thousand leftists were herded into the bullring and cut down by machine guns. It was a colonial campaign, fought by the Nationalists against their own people. With Mola and Franco heading toward a rendezvous in Madrid, the Republican government fled to Valencia and a rebel victory by Christmas appeared certain. Italy and Germany recognized the Nationalists in November 1936. The Rubicon was crossed and Franco could not be allowed to lose.

But Madrid unexpectedly held, after the arrival in October of Soviet arms and the international brigades. The people of the capital fought a desperate defense under banners that read: "Madrid Will Be the Tomb of Fascism." Nationalist troops were halted on the campus of the University of Madrid, and both sides fought ferociously over philosophy and science classrooms. The city would resist for another two and a half years.

As well as the illusory nature of international nonintervention in the Spanish Civil War, there was a second problem with Washington's moral embargo. It lacked any method of enforcement, and if an American arms dealer was determined to sell weapons to either side in Spain, there was

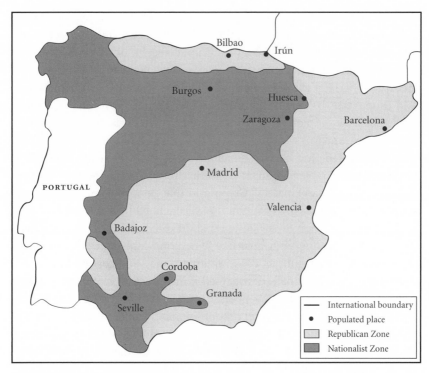

Spain, August–September, 1936

little that the administration could do about it. On 24 December Robert Cuse simply ignored the moral embargo and requested licenses to directly export almost $3 million of arms to the Loyalists. The Spanish government had apparently decided that a direct challenge to the moral embargo was preferable to the unreliable and surreptitious delivery of weapons, even at the risk of provoking a legal embargo. Joseph C. Green, head of the Office of Arms and Munitions Control, called Cuse "the most engaging rascal he had ever met."[43] Cuse was Russian by birth, which led to considerable but probably unfounded speculation that he was a Soviet agent. In fact Cuse was a New Jersey aircraft dealer, who, as he reported it, "preferred to play the game openly."[44]

Cuse's efforts were joined by those of Richard Dinely, who attempted one of the most extraordinary scams in American history. Dinely, an ex-marine, warmed up by selling $77,000 of arms to Cuban revolutionaries who obtained the money by kidnapping wealthy Cubans. Dinely received the money but never exported the arms, knowing that Mexico would deny the necessary permits. Using this successful swindle as a model, Dinely gained an armaments contract for $9 million with the Spanish government. The plan was to have the money paid upon receipt of an export permit, in the knowledge that a subsequent congressional embargo would revoke all existing permits and leave Dinely $9 million richer. When Joseph Green told Dinely that he was trying to swindle a friendly government, Dinely replied that he did not care, "as long as he received his nine million dollars." Dinely, who was vice-president of the Anti-Communist League of California, professed that he was reluctant to violate American policy: "but he thought that he was doing a patriotic thing in obtaining nine million dollars for American citizens." Green said that he would contact the staff at the Spanish embassy to caution them. Dinely had no objection to this, "although such action might put a crimp in the deal."[45] That the Spanish Republic was dealing with men like Dinely indicates its desperation for weapons and, as a result, its vulnerability to fraud and corruption.

Roosevelt was personally determined to introduce legislation that would frustrate Cuse's and Dinely's plans. In December 1936 the British and French hoped that foreign intervention in Spain could be curtailed. Thus it was a particularly unpropitious moment for large-scale American arms sales to the Loyalists. The United States was aware that Berlin was using Cuse's shipment to justify continuing its own intervention in Spain.[46] The movement to legislate the moral embargo was not based on considered analysis; instead it represented a desperate attempt to enact a law before Cuse could physically ship the weapons from the United States. The popular image at the time was of a race between Cuse and Congress. Green later wrote: "It is certainly true that the obligatory and reluctant issue of these export licenses to Cuse and Dinely and the great publicity which was given to their issuance made the passage of the Joint Resolution of 8 January almost inevitable."[47]

In December 1936 Green wanted to release details to the press about Cuse's application to export arms, but Assistant Secretary Moore had doubts. FDR, however, had none: "Tell Joe Green to go ahead."[48] Moore publicly tapped into the widespread hostility toward war profiteers by comparing Cuse to Mammon in *Paradise Lost*. Moore added that every other American aircraft manufacturer had patriotically resisted the temptation to profit from the Spanish Civil War. The reality was somewhat different: by the third week of September 1936, the Spanish Republican ambassador to Mexico had received offers from the United States of at least 128 aircraft, as well as unlimited mountain guns, 450,000 rifles, and 5,400 machine guns.[49]

At a press conference on 29 December Roosevelt offered his own opinion of Cuse, describing the export request as "a perfectly legal but thoroughly unpatriotic act." It was, he said, "a rather good example of the need of some power in the Executive." Roosevelt declared that rapid legislation was required to defeat Cuse and favored granting the president discretionary powers to introduce an arms embargo in cases of civil war. "Obviously," Roosevelt said, "there should be further discretion invested in the President with the appropriate penalties to take care of internal strife . . . civil war means anything or nothing; and the circumstances and the particular case must be decided on by somebody who has authority 365 days of the year." When a reporter noted that selling arms to Spain would create jobs, Roosevelt responded with an analogy to the First World War: "Of course, that particular plea was made in 1914 and 1915 and 1916, in just the same way. They said that the export of machine guns would give work to Americans. That does not mean it was the right thing to do." The State Department apologized to the German government for Cuse's shipment, but said that because of ongoing repairs, the export of the arms would likely be delayed by up to six months.[50]

It soon became apparent that instead of months, the shipment would be ready in a matter of days. As a result FDR shifted his position and now supported a mandatory embargo on arms sales to Spain, with no executive discretion. Key Pittman, head of the Senate Foreign Relations Committee, suggested that otherwise proposals could be delayed "for a day or so."[51] This hurried administration decision would prove in the end to be far more important than Roosevelt at the time realized, because it placed the embargo under congressional control. The president was willing to sacrifice executive discretion because time was of the essence. He also wanted to avoid an argument with congressional isolationists given the coming "court-packing" controversy, which arose when Roosevelt tried and failed to expand the size of the Supreme Court after a series of legal rulings against New Deal legislation. The president does not appear to have envisaged in January 1937 that he might later want to lift the embargo. His hasty choice was to have unexpected consequences when he radically altered his views of the Spanish Civil War in 1938.

The congressional debate on the Spanish embargo on 6 January 1937 was interrupted by Roosevelt's Annual Message to Congress, in which he briefly mentioned the need for legislation in regard to Spain before focusing on domestic matters.[52] The debate on the arms embargo was limited partly because at that very moment, in New York harbor, Cuse's arms were being hurriedly placed on the freighter *Mar Cantabrico*, destined for Spain. The bill passed unanimously in the Senate and by 411 votes to 1 in the House, but opinion was less nearly unanimous than the votes suggested. Senator Nye, for example, was prepared to vote for the bill to keep the United States out of a European war, but he made it clear that in his view the embargo was an attempt to align with Britain and France, would advantage the rebels, and was not therefore a neutral measure. This was one of the first indications of the fragility of liberal isolationist support for the Spanish embargo.

Senator Pittman, by contrast, emphasized that his colleagues should "not . . . think of either of the opposing forces in Spain but think of our peace and our own country." For Pittman, both sides in Spain represented "foreign theories of government." Representative John T. Bernard was the only congressman who voted against the embargo. Bernard deliberately raised technical issues to delay proceedings until 8 January, thus allowing the *Mar Cantabrico* to slip away. The Loyalist victory was short-lived, because Franco's forces captured the ship en route and executed her Spanish crew.[53] Meanwhile, Richard Dinely was aghast at the collapse of his scheme. "After we've been working on this deal for months, the President starts shooting off and the thing gets all screwed up."[54]

Four months later, on 1 May 1937, Congress introduced a permanent Neutrality Act. It was the product of a two-year search for legislation to prevent American entry into foreign wars. Whenever the president found a state of war to exist, he would prohibit arms sales and loans to combatants, as well as travel by American citizens on belligerent ships. In an attempt to guarantee peace for the United States while enabling American businesses to trade in wartime, the Neutrality Act gave the president discretionary power to introduce the "cash and carry" clause, which would restrict nonmilitary trade with belligerents to foreign ships, with payment to be offered immediately. In accordance with Roosevelt's original preference back in December, the new act also gave the president discretionary power to impose arms embargoes in civil wars.[55]

There was one exception: the Spanish Civil War. Sam McReynolds, the chairman of the House Committee on Foreign Affairs, explicitly told the House that the new bill did not repeal the Spanish embargo of 8 January, a statement that was politically rather than legally binding.[56] Despite certain elements in the neutrality bill which dissatisfied Hull and FDR, the president was unwilling to begin a major political fight in Congress in a period when his influence was declining. The president immediately applied the new law to Spain. "A state of civil strife unhappily exists in Spain,"

Roosevelt wrote, and "the export of arms from . . . the United States . . . would threaten and endanger the peace of the United States."[57] The Spanish embargo had now been proclaimed on three separate occasions inside ten months: once as a patriotic duty, again as a congressional resolution, and yet again at the discretion of the president.

Realizing that FDR sympathized with the Loyalists but had at the same time introduced an arms embargo undermining the Spanish Republic's war effort, several commentators concluded that the president must have been coerced into the nonintervention policy.[58] Yet Roosevelt saw no important conflict in 1936–37 between his moderate sympathy for the Loyalists and his support for the American embargo. That this conflict did not necessarily arise is indicated by the stance of the ambassador to Spain, Claude Bowers. In 1936–37 Bowers favored the Spanish Republic far more resolutely than Roosevelt did, consistently perceiving the fight as one between fascism and democracy. But Bowers also thought that the Spanish Civil War was a European rather than an American problem. On 26 August 1936 the ambassador wrote: "we must not become involved by any kind of meddling with the domestic quarrel of Spain." On 23 September he added: "this is a serious European quarrel in which we have no proper part." To maintain the image of American neutrality in Spain, Bowers thought that political leaders in the United States should avoid making any comments at all on "the merits of the [Spanish] controversy."[59]

"What an unfortunate and terrible catastrophe in Spain!," replied Roosevelt to Bowers in September 1936. Still, the president had no desire to intervene and no intention of doing so. Roosevelt personally sought to introduce an embargo on arms sales as a means of limiting the Spanish conflict and cooperating with the European states, and, as a secondary benefit, gaining the political support of isolationists. After Bowers stressed the necessity for the United States of staying out of the conflict, FDR could not agree more. "You are absolutely right . . . about what you say of our complete neutrality in regard to Spain's own internal affairs."[60]

British and French pressure only reinforced Roosevelt's wish to contain the Spanish Civil War. Indeed, the nonintervention framework mirrored in some respects FDR's own idea for an international conference on Spain. In Roosevelt's correspondence with Norman Thomas, the president set out his "entire approval" for the embargo policy: "The civil conflict in Spain involves so many non-Spanish elements and has so many international implications that a policy of attempting to discriminate between the parties would be dangerous in the extreme." Roosevelt signed the Spanish embargo act in January 1937 without offering any of the reservations about executive discretion that accompanied his signature of the Neutrality Act in 1935.[61]

Some historians have suggested that anticommunist American bureaucrats engineered the embargo policy to deliberately undermine the leftist Spanish Republic.[62] But there is little evidence for this argument. Of the central players, Hull was genuinely neutral as to the outcome of the war and Roosevelt was a moderate Spanish Republican sympathizer. Joseph Green, responsible for enforcing the embargo, was also privately pro-Loyalist.[63] Far from being the work of anticommunists in the State Department, the strongly worded defense of nonintervention in the letter to the Glenn Martin Company in August 1936 was produced by the pro-Loyalist president himself. Many American officials found the potential international consequences of the Spanish Civil War to be far more worrying than the specter of the red peril. As William Phillips noted on 4 August 1936, "everyone realizes the acute danger of a European conflagration."[64] That anticommunism was not a necessary condition for supporting the embargo in 1936 is demonstrated by Claude Bowers's resolute advocacy of nonintervention in Spain.

As for domestic politics, there were occasions in 1936–37 when Congress overrode Roosevelt's clear policy preferences, for example with the terms of the Neutrality Act in May 1937. But domestic politics did not determine either Roosevelt's sympathy for the Spanish government or his support for nonintervention, both of which were soon evident. If the nonintervention policy had been driven by Roosevelt's fears about the upcoming election, then his landslide victory in November 1936 would have represented an admirable opportunity to end the moral embargo. Yet after his triumph, far from considering a revocation of the moral embargo, FDR asked for strengthened legal powers to prevent arms sales to Spain, if necessary under congressional control. During the first months of the Spanish Civil War, international and domestic winds were blowing Roosevelt in the same direction in which he wished to travel.

CHAPTER 5

American Men, American Oil, American Arms

With the failure of the Nationalist attack on Madrid in late 1936, the Spanish Civil War descended into a war of attrition. For many of the leaders involved, this was quite satisfactory. Franco recognized the merits of a protracted campaign in which the Nationalists could purge captured territory by systematically murdering working-class leaders. Stalin and Hitler both desired above all to avoid defeat and prolong the war, rather than win quickly. Stalin wanted to keep Hitler bogged down in the Spanish quagmire. Hitler sought to deepen the splits between Britain, France, and the Soviet Union, fuse together his own alliance with Mussolini, and ensure that Italian attention remained focused on Spain rather than on German expansion in central Europe. Hitler remarked that he would quite like a communist Catalonia to survive so that Mussolini would keep "gnawing at it, while he does not trouble himself worrying about other things in Europe."[1] The leftist parties in Spain were often consumed as much by internecine hostility as they were by the Nationalist threat. In May 1937 divisions within the Spanish Republic erupted into open violence in Barcelona as the communists crushed rival Trotskyite and anarchist factions. Overall, Mussolini appears to have been exceptional in his commitment from the start to a rapid victory.

In early 1937 Franco made a series of attempts to encircle Madrid. In March he gathered a force of 50,000 troops, including 30,000 Italians and 250 tanks, to attack Guadalajara, forty miles northeast of the capital. Caught in a heavy snowstorm, the Italians were routed. The result provided a major morale boost for the Spanish Republic. At Alicante, a Loyalist city on the southern Mediterranean coast, Ernest Hemingway's plane touched down into a victory fiesta, with people crowding the sidewalks, playing accordions and guitars.[2]

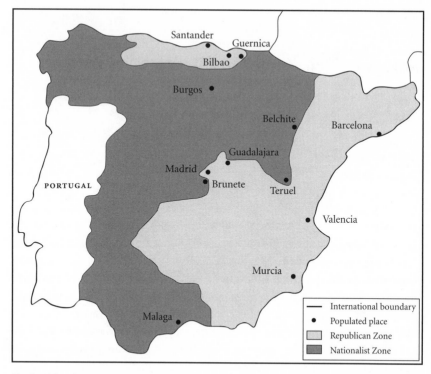

Spain, March, 1937

But the Loyalists continued to be hampered by internal divisions and the stifling effects of nonintervention. The Nationalists maintained the initiative and shifted their strategy toward capturing the northern Basque region, which was separated from the main Republican zone in eastern and southern Spain. Mola gathered an army of forty thousand men supported by the German Condor Legion. German forces were led by Wolfram von Richthofen, the cousin of the famous First World War air ace, the "Red Baron." Richthofen developed strategies of saturation bombing that he later employed against Poland. On 26 April 1937 the town of Guernica, the spiritual home of Basque nationalism, was destroyed from the air. By October the Nationalists had successfully completed the conquest of the Basque region, as well as neighboring Cantabria and Asturias, depriving the Spanish Republic of critical heavy-industry resources.

Republican counterattacks followed a similar pattern. In July 1937 Loyalist forces struck at Brunete, fifteen miles west of Madrid. They achieved initial surprise, but lacking reserves and weapons, and weakened by political divisions, the Loyalists were eventually pushed back. The story was the same with the offensive at Belchite in August. In great heat, and with poor communications, the Loyalists were unable to convert a breakthrough into a significant victory. In the bitter winter of 1937–38 they launched another attack at Teruel. The city fell to the Loyalists in January, but was lost again to the Nationalists in February.[3]

As these military events in Spain unfolded during 1937, Roosevelt encountered a series of problems related to the enforcement of the non-intervention policy. How should the administration deal with Americans who volunteered to fight in the Spanish Republic's international brigades, or provided medical services for the Loyalists? What about the Texaco Oil Company's massive provision of oil on credit to the Spanish Nationalists? Most significantly, should Roosevelt extend the arms embargo to Germany, Italy, or even the Soviet Union, because their intervention in Spain amounted to an act of war? In deciding these issues, a new and increasingly important policy dimension emerged. The Spanish Civil War sparked a domestic storm in the United States that threatened to fracture Roosevelt's New Deal coalition.

Despite FDR's landslide election victory in 1936, the president's political standing entered its lowest point between 1937 and 1939. In early 1937 he initiated the disastrous "court-packing" controversy. "The Court fight wasted a congressional session, helped destroy the Roosevelt myth of invincibility, disillusioned many of his former disciples, divided the Democratic party, gave the Republican party a new lease of life, and left Roosevelt bitter and hurt."[4] Many Americans began to fear an excessively dictatorial executive, and after 1936 Congress became increasingly hostile to legislation expanding the New Deal. FDR showed signs of becoming a lame duck president; few were certain that he would stand for a third term. To Harold Ickes, Roosevelt seemed "a beaten man."[5]

In this general context of declining political support for the president, the Spanish Civil War produced one of the great foreign policy controversies of the interwar period. The domestic debate over Spanish policy was slow to develop; indeed Washington's moral embargo won almost unanimous support in the summer and fall of 1936. Cordell Hull remarked: "Isolationists approved because we were keeping aloof from the conflict. Internationalists approved because we were cooperating with Britain and France."[6] At this time, a majority of Americans were largely uninterested in foreign affairs and sought to remain a safe distance from the horrors of war. The news from Spain was also confusing and included reports of atrocities by both sides. Opinion polls in the spring of 1937 indicated that twice as many Americans sympathized with the Spanish Republic as with the Nationalists, but between 65 percent and 79 percent had no opinion.[7]

Spain soon had a dramatic impact among the minority who followed international politics. J. David Valaik wrote that the Spanish Civil War caused "one of the most bitter debates in American history."[8] The conflict had a far more profound effect on the American consciousness than the wars in Ethiopia and Manchuria. Motion pictures and writings tended to present the conflict as a stark battle between good and evil, with the battles at Madrid and elsewhere representing a deciding moment in world history. "More than any other event of the 1930s, the Spanish Civil War vividly aroused the American people to the compelling pattern of European affairs. It was not merely a tragedy to be mourned from afar; it was an experience that touched the lives and the hearts of millions of Americans."[9] Newspapers were divided: the Hearst and Catholic press were pro-Franco; the *New York Times* and the liberal press sympathized with the Loyalists. The *Chicago Daily News* was pro-Republican; the *Chicago Tribune* was pro-embargo. *Newsweek* originally favored Franco but later moved toward neutrality. Journals such as *Esquire, Harper's*, and the *New Yorker* sympathized with the Republic, as did the *Daily Worker*, which may have given more coverage to Spain than any other paper.[10]

The Spanish Civil War was like a Rorschach test, perceived by Americans in terms of their own personal beliefs and concerns. Pro-Republican activists represented a loose coalition of Protestant, Jewish, liberal, and leftist groups. At first, in 1936, many of America's liberals drew an analogy between the Spanish Civil War and the First World War, supporting an embargo against the activities of the arms-trading "merchants of death." But liberals quickly viewed the Spanish Civil War in idealized terms. Loyalist sympathizers either perceived the Spanish Republic as an attempt to modernize and reform a feudal and backward society, or in contrast, as virtuous primitivism fighting against brutish modernity. The Republic's repeated defeats encouraged a pure image of the heroic lost cause. The American poet Edna St. Vincent Millay wrote "Say That We Saw Spain Die," originally published in *Harper's* in 1938, which opened: "Say that we saw Spain die. O splendid bull, how well you fought! Lost from the first."[11]

For many Americans on the left it seemed, for a while at least, to be the "good war." This emotional reaction to the Spanish Civil War, and a tendency toward a black-and-white interpretation of the conflict, were both captured in a conversation between the pro-Loyalist lawyer Ernest Cuneo, and the Supreme Court justice Louis Brandeis:[12]

The Justice turned towards me. The effect was like a wave of air which precedes the shock of an explosion. It was like Michelangelo's Moses come to life . . . He spoke.

"I am told," he said, "that Mussolini's tanks have landed at Malaga."

"That is true," I said.

"I am also told," he said, "that the unarmed people of Malaga stood in their path and threw stones at them."

"That is true also, Mr. Justice," I said.

Then he said very gently: "To see men go forth to die in the streets for their liberty is like watching the first furze of spring come to the tree tops. One knows that the tree of life will live again."

The Spanish Civil War occurred at a time when communism was at the height of its attractiveness in the United States. The Great Depression had shaken the faith of many Americans in capitalism. Yet most American supporters of the Spanish Republic campaigned for what they saw as a liberal democratic cause. The Spanish Republicans were the men of 1776, not 1917. The communist leader Earl Browder remarked: "Let us ask Jefferson where he stands on the issue."[13] From the start Loyalist sympathizers identified the Nationalists with international fascism, despite the war's origins in Spanish social divisions. In the 1920s many Americans perceived that Mussolini's corporate state was Americanizing Italy. But the experience of the Italian war against Ethiopia and Italy's association with German National Socialism created a perception of fascism as an aggressive international conspiracy.[14]

During 1937–38 there emerged a broad pro-Loyalist movement that included Albert Einstein, Dorothy Parker, Helen Keller, and Gypsy Rose Lee. Thousands of Americans joined Spanish relief organizations, with pro-Loyalist groups raising at least $2 million and pro-Franco groups rather less.[15] Other Americans campaigned vigorously for the repeal of the arms embargo. Hollywood tended to rally behind the Spanish Republic: performers such as Orson Welles, James Cagney, Bing Crosby, Rudy Vallee, Joan Crawford, and Bette Davis gave their time, blood, money, and signatures to the Loyalist cause. American artists mainly favored the Loyalists, although a few such as Gertrude Stein and Ezra Pound sympathized with the Spanish Nationalists. Pound thought that "Spain is an emotional luxury to a gang of sap-headed dilettantes."[16]

The Spanish Civil War captured Ernest Hemingway's imagination like few other events in his life. Hemingway spent much of the war in rooms 108 and 109 at the Hotel Florida in Madrid. He had access to food supplies that were almost impossible to find in Madrid, and because he was generous with his provisions, his rooms became a meeting place for a wide and varied cast of Spaniards and non-Spaniards. Hemingway thought that Franco was "a son-of-a-bitch of the first water," and despite his long-standing hatred of war he became a partisan for the Loyalists. Hemingway saw the Republic as a heroic underdog combating the tyranny of fascism, epitomized by the Nationalists' aerial bombing of cities such as Guernica. He loved the land and the Spanish people, and held an idealized image of peasant life. If fascism were not stopped in Spain, the domino effect would propel aggression toward Paris, London, and Washington. The hero of Hemingway's *For Whom the Bell Tolls* pronounces: "as long as we can hold them here we keep the fascists tied up. They can't attack any other country until they finish with us and they can never finish with us."[17] As well as writing pro-Republican articles, Hemingway ventured out to visit the young international brigade volunteers, and showed them how to hold and fire their rifles.

The president's wife, Eleanor Roosevelt, was strongly committed to the Loyalists, and helped to keep the Spanish Civil War in the forefront of FDR's mind. Eleanor was active in the women's peace movement, but she deviated from a number of pacifist positions, supporting collective security and military preparedness. Joseph Lash, a student organizer and socialist activist in the 1930s, described Eleanor as "passionately engaged upon the Loyalist side. She loved to hear the 'Six Songs of the International Brigade' and for many years kept on her desk a little bronze figure of a youthful Spanish militiaman in coveralls that was a symbol of the Republican cause." Eleanor wrote many columns on the horrors of the Nationalist bombings and donated money to pro-Loyalist groups. One day, traveling on a train up the Hudson, she found herself unable to work, unable to do anything in fact except think about the Spanish Civil War. She wondered: "If this were Spain would I be sitting so calmly and with such security?"[18] Eleanor maintained contacts with a range of figures in the pro-Loyalist movement, including Hollywood actors, writers such as Hemingway, and prominent Spaniards. One of her friends was Martha Gellhorn, a journalist, writer, and future wife of Ernest Hemingway, who traveled to Spain in 1937 to cover the war for *Collier's Weekly*. Gellhorn came to passionately believe in the Loyalist cause: "We knew, we just *knew* that Spain was the place to stop fascism."[19]

Idealistic impressions of the Spanish Civil War created a huge dilemma for liberal isolationists. The Spanish embargo was precisely the type of policy generally favored to avoid entangling the United States in foreign wars, but here it was undermining a cause in which they fervently believed. Senator Gerald Nye was a progressive isolationist who had orchestrated the enactment of wider neutrality legislation. But Nye ended up leading the congressional efforts to lift the Spanish embargo, convinced that American nonintervention aided Franco. The argument that the United States should check the aggression of the European dictators, and the contrary position that Washington should distance itself from dangerous international events, were as manifest as ever. On this occasion, however, Nye upheld the fascist danger while the administration justified its policy by employing the whole repertoire of isolationist language.[20]

By making an exception for Spain, liberal and pacifist isolationists weakened their wider argument that the United States should stand aside from international conflicts. Norman Thomas, a former Presbyterian minister from Ohio, was a socialist and pacifist. He wrote to Roosevelt in December 1936, arguing with some difficulties of logic: "In the long run, it is not peace for the world, or even America which will be served by applying to the Spanish rebellion a general principle which should be asserted more rigorously than is yet the case in Congressional legislation concerning neutrality in international war."[21]

If selling arms to combatants would draw the United States into foreign wars, why would this not happen with the Spanish Civil War? If Spain was an exception, were there other cases in which the United States should aid the victims of aggression? When Thomas helped to organize the recruitment and financing of five hundred American Loyalist volunteer fighters, there was an outcry from his pacifist colleagues. John Haynes Holmes urged Thomas to resist the temptation to support the Spanish Republican war effort: "[In the First World War] we stood fast when the Belgians lifted cries as pitiful as those lifted by Spaniards today, and when Paris was beset no less terribly than Madrid."[22] For Thomas, fighting the Nationalists was the lesser evil: the defeat of Franco was the only way to stop a second world war. These clear value conflicts were rarely resolved. In May 1938 Nye had two resolutions in the Senate. One was designed to facilitate the sale of arms to the Spanish Loyalists; the other would effectively end the export of arms altogether.[23]

In sharp contrast, American Catholics tended to identify with the Spanish Nationalists. The Spanish Civil War intensified the anticommunism of many Catholics, who had earlier been mobilized in a campaign against anticlericalism in Mexico. Leftist violence in Spain led many American Catholics to interpret events as part of a communist war against religion. The National Catholic Welfare Conference, the major source of news for diocesan weeklies, focused overwhelmingly on the raping of nuns, the murder of bishops, and the burning of churches. Catholic publications depicted the Spanish Civil War as the product of an international Bolshevik conspiracy. At the same time, very few Americans supported Spanish fascism, and there was considerable debate among Catholics on the merits of General Franco. For some it was sufficient that Franco was against the persecutors of their faith. But given the scale of Nationalist atrocities, with the victims including the deeply religious Basque people, other American Catholics adopted a "plague on both your houses" approach. Like the pro-Loyalists, Catholic supporters of Franco attempted to place the war in the American tradition. Franco was likened to George Washington in a revolt analogous to that of 1776. The American Catholic stance was strengthened at the end of 1937, when the Spanish bishops published a pastoral letter in the United States supporting Franco. The letter drew a reply from 150 Protestant leaders, who disputed the Catholic hierarchy's attempt to justify rebellion against a legal government. Over 170 Catholic priests and laymen responded by querying how anyone could support a government that persecuted Christians.[24]

Not all American Catholics supported Franco. The opinion polls suggest that as many as 30 percent favored the Spanish Republic. A young John F. Kennedy traveled to southern France in the summer of 1937, describing his sympathies as "rather governmental." But the stories that JFK heard from pro-Franco refugees about the horrors of Republican Spain tempered his support for Madrid. Perhaps, Kennedy wrote, it would be better for Spain if Franco won. But the Loyalists were "in the right morally speaking," because the Spanish Popular Front was similar to the New Deal. Kennedy believed that Republican anticlericalism was simply a reaction to the overly close relationship between Spanish church and state—a view not shared by the American Catholic hierarchy.[25] Yet back in the United States few pro-Republican Catholics were willing to challenge the Catholic hierarchy and publicly support the Loyalists. The vocal response of pro-Franco American Catholics, and the relative silence of pro-Republican Catholics, created the undeserved impression that Catholics were united on the subject.

And at the same time, not all pro-Franco Americans were Catholic. Jane Anderson was brought up as a Presbyterian and lived a remarkable life, reporting as a journalist from the Western Front in the First World War, becoming the first women to travel in a submarine, and working in the

1920s with H. G. Wells and Joseph Conrad, all the while pursuing a series of torrid love affairs. Having been arrested in Republican Spain in 1936, Anderson devoted her time upon release to telling increasingly outlandish tales of the murderous brutality of the Spanish Republicans. She toured America from 1937 to 1939, speaking at over one hundred Catholic gatherings about the horrors of Loyalist Spain. Anderson eventually moved to Nazi Germany, where she praised Hitler in radio broadcasts as the savior of world Christianity.[26]

Still, Catholics were certainly the backbone of the pro-Nationalist movement in the United States, which was a cohesive and well-mobilized pressure group. It included prelates such as Cardinal William O'Connell, Catholic politicians such as Representative John McCormack, publications such as *America* and the *Boston Pilot* (which gave more attention to the Spanish Civil War than to any other topic), the radio voice of Father Charles Coughlin, the Catholic University of America, and the National Catholic Welfare Conference. In 1937 Catholic politicians, led by McCormack, successfully opposed a proposal backed by the ambassador to Spain Claude Bowers and Eleanor Roosevelt, to bring Basque refugee children to the United States. Similarly, in January 1938, when sixty congressmen sent congratulations to the Loyalist Spanish Cortes, Catholic pressure induced many to recant.[27]

Class was not a major predictor in the United States of affiliation to the Spanish Loyalists or Nationalists. One might expect American workers to have backed the Republic and more prosperous Americans to have backed Franco. In fact, American businessmen and professionals were more strongly pro-Loyalist than skilled and unskilled workers. Religious beliefs were, however, strongly correlated with allegiances in the Spanish Civil War. In one poll 39 percent of American Catholics supported the Spanish Nationalists, compared with only 9 percent of American Protestants and 2 percent of Jews.[28]

The embargo debate thus tapped into the sensitive domestic issue of religious intolerance. For some American Protestants, the Spanish Civil War reinforced their prejudices about the place of Catholics in American society. The belief that Romanism and Americanism were somehow incompatible had been a tenet in Protestant discourse since the Revolution, and produced a wave of bigotry against the Catholic Democratic Party candidate Al Smith in the presidential election of 1928. The Spanish Civil War introduced further tensions, because many Protestants placed the blame for the continuation of the embargo firmly at the feet of America's bishops. Fearing that this division could have far-reaching consequences, Senator Pittman in 1939 stated that a continuing "discussion of the Spanish embargo would stir up a religious controversy in each one of the forty-eight states with political results that no one could foresee."[29]

From Roosevelt's perspective, the debate over the Spanish embargo, by setting in opposition liberal against Catholic, divided two key constituents of the New Deal coalition. In the election of 1936 FDR had "forged a new political coalition firmly based on the success in the great northern cities, and led in Congress by a new political type: the northern urban liberal Democrat."[30] It was in the northern cities that the Catholic population was concentrated, and between 70 and 80 percent of Catholics voted for Roosevelt in 1936. Individual Catholics also played a significant role in undermining the belief that FDR was pro-communist. Cardinal Mundelein of Chicago was particularly close to Roosevelt, and the chairman of the Democratic National Committee, Jim Farley, also kept the president in contact with Catholics. Roosevelt's wider interest in Catholic opinion was evident in 1939, when he sent Myron C. Taylor as his personal emissary to the Vatican. The domestic controversy over the Spanish Civil War dramatically raised the stakes for American policy toward Spain. In addition to its diplomatic repercussions, Roosevelt's political future was now on the line.[31]

Offering the greatest commitment to either side in the Spanish Civil War were the 2,600 Americans who volunteered to fight in the Loyalist international brigades between 1937 and 1938. They formed the "Abraham Lincoln Battalion," the "George Washington Battalion," and the "John Brown Battery," all part of the Fifteenth International Brigade. They were the first racially mixed units in American history and the first to have a black commander. Nearly nine hundred Americans died in Spain, the volunteers suffering a higher casualty rate than American troops later would in the Second World War.

Their motives for fighting were often complex and shaped by personal experience. Most of the volunteers were members of the Young Communist League or the Communist Party, and some were committed ideologues eager to strike a blow for the international proletariat and build a people's republic in Spain. Other volunteers traveled to Spain primarily to fight fascism. In May 1938 James Lardner wrote to his mother from Spain, listing the five most important reasons for his decision to join the international brigades: "Because I believe that fascism is wrong and must be exterminated, and that liberal democracy or more probably communism is right . . . Because my joining [the international brigades] might have an effect on the amendment of the neutrality of the United States . . . Because after the war is over I shall be a more effective antifascist . . . Because in my ambitious quest for knowledge in all fields, I cannot afford in this age to overlook war . . . Because there is a girl in Paris who will have to learn that my presence is not necessary to her existence."[32]

Hank Rubin was studying at the University of California, Los Angeles, when a fellow student sat down next to him and asked: "Hank, how would you like to go to Spain and fight with the International Brigades against Franco?" Partly because of his political sympathies, partly because he was Jewish and wanted to fight back against anti-Semitism, and partly because he saw the opportunity for a heroic gesture to find out who he was, Hank said "sure" and worked as a medical volunteer for the Loyalists.[33]

Joe Dallet was brought up in a privileged and conservative American family, but gave it all up to become a longshoreman in New York City and a Communist Party organizer. In 1937 Dallet traveled to Spain to join the Abraham Lincoln Battalion and was appointed as a political commissar. Dallet died in 1938 at the Battle of the Ebro, cut down by machine-gun fire in a charge against superior forces. Dallet's wife, Katherine, would later marry J. Robert Oppenheimer, the "father" of the atomic bomb. Oppenheimer also identified with the Republican cause in the Spanish Civil War: "the matter which most engaged my sympathies and interests."[34]

The roughly ninety African American volunteers were partly motivated by a desire to strike back against Italy after its recent invasion of Ethiopia. As one writer commented: "This ain't Ethiopia but it'll do."[35] At least one-third of the volunteers were Jewish—men who felt a special commitment to fighting fascism. In November 1937 Hyman Katz wrote to his family in the United States: "I took up arms against the persecutors of my people—the Jews—and my class—the oppressed."[36] American mercenary pilots were also in demand in Spain. The Spanish Republic paid Frank Tinker $1,500 a month and $1,000 for each kill: he achieved eight and became an ace.[37]

In contrast to the forty to fifty thousand members of the international brigades, a total of about one thousand to fifteen hundred foreign volunteers fought for Franco. They were a diverse group, united by the belief that the communists dominated the Republic, and in most cases appalled by the killings of religious figures in Spain. Among the volunteers were a handful of Americans. One was Vincent Patriarcha, who enlisted in 1936 in the Nationalist air force. Patriarcha was motivated by his love of flying more than anything else. Unable through lack of funds to get his pilot's license in the United States, Patriarcha noticed an advertisement offering free flying lessons in Italy for the sons of Italians living abroad—a scheme designed to encourage greater identification with the mother country among Italian expatriates and their descendents. Patriarcha received training in Italy and eventually agreed to fly missions for Italian troops in Ethiopia before participating in the airlift of Franco's forces from North Africa to Spain.[38]

The American volunteers presented a conundrum for an administration that was committed to nonintervention. The State Department released a statement to the press on 13 January 1937 declaring that "the enlistment of American citizens in either of the opposing sides in Spain is unpatriotically inconsistent with the American Government's policy of the most scrupulous non-intervention in Spanish internal affairs." Indeed, since the start of the Spanish Civil War all passports, except to accredited journalists, had been stamped "not valid for travel in Spain." The Department of Justice considered prosecuting those who had recruited Americans for the international brigades, under an old statute.[39]

That option was foreclosed when FDR intervened and ordered the administration not to go "over strong" on prosecuting the recruiters, "as this happened before anyone realized what this Spanish thing meant."[40] Ernest Cuneo, general counsel for the pro-Loyalist North American Committee to Aid Spanish Democracy, defended two Spaniards about to be indicted for recruiting. Cuneo planned to surrender the two men to arrest, "at a Madison Square Garden rally before 25,000 people . . . I was morally certain that a great American [Norman Thomas] would step forward and ask that he be arrested at the same time . . . it was my best guess that 250,000 people in New York would be in Foley Square to protest the arrest of Norman Thomas the day he was arraigned." Cuneo was told that the President was impressed by Thomas's willingness to be arrested: "The President said Norman Thomas never broke a law in his life."[41]

FDR probably found that in this case his own sympathies and political considerations coincided. The American communist leader Earl Browder admitted that he broke the law by helping to organize American volunteers for Spain: "but for this instance when I was clearly guilty I was never even officially questioned, not to mention indicted." Browder believed that "no official wanted to test how deep American sympathy was for the beleaguered Spanish Republic."[42] Gardner Jackson wrote to the administration arguing that any prosecutions would in political terms "be most unfortunate from the President's point of view quite as much as from the Spanish Government's."[43]

Roosevelt began to distinguish sharply between American volunteers who fought for the Loyalists and the handful who fought for Franco. At a press conference in 1938 he proposed removing licenses from pilots who "aid revolutionists." When asked whether this would apply to those fighting "on the side of an accredited government," the president replied: "Normally speaking, no." Roosevelt was immediately asked if the Spanish Civil War was a revolution. "Oh, I don't know," he replied, "that has been characterized already. It is a war and of course it is a revolution."[44] As one critic argued: "the statement is obviously designed as an expression of preference for the Spanish Loyalists-to-Moscow and an objectionable dig at the millions of his fellow citizens whose sympathies are with the Nationalists."[45]

Roosevelt also favored the Spanish Republic's position on the issue of passports for American medical volunteers. In the spring of 1937 the State Department denied passports to relief workers because they were only going to Republican territory. Cordell Hull in February told the Spanish ambassador: "I could not hold out any particular hope that our decision would be changed."[46] FDR personally forced a reversal of policy. On 13 March, James Roosevelt, the president's son and secretary, telephoned R. Walton Moore to say that his father disapproved of the State Department's stance. Moore was doubtful but Roosevelt pressed the issue. Ernest Cuneo was ready to pursue legal action based on the premise that the U.S. government did not have the right to deny passports. Hull was also ready to fight it out in court. But before Cuneo could appear in court he was telephoned by a source in the White House: "Don't go yet. The President will raise the question in Cabinet meeting this afternoon, wait." Several hours later Cuneo was called again: "The President has reversed State. You people can go." If the American Red Cross could vouch for the applicant, the passport would be given.[47] Roosevelt may once again have been partly motivated by a desire to avoid bad publicity resulting from a denial of passports to relief workers. Iz Feinstein sent a telegram to Roosevelt's advisor Tom Corcoran: "if it does come to an open fight the issue is swell and it is going to hurt [the] new deal and show up our whole stinking Spanish neutrality policy."[48] In the end about 150 American medical volunteers served in Spain.

FDR's tendency to back the Loyalists in private on borderline issues that did not significantly challenge the overall policy of nonintervention was again evident at a cabinet meeting in September 1937. Roosevelt told Hull that the Spanish Republic was eager to be retained as a member of the League of Nations Council. Hull was hostile to American involvement, but FDR ordered him to exert influence in Latin America to help the Republic keep its seat. But in the end Latin American countries ensured that Spain would fail to be reelected to the Council, because the Loyalists would not allow the evacuation of Franco supporters from Latin American embassies in Spain.[49]

Roosevelt was particularly annoyed by the activities of the Texaco Oil Company. The pro-fascist head of Texaco, Colonel Thorkild Rieber, met General Franco in August 1936 and promised to provide all the oil the Nationalists needed, on credit, for the duration of the war. Texaco tankers would ostensibly sail for Antwerp, but when the captain opened his orders he would find that a rebel port was his destination. Elliott Roosevelt wrote: "Father was incensed when he learned of the trick. Any captain joining in the deception should have his license revoked, he ordered, and their employers could possibly be indicted for conspiracy."[50] Selling oil to Franco was legal because the embargo exempted nonmilitary materials such as oil or trucks despite their obvious strategic value. Ford, Studebaker, and General Motors, for example, sold twelve thousand trucks to the Spanish Nationalists. The Firestone company advertised its products in the Nationalist zone: "Victory smiles on the best. The glorious Nationalist army always wins on the field of battle. Firestone Tires has had its nineteenth consecutive victory in the Indianapolis 500." In 1937–38 the Loyalists spent around a million dollars a month on American trucks, tires, and machine tools.[51]

But Texaco's credit arrangements for Franco were illegal. FDR met Rieber in June 1937 and threatened to embargo further oil shipments if credit to Franco continued. Texaco eventually received a fine of $20,000 for contravening the Neutrality Act of January 1937, but Rieber displayed contempt for the decision and continued to supply oil to the Nationalists on credit. The 3.5 million tons of oil that Franco received represented over twice the Republic's entire oil imports. These supplies were strategically vital, contributing to Franco's "ultimate victory."[52] *Life* magazine offered a glowing portrait of Rieber in 1940: "Rieber's dealings with the Franco Government in Spain were a shrewd gamble. When the Spanish civil war broke out in July, 1936, Texaco had five tankers on the high seas bound for Spain. Rieber was in Paris. He flew to Spain, took a good look around and forthwith ordered the tankers to deliver their oil to the Insurgents . . . For the next two years Texaco supplied Franco with all the oil he needed, while the Loyalists never had enough. If Franco had lost, Texaco would have been out some $6,000,000. But the gamble won and not only did victorious Franco pay his bill but the Spanish monopoly is currently buying all its oil from Texaco. For ambitious young men Rieber is a prime example of what it takes to be a successful tycoon."[53] Shortly afterward, however, Colonel Rieber's oil deals with Berlin enabled the German agent Niko Bensmann to obtain information on the American aircraft industry. When British intelligence broke this spy ring, a disgraced Rieber was forced to resign.[54]

As the full extent of fascist intervention in Spain became clear in early 1937, there were voices in London and Paris urging a stronger stance. The British foreign secretary, Anthony Eden, became concerned that a victory by a fascist-backed Franco would produce German and Italian strategic gains. Eden suggested a unilateral British blockade of Spain in January 1937, but the cabinet and the prime minister opposed him. From this point onward Eden favored a Spanish Republican victory. There followed periods of occasional British resolve in Spain. In the summer of 1937, after a spate of attacks on ships by "pirate" (Italian) submarines, the British navy was ordered to sink suspects, and the subsequent conference at Nyon established a successful international antisubmarine patrol.[55]

Such episodes were exceptional. When Neville Chamberlain replaced Stanley Baldwin as prime minister in May 1937, British foreign policy shifted decisively in favor of appeasement. Chamberlain strongly believed that the road to peace lay in satisfying the legitimate demands of the dictators. The chances that Britain would take a firm stand in Spain against foreign intervention dwindled. Indeed, Chamberlain was confident that if and when Franco won, he would prevent Italian or German domination of Spain. The British Labour Party supported nonintervention in Spain for over a year, although by the end of 1937 it, along with the trade unions, argued for lifting the Spanish embargo. Yet overall, Baldwin and later Chamberlain, with huge majorities in Parliament, were little troubled by public opinion.[56]

During this period Roosevelt became interested in a potentially significant foreign policy proposal: to extend the arms embargo to the European fascist dictators because they were militarily engaged in the Spanish Civil War. Roosevelt considered widening the application of neutrality legislation to deter foreign intervention in Spain. The extension idea originated with pro-Loyalists who recognized that denying the sale of weapons to Germany and Italy would be more popular in the United States than selling arms to the Spanish Republic. In Congress, Nye began pressing for a resolution to widen the embargo.[57]

FDR sympathized with the notion of extending the embargo. Information available to the president in the fall of 1936, and especially in 1937, made clear the large-scale nature of German, Italian, and Soviet intervention. But Hull concluded that extending the embargo would threaten the conciliation policies of Britain and France and increase the chances of a general war. The situation was also complicated by the existence of the

Non-Intervention Committee, as well as the lack of a formal state of war between the fascist states and the Spanish Republic. Roosevelt ordered Hull to probe Ambassador Robert Bingham in London on the British reaction to an avowed Italian move in the Spanish Civil War. Bingham stated that Britain wanted to avoid a decisive victory by either side and would certainly not intervene with arms if the Italians acted officially in Spain.[58]

Roosevelt's interest in the issue gained fresh impetus from the German Condor Legion's bombing of Guernica in April 1937, which left hundreds dead.[59] It was the first time in the western world that an open town had been attacked from the air. The Basque government and most of the foreign correspondents in Bilbao revealed the true story that fascist aircraft had destroyed Guernica. In contrast, the American reporter H. Edward Khoblaugh, and much of the American Catholic hierarchy, argued that anarchist dynamiters had razed the town. Alfred M. Landon, the Republican presidential candidate in 1936, joined seven senators, two state governors, and the former secretary of state Henry Stimson in signing an official protest against the attack. In Congress, Representative Jerry O'Connell argued that Guernica necessitated embargoing the fascist dictators.[60]

Roosevelt was clearly in a receptive mood when Norman Thomas wrote on 9 June with a request to discuss an extension of the embargo: "In its practical effects our neutral policy thus far in the Spanish situation has tended not toward genuine non-intervention but toward a kind of left-handed aid to Franco." Roosevelt ordered his secretary to "get hold of Norman Thomas right off," and the two men met on 29 June.[61] Thomas gave the president a Loyalist document describing the extent of fascist intervention in Spain and requested an extension of the embargo as an act of "moral principle." Roosevelt replied that he would be compelled to act if intervention were officially acknowledged or proved beyond any doubt. But Thomas later recalled being rebuffed after pleading with the president: "[Roosevelt] told me we didn't send many arms [to Germany and Italy] anyway and rather brushed off my suggestion that the moral weight of the embargo would be important. In his own inimitable way he changed the subject." Roosevelt "nodded" at Thomas's discussion of the fascist threat and then suddenly said "what a great man Cardinal Mundelein was." Thomas perceived this as a reference to Catholic pressure. "The major thing in Roosevelt's mind was not so much foreign policy but a belief that in his whole policy, domestic and foreign, it was necessary to carry along the Catholic Church."[62]

This cannot have been FDR's primary consideration, because on the very same day, he wrote to Hull arguing that an extension of the embargo would be necessary if an official move were made by Germany or Italy (although not, significantly, by the USSR). Roosevelt was thinking about "precedents and the future," and concluded: "I do not think that we can compound a ridiculous situation if after the fight is established, Great Britain and France continue to assert solemnly that they 'have no proof' of Italian or German participation in the Spanish War . . . According to some of the newspapers, Mussolini has personally directed participation by the regular Italian armed forces—and Hitler has also made the same kind of statement."[63]

Almost the entire foreign policy bureaucracy opposed the extension proposal. This included Hull, who had himself asserted the "no proof" argument in a letter to Jerry O'Connell in May 1937. The Office of Arms and Munitions Control argued against extension based on the lessons of history. The "Ethiopian experience" suggested that extending the embargo would force the dictators to step up their intervention in Spain to gain a rapid victory. And the Hoare-Laval Pact was invoked by analogy to suggest that extension could lead the British to compromise with the dictators to avoid a general war. The initiative would therefore be an "unwise gesture" and could "injure most those people—the Spanish Loyalists—on whose behalf the action has been sought."[64]

In spite of this, Roosevelt ordered the canvassing of diplomatic opinion in Europe about the idea. In the end the extension policy was never introduced, primarily because the European reaction, which FDR had never been certain about, was universally hostile. According to Ambassador William Phillips in Rome, the Italians would regard widening the embargo as a hostile act, and the move could spread the conflict beyond Spain. In London, Eden told Ambassador Bingham that extending the embargo would be, "to say the least, premature." Bingham added that the proposal would be viewed as a "gratuitous interference in continental affairs," complicating British efforts to have foreigners withdrawn from Spain. According to Hull, he phoned FDR with these responses, and the president "readily agreed to continue" the American position.[65] Extending the embargo could interfere with British efforts to reduce international intervention in Spain, and thereby undermine Roosevelt's original aim.

When Norman Thomas again lobbied for extension on 26 August, FDR replied that he was giving careful attention to the neutrality legislation, but added that arms sales from the United States to Italy during 1937 totaled only $190,000. Extending the embargo thus might have symbolic value, but it would not be effective. German arms purchases in the United States in the first half of 1937 totaled only $440,000, mostly aircraft parts for re-sale abroad. The Johnson Act of 1934 already prevented Germany and Italy from raising loans in the United States. As the domestic controversy over Spanish policy grew in 1937–38, the debate about extending the embargo disappeared, to be replaced by the more fundamental question of the validity of the embargo itself.[66]

In the summer and fall of 1937 Roosevelt's sympathy for the Loyalists was stronger than ever. On 19 September the president discussed a conversation with the Spanish Republican ambassador about an Italian submarine that the Loyalists had captured. FDR remarked that "the Spanish Government did not have a sense of publicity," and suggested that if the Loyalists photographed the submarine and crew, they could make the front page of every newspaper in America.[67] But Roosevelt still did not view the outcome of the Spanish Civil War as a matter of major national interest for the United States. He seemed satisfied with the workings of the embargo, telling Sumner Welles on 3 July: "The United States has honestly maintained not only the letter but the spirit of neutrality."[68]

In the summer of 1937 the writer John Dos Passos discussed Spanish policy with an American diplomat—left unnamed—who believed that if the embargo were lifted there was still a chance to stop fascism in Europe. The diplomat had an appointment to see FDR at the White House, and was "jumping up and down with determination" to confront the president. If policy were not changed, the diplomat had a resignation letter ready in his pocket. A few days later Dos Passos met the same diplomat, and asked how the meeting had gone. There was no more talk of resignation. The diplomat had come under the spell of Roosevelt's "virtually hypnotic" powers of persuasion. After Roosevelt described "the larger view," the president and the diplomat "agreed perfectly about everything."[69]

The president's famous "Quarantine" speech at Chicago in October 1937 reflected developments in both Spain and Japan: "Without a declaration of war and without warning or justification of any kind, civilians, including vast numbers of women and children are being ruthlessly murdered with bombs from the air." Other parts of the speech clearly referred to Spain: "Nations are fomenting and taking sides in civil warfare in nations that have never done them any harm . . . In time of so-called peace, ships are being attacked and sunk by submarines without cause or notice." Roosevelt suggested that the United States could not be isolated from a breakdown in international law and morality, and that therefore aggressive states should be "quarantined," a policy he never specified.[70]

The Quarantine speech was not a departure from previous policy. The president had examined similar ideas before the speech, and he did so afterward as well. Rather, Roosevelt was seeking to shape American public opinion and warn the dictators, preparing the ground for future collective action against international aggression.[71] Crucially, the speech did not herald a new Spanish policy. FDR told Ickes that there would be no quarantine for either Spain or China, "because what has happened in those countries has happened." Roosevelt's resigned and somewhat detached attitude toward the Spanish Civil War was also apparent in his comment to Martha Gellhorn in July 1937: "Spain is a vicarious sacrifice for all of us."[72]

In 1936–37 FDR maintained a consistent sympathy for the Spanish Republic but never pursued a determined pro-Loyalist policy. This apparent tension has often been explained by Roosevelt's deference to British, bureaucratic, Catholic, or congressional pressure. According to Eleanor Roosevelt: "In the case of the Spanish Civil War, for instance, we had to remain neutral, though Franklin knew quite well he wanted the democratic government to be successful. But he also knew he could not get Congress to go along with him."[73] But American policy toward Spain in 1936–37 correlated very closely with FDR's personal beliefs about the conflict. For the president, promoting international nonintervention in the Spanish Civil War was more important than aiding the Loyalists. Maintaining the European peace was a far greater imperative than the question of who governed Spain. The arms embargo was part of a wider international effort to contain the Spanish Civil War that FDR had supported from the start. The notion of extending the embargo to the fascist states was consistent with these aims. If successful, it might pressure the Germans and Italians into reducing their aid to Franco, once their intervention had given rise to a "ridiculous situation."

International factors were evident in Roosevelt's concern in 1936 that European conflict could be sparked by Franco's revolt. Furthermore, the accession in Britain of Neville Chamberlain as prime minister in 1937 complicated any potential initiatives in the Spanish Civil War by Washington, because the British reaction to an American provocation of the fascist states became more uncertain. Yet objective international constraints did not force Roosevelt's hand. Indeed, Americans perceived diplomatic pressures in widely varying ways. FDR's desire for mildly biased neutrality can be contrasted with Moore's support for strict isolation. Left-wing critics interpreted the same international events very differently, believing that the United States ought to aid the antifascist forces in Spain.

Roosevelt's decision making demonstrated his reluctance to simply follow the State Department line. Policies on medical volunteers, the prosecution of recruiters for the international brigades, and Spain's seat on the League of Nations Council all occurred in spite of, rather than because of, American bureaucrats. It is true that FDR rejected the idea of extending the embargo when he received evidence from American officials about likely international complications. But Roosevelt pursued the proposal in the face of a hostile State Department, and despite vague references to Catholic pressure, FDR decided to put the idea before the European ambassadors. The initiative was abandoned when new evidence suggested that a wider embargo would fail to achieve any of the president's foreign policy goals.

The domestic controversy over the Spanish embargo has led many writers to suggest that Catholic opinion crucially shaped Roosevelt's policy making.[74] But establishing the causal link between domestic politics and decision making toward the Spanish Civil War in 1936–37 is difficult. Domestic factors did not so much constrain Roosevelt as reinforce the president's own preference for nonintervention. In 1938–39, in the context of Roosevelt's rapidly changing perceptions of Spain, the domestic controversy would emerge as an important factor, shaping the methods used by FDR to aid the Spanish Republic, as well as the success and failure of his initiatives.

CHAPTER 6

Roosevelt's Perceptions of the Spanish Civil War, 1938–1939

In January 1939 President Roosevelt declared that events in Spain were occupying his "thoughts to an astonishing degree," signifying a transformation in FDR's views of the international situation and the Spanish Civil War.[1] During 1936–37 Roosevelt's emphasis shifted from viewing Spain as a potential spark or catalyst for wider European conflict, toward focusing on the danger of German and Italian intervention. In 1938 this evolution in thinking continued, with Roosevelt increasingly believing that a victory by Franco ran counter to American interests. Roosevelt's changing perceptions of Spain are the crucial explanation for the president's greater engagement in Spanish policy in 1938–39.

To understand Roosevelt's reevaluation of the Spanish Civil War in 1938 we first need to examine the president's wider thinking about international affairs in this period. At the start of 1938 the international security environment was disturbing but highly ambiguous. By the end of the year a major European or world conflict appeared increasingly likely, although not yet certain. In the Far East the war continued between Japan and China, with the Japanese steadily gaining the upper hand and advancing into southern China. Border skirmishes also began at this time between the Japanese and the Soviet Union. FDR's suggestions for a firmer stance against Japan, involving orchestrated Anglo-American naval maneuvers, were rebuffed by Chamberlain, who thought it rash either to provoke Japan or to rely on the United States. By 1938 Roosevelt linked Japanese aggression with German gains in Europe. But it was not until 1940 that firm American resistance in the Far East began, after Japan's occupation of Indochina and the Tripartite Pact between Tokyo, Berlin, and Rome.[2]

It was the European rather than the Far Eastern situation that changed fundamentally in 1938. Sensing the weakness of the western democracies and with German rearmament now in an advanced state, Hitler in February and March 1938 forced Chancellor Kurt von Schuschnigg of Austria to agree to a union with Germany, an act specifically forbidden in the Versailles Treaty. Hitler also began making demands for the annexation of the German-speaking Sudetenland from Czechoslovakia. In May, Hitler instructed Germany's top generals of his "unshakeable will to wipe Czechoslovakia off the map."[3] The French were obliged to defend Czechoslovakia under the Treaty of Mutual Assistance of 1925, but meaningful support would require full-scale war against Germany.

There were some in Britain urging a strong antifascist policy. Winston Churchill, a man at the time in the political wilderness, advocated a "grand alliance" of Britain, France, and the USSR against Germany. The foreign secretary, Anthony Eden, also criticized Italian aggression in Spain. But once Eden resigned in February 1938 and was replaced by Lord Halifax, Prime Minister Neville Chamberlain began to dominate British foreign policy. Chamberlain stepped up his efforts to appease what he considered the legitimate grievances of the fascist states, and hoped by this policy to split the Axis powers and avoid war. On 20 March Chamberlain announced that Britain would not back Czechoslovakia or the French in a war with Germany over the Sudetenland. Chamberlain recognized Italian Ethiopia and extolled the "new vision" of fascist Rome.[4] It was, according to Churchill, a "complete triumph for Mussolini, who gains [British] cordial acceptance for his fortification of the Mediterranean against us, for his conquest of [Ethiopia], and for his violence in Spain."[5]

Chamberlain was deeply uncertain about the wisdom of closer relations with the United States. He sought "Anglo-American cooperation in principle, but only where it was consonant with his overall diplomatic goals and where U.S. support could be guaranteed."[6] As Chamberlain saw it, just as his carefully laid appeasement plans were gaining momentum, an ill-thought-out American proposal would suddenly arrive—an unexploded "bombshell" in his lap. All too aware of the restrictions provided by American neutrality legislation, Chamberlain believed that the United States would be unable to offer significant aid in protecting British interests.[7]

During the first months of 1938 FDR received mounting evidence of German preparations for war. Charles Lindbergh, American flying ace turned aviation envoy, sent a memorandum in February 1938, which concluded that German air development was "without parallel."[8] At press conferences on 20–21 April, Roosevelt highlighted the new vulnerability of the United States to air attack and the possibility that the United States might face enemies in both the Atlantic and the Pacific. Roosevelt privately feared that appeasement would not succeed in preventing war. In March, when analyzing British foreign policy, FDR compared the European dictators to gangsters: "If a Chief of Police makes a deal with the leading gangsters and the deal results in no more hold-ups, that Chief of Police will be called a great man—but if the gangsters do not live up to their word the Chief of Police will go to jail. Some people are I think taking very long chances."[9] Speaking frankly to the Spanish Loyalist ambassador, Roosevelt sharply criticized Chamberlain's appeasement policies and "said that he did not trust the English."[10]

In the spring of 1938, however, FDR was not yet certain that appeasement would fail, and with the British still hopeful, he was willing to offer limited public support for conciliation efforts. In January 1938 he suggested an international conference to negotiate arms reduction and a framework of economic opportunity for all states. In part because of British doubts, and in part because of the president's unwillingness to take a lead on the initiative, it never got off the ground.[11] FDR seems to have viewed the Anschluss of Germany and Austria as concerning but perhaps inevitable. He was also willing to approve British recognition of the Italian conquest of Ethiopia. A mixture of uncertainty and fear that war could break out any day meant that the president was initially determined to stay out of the gathering crisis over the Sudetenland. As he complained at a press conference on 6 September, reporters cannot get "the dope, the plain facts. The same thing happens to us. While our State Department dispatches are not as wild as the newspaper stories, they are darned near, and that is saying a lot."[12]

Despite his caution in the spring and summer of 1938, Roosevelt searched for effective ways to reinforce the resolution of Britain and France. In early 1938 he described to a French representative how aircraft could be built in Canada from American parts and then shipped to France, if neutrality legislation were invoked in a European war. In August the president outlined a plan to deposit British gold in the United States for the purchase of war materials. A few weeks later he suggested that Britain should fight defensively in any European conflict. If London could avoid an actual declaration of war, he might be able to ignore the Neutrality Act and continue arms sales, as he was doing with China. The president added vaguely that "somehow or other" the Americans might ultimately be drawn in. It is fair to say that Roosevelt in his advice did not fully appreciate the triple threat posed to British home and imperial strategic interests by Germany, Italy, and Japan, or the extent to which the British were skeptical about his unclear private promises.[13]

Chamberlain sought to avoid war by enacting a peaceful transfer of the Czechoslovakian Sudetenland to Germany, and he traveled to meet Hitler at Berchtesgaden and Bad Godesberg. But Hitler's insistence on humiliating terms for the transfer of Czech territory threatened to undermine these efforts. After being largely inactive in the crisis, Roosevelt sent two diplomatic notes urging further negotiation. In Spain, Franco announced that if conflict came he would be neutral. More important in averting hostilities, however, was the warning given to Hitler by his generals that the German army was unready for immediate conflict, and the German public was unenthusiastic about war. At the subsequent conference in Munich on 29–30 September 1938, Chamberlain agreed to satisfy almost all of Germany's demands. In return he gained Hitler's written pledge of peaceful intentions.[14]

In Chamberlain's eyes Munich had achieved the fundamental goals of British appeasement: first by avoiding war through the establishment of a four-power entente of Britain, France, Italy, and Germany, and second by excluding the USSR. But the achievement was illusory. Hitler learned from his triumphant destruction of the Czechoslovakian state that the democracies would not resist further aggressive policies. With the powerful Czechoslovakian army neutralized, the Soviet Union lost one of the major buffers between Hitler and his avowed goal of destroying Bolshevism. Stalin, facing isolation, became amenable to cutting a deal with Germany, a process that resulted in the Nazi-Soviet pact of August 1939. Churchill described Munich as "a total and unmitigated defeat." But it was "only the first sip, the first foretaste of a bitter cup which will be proffered to us year by year unless, by a supreme recovery of moral health and martial vigor, we arise again and take our stand for freedom as in the olden time."[15]

For Roosevelt the Munich crisis produced a significant clarification of Hitler's motives and the necessity for American action. FDR was initially relieved that war had been averted, and was quite optimistic about the future prospects for peace. Yet privately he compared Britain and France to Judas Iscariot, betraying the smaller European states. His post-Munich confidence had largely evaporated by the second week of October, when FDR predicted new demands from Germany.[16] On 14 November Roosevelt declared that Munich "may have saved many, many lives now, but . . . may ultimately result in the loss of many times that number of lives later." Hitler's obduracy and aggressive posturing particularly influenced Roosevelt: the Führer was a man who had little regard for FDR's core belief in negotiation. No longer did the president think that Germany could be satisfied by diplomatic adjustments; instead he felt that Hitler's intentions were definitely warlike. Roosevelt also believed at this time that German air power could defeat Britain and France. This represented an exaggerated view of German air strength. William C. Bullitt, for example, erroneously told the president in October 1938 that the German air force was ten times the size of the French air force.[17]

From the fall of 1938 Roosevelt became convinced that Germany posed a major threat to national security. Latin America could become a target for the fascist countries, and the United States might be directly threatened militarily, or end up isolated in a world dominated by Germany. In January 1939 Roosevelt told the Senate Military Affairs Committee that Hitler's aim was world domination. The barbarism of German National Socialism was starkly illustrated by the Kristallnacht pogrom against the Jews in November 1938. Roosevelt publicly remarked: "I myself could scarcely believe that such things could occur in a twentieth century civilization."[18] The president subsequently recalled the U.S. ambassador from Germany. Roosevelt began to differentiate sharply between Hitler and Mussolini, maintaining his belief that the Italian dictator was a potential partner for negotiation until Mussolini declared war on France in 1940.[19] At the same time, Roosevelt was worried by coordination among the fascist states, especially German attempts to create a tripartite military alliance with Italy and Japan. In December 1937 FDR had already described the anti-Comintern pact as a global conspiracy to coordinate aggression.[20]

This clarification of his beliefs in October and November 1938 led the president to seek to aid Britain and France by providing thousands of American aircraft. Without risking direct American involvement in war, the United States would become the arsenal of European democracy, thereby deterring, or if necessary defeating, Hitler. In addition, the expansion of aircraft production would offer a welcome boost for American industry. Airpower was widely believed to dominate modern warfare, in part because of the role of aerial bombing in Spain and China. Bullitt wrote to Roosevelt on 20 September: "The moral is: If you have enough airplanes, you don't have to go to Berchtesgaden." FDR told his ambassador to Mexico, Josephus Daniels, that knowledge of German air strength "made Chamberlain capitulate at Munich."[21] On 14 November FDR declared that the "recrudescence of German power at Munich" meant that the United States required a "huge air force" so that it "did not need to have a huge army to follow that air force."[22]

The president wanted ten thousand planes a year, and on 12 January

1939 he called for an additional half-billion dollars of defense expenditure. He told Daniels that the most important thing he was working on was "national defense, especially mass production of planes."[23] Roosevelt supported this policy in the face of domestic challenges from both congressional isolationists and the War Department. FDR's demands were eventually scaled back to three thousand planes a year, and although France ordered a thousand planes by July 1939, production problems prevented their arrival. The French had only two hundred of these American planes by September 1939, an insufficient force to either deter or defeat Hitler.

At the start of 1938 Roosevelt demonstrated his sympathy for the Spanish Republic by telling his wife Eleanor that he was in agreement with the Loyalist cause.[24] Throughout the year, the president's attachment to the Spanish Republic grew steadily more resolute. There were three major reasons for this. First, Roosevelt's stark reevaluation of Hitler's power and intentions after the Munich crisis helps to explain why the president viewed a victory by Franco as a substantial defeat for American interests. In 1936–37, when FDR was unsure about German aims, his major concern about the Spanish Civil War was the possibility of escalation, not the character of the government in Madrid. After Munich, once Roosevelt believed that Hitler intended to fight, the outcome in Spain became more significant in strategic terms. If Franco won, he might ally with Germany and Italy in a future European conflict. In this case France would face a war on three fronts, and British Gibraltar would also be threatened. On 7 December 1938 Sumner Welles passed highly confidential information to the president that detailed "the establishment of nineteen German and Italian bases in the Basque provinces of Spain" and indicated "the exact distance from these bases to strategic positions in France." On 9 January 1939 Welles forwarded intelligence on German submarine bases in Spain.[25]

The second reason for Roosevelt's growing pro-Loyalism was his fear that a victory by Franco would lead to increased fascist subversion and intervention in Latin America. Although the largest contingent of foreign troops in Spain had been sent by Rome, it was not Italian expatriates, or likely Italian military intervention in Latin America, which concerned Roosevelt. As the president remarked to Francis Biddle, "I don't care so much about the Italians. They are a lot of opera singers, but the Germans are different, they may be dangerous."[26] Many in the government considered Berlin's penetration of Latin America to be the most direct threat to American security. By 1938 Germany had organized fascist parties in Latin America, established propaganda organizations, underwritten arms sales, and engaged in barter trade agreements. In May 1938 a fascist group in Brazil attempted an unsuccessful coup d'état. Roosevelt perceived American security as being intrinsically tied up with that of the western hemisphere as a whole and saw German activities as a threat to the Monroe Doctrine. Roosevelt encouraged closer military contacts with Latin American states, including a Standing Liaison Committee established for this purpose in March 1938.[27]

In Roosevelt's mind the model for a fascist assault on the western hemisphere was the Spanish Civil War. Germans in Latin America would incite a civil conflict and then fascist aircraft would decisively intervene, as they had done in Spain. Several Americans had already noted this potential analogy between Spain and Latin America in 1936–37. For example, the journalist Livingston Hartley wrote in 1937 of the "imminent eruption of civil conflict all over Latin America, patterned after the carnage in Spain." At the time, the president and his administration tended not to take this threat seriously.[28]

The situation had changed by 20 April 1938, when Roosevelt voiced his fears: "Suppose certain foreign governments, European governments, were to do in Mexico what they did in Spain. Suppose they would organize a revolution, a Fascist revolution in Mexico. Mexico is awfully close to us, and suppose they were to send planes and officers and guns and were to equip the revolutionists and get control of the whole of Mexico and thereupon run the Mexican Government, run the Mexican army and build it up with hundreds of planes. Do you think that the United States could stand idly by and have this European menace right on our borders? Of course not." It was not Soviet intervention in Spain that concerned the president: the only foreign governments mentioned were the "Italian flag or the German flag." FDR thought that such a situation could happen anywhere in Latin America. When asked by an interviewer if there was any reason why European states would establish a conflict in Mexico, FDR shot back: "They did it in Spain." "I know," the interviewer pointed out, "but that is across the Atlantic." The president responded that Spain "is three days from Germany and Mexico is only seven days from Germany."[29]

Roosevelt's ambassador to Spain reinforced such ideas. On 9 May Bowers wrote to FDR: "If fascism wins in Spain, it will mean a tremendous impetus to fascism in Latin South America." After reading the letter the president asked to discuss the matter with Welles.[30] Later in the summer he warned Prime Minister W. L. Mackenzie King of Canada that Germany and Italy were fomenting revolution in South America.[31] Evidence of fascist attempts to engender civil conflict in Latin America mounted in the wake of the Munich crisis. After an attempted rightist coup in Chile, the *Nation* wrote: "Just as Spain was invaded because of its strategic importance in a possible war of the fascist powers against France and Great Britain, so Latin America is being contended for as a base of operations from which Germany's military, naval, and air forces might launch a decisive attack on the United States and the Panama Canal in the upcoming world war."[32]

On 24 October 1938 Bowers told FDR: "Hitler and Mussolini are working on South America as you know. They are now organizing a fascist organization in Franco Spain of all South and Central Americans living in Spain."[33] The Brazilian foreign minister wrote to Welles on 8 November, outlining a grave political situation. Germany planned to dominate Latin America, initially by "fomenting disorder, revolution and civil wars, in order to justify an intervention similar to that in Spain."[34] On 14 November the U.S. Standing Liaison Committee reported that it expected rebellions backed by Germany to break out in Uruguay, Argentina, and Brazil, and on the same day Archibald MacLeish, poet and friend of FDR, wrote to the president, arguing that a victory by Franco in Spain would lead to a chain of fascist coups in Latin America. FDR summoned him to report to the White House.[35] On 15 November Roosevelt stated at a press conference that he foresaw a potential German invasion of Brazil, "via the unprotected bulge of South America."[36]

Two days later, on 17 November, Breckinridge Long, who had formerly been a lobbyist for the Spanish Loyalists and had recently become Roosevelt's secret ambassador to South America, reported on the extent of fascist penetration in the region. The Brazilian foreign minister had told Long that the attempted coup in May 1938 had been "sponsored by the activists of the German embassy." According to the minister, a future insurrection in the German-populated parts of Brazil was almost certain, and he requested help from Washington to combat this internal threat.[37] More worrying news came on 15 December, when Welles passed on to Roosevelt, in the "utmost confidence," an intercepted communication from the German general Heinz von Horntz in Brazil to Foreign Minister Joachim von Ribbentrop in Berlin. According to von Horntz, Brazil was divided, communists represented the largest party, and German agents were about to begin a coup. "The preparations for the armed movement are already well initiated . . . If civil war is brought about, everything will take care of itself."[38]

The very next day, on 16 December, Roosevelt's cabinet discussed the danger of fascist intervention in Latin America and emphasized the importance of the ongoing Pan-American Conference in Lima in forging hemispheric unity. According to Ickes, the president wanted the Conference to reach "an understanding that one country will not encourage or support an attempt at revolution in another."[39] FDR contacted Cordell Hull in Peru, via Sumner Welles, to ask him if it was possible to address these concerns in the Lima Declaration: "The President asked me to let you know that he believes that it would be highly desirable to have included in the proposed declaration of continental solidarity a statement to the effect that the American republics declare they QUOTE shall not permit any non-American state to assist or abet in the fomenting of internal disorder in any American republic UNQUOTE." Roosevelt realized that this principle was implied in the current wording, but he wanted stronger and more specific language. Yet he also recognized the great problems involved in altering language agreed to by over twenty states, and Hull replied that the final wording could not be predicted.[40]

On 4 January 1939 Roosevelt addressed Congress about the world situation and described the emergence of a model of fascist aggression: "We have learned that long before any overt military act, aggression begins with preliminaries of propaganda, subsidized penetration, the loosening of ties of good will, the stirring of prejudice and the incitement to disunion."[41] Hull believed that these tactics had been used in Austria and the Sudetenland, with German minorities destabilizing these states from within.[42] However, in relation to Latin America Roosevelt's principal analogy was the Spanish Civil War. In his conversation with Josephus Daniels on 14 January, the president expressed his fear that Spain today provided a glimpse of Brazil tomorrow: "FDR, speaking of our obligations under the Monroe Doctrine, indicated that the first danger to us would come from Brazil. I asked if it was because there were nearly a million Germans in Brazil, he answered 'there are a million and a half.' When . . . armadas of bombing planes from Africa (look how Africa juts out on the map) [are] ready to fly to Brazil a civil war would be started there and German planes will swoop down from Africa on Brazil to decide the war in favor . . . Germany. He spoke as if that might be the real danger to the continent."[43]

The Spanish Civil War as a potential model for fascist aggression was also in Roosevelt's mind when he spoke to an assembled group of senators on 31 January. FDR claimed that Germany might threaten Latin America by inciting a coup and then employing airpower. According to Roosevelt, Berlin could press a button and Germans in Brazil would attempt a revolution: "a very serious threat to the Brazilian government." He continued: "You would have a new government in Brazil completely dominated by Germany and Italy and Japan. There are a great many revolutionists in Brazil with a very excellent organization from the military and revolutionary viewpoint, and they are right in with the Germans and Italians." Venezuela and Colombia were also vulnerable. Indeed, a foreign power could spark a revolution in any Latin American country for "between a million and four million dollars." The threat was not simply internal revolution but also fascist intervention: "The Germans have 1,500 bombing planes that can go from Germany to Colombia inside of forty-eight hours."[44]

With the benefit of hindsight, these fears that the Spanish Civil War would be a prototype copied in the western hemisphere seem exaggerated. Roosevelt clearly thought that Germany and Italy had fomented revolution in Spain and that German minorities would act as a fascist vanguard in Latin America. In fact, neither Hitler nor Mussolini had directly engineered Franco's revolt, and German minorities in the western hemisphere were considerably less well orchestrated than FDR supposed. The plots in Brazil and Chile were largely unconnected to Berlin. A purported secret Nazi map published in the United States in 1938, showing Latin America divided up into five German vassal states, is now thought to have been the work of British intelligence.[45] In addition, arguments about German subversion and intervention in Latin America were undoubtedly an effective tool against isolationist opponents. Yet Roosevelt's consistent discussion of this menace, both in public and in private, suggests that on the basis of the available evidence he was personally convinced that the threat existed.[46]

The third reason for the president's increasing support for the Spanish Republic in 1938 was the scale of fascist intervention in Spain and the brutality of Franco's war effort. Italy continued to provide massive military assistance to Franco with few preconditions, including six thousand new troops, as well as new aircraft in June 1938. What had begun with the provision of a few transport planes in 1936 had turned into a huge, open-ended commitment. Mussolini's son-in-law, the foreign minister Galeazzo Ciano, told Hitler in 1940: "Franco had declared that if he received 12 transport planes or bombers he would have the war won in a few days. Those 12 airplanes became more than 1,000 airplanes, 6,000 dead and 14 billion lire."[47] Germany also continued to provide substantial military aid, although in return Berlin demanded access to Spanish mineral resources. In the fall of 1938 Franco grudgingly accepted greater German economic penetration in return for arms required to win the war.

On 20 February 1938 Bowers wrote to the president detailing German and Italian intervention in Spain. At the bottom of the letter Bowers scrawled the handwritten note: "Word has just reached us that an enormous shipment from Germany of 1000kg bombs is on its way. If so thought to mean an utterly ruthless bombing of Barcelona, Valencia and Madrid."[48] On 28 February Roosevelt personally forwarded information to the secretary of war to be kept "extremely secret" regarding German-Italian air supremacy in Spain.[49] Roosevelt wrote to Bowers on 7 March: "I hate to think of the war in Spain as a mere laboratory which continues to be financed for [fascist] experimentation."[50] On 21 April the president attacked the "terrible, inhuman bombing of the civilian population in Barcelona."[51]

Wider threats in Europe and Latin America, and the brutality of fascist intervention in Spain, all served to heighten Roosevelt's desire to aid the Spanish Republic. The battlefield fortunes of the Loyalists shaped his ability to do so. The new year began with a Republican success—the taking of Teruel. But Franco reoccupied it on 20 February, and followed through with a massive Nationalist offensive through Aragon. Alvah Bessie, an American member of the international brigades, wrote in his notebook on 18–19 March 1938: "Things look hard, here; the men are worn and discouraged, individualistic. It appears the brigade took a terrific licking . . . They have by dint of long months in the lines been reduced to a truly animal level."[52] On 15 April Franco's troops reached the Mediterranean and split the Republican zone in two, threatening the capital, Valencia.[53] Roosevelt and Hull believed that the Spanish government was virtually defeated. In February and March FDR sought to bolster Loyalist morale by sending Bowers on periodic trips to Barcelona from France, where the American embassy had moved. Roosevelt "rejected the arguments that [the State Department] put forward that this would be construed under present conditions as a move to bolster up the Loyalist Government despite our policy of noninterference and nonintervention which we had pursued to date." It was discovered, however, that only two roads were open and both were constantly shelled.[54]

The French decision to open the frontier to Loyalist military supplies in March helped to ward off an immediate Republican defeat. This recovery created the possibility for American intervention in the Spanish Civil War. By the summer, the military situation had stabilized sufficiently to enable a Loyalist offensive on the Ebro River.[55] Bowers wrote on 18 August that there had been a "radical, even sensational change" in the military situation, with divisions growing in Franco's coalition. Roosevelt's reply on 31 August noted that Bowers's summary checked with his other sources: "I

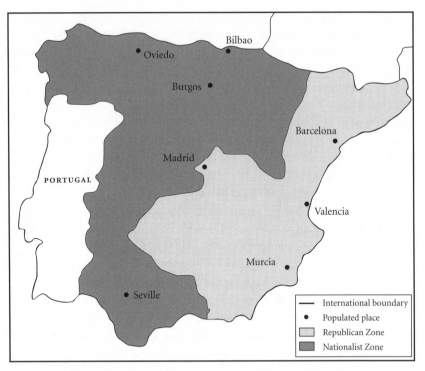

Spain, October 1937

am particularly interested in what you say about the situation in rebel territory." Nationalist disagreement would facilitate the mediation proposals
that Roosevelt was already formulating.[56]

Having radically reevaluated what was at stake in the Spanish Civil War,
on 27 January 1939 FDR spoke before his cabinet and explicitly characterized a victory by Franco as a defeat for American national interests. Roosevelt said that he had previously acted in "the belief that" Washington was
working in its "own interests" over Spain, but this had now become un-
tenable: "He very frankly stated, and this for the first time, that the embargo had been a grave mistake . . . The President said that we would never
do such a thing again . . . He agreed that this embargo controverted old
American principles and invalidated established international law." Roosevelt then suggested that the Spanish Civil War could be the first round
of a larger European or world conflict: "The President said the policy we
should have adopted was to forbid the transportation of munitions of war
in American bottoms. This could have been done and Loyalist Spain would

still have been able to come to us for what she needed to fight for her life against Franco—to fight for her life and for the lives of some of the rest of us as well, as events will very likely prove."[57] Roosevelt's hostility was now focused on the fascist-dominated Nationalists. Gone were references to the Loyalists as dangerous radicals. By 1940 FDR had come to see the Spanish Civil War as a conflict between "democracy" and "other forms of government."[58]

The relationship between Roosevelt's perceptions of the Spanish Civil War and his beliefs about the broader international environment was reciprocal, with Iberian events influencing the president's wider thinking. That Spain could be a model for fascist expansion shaped his views of the threat to Latin American security. The Spanish Civil War also consistently demonstrated the aggressive nature of the German and Italian regimes.

In addition, events in Spain influenced Roosevelt's views of Britain. In FDR's eyes the British were failing to fulfill the role traditionally assigned to them by American statesmen: that of protector of global order. Roosevelt told Bowers in March 1938 that he hated compromise with principle and suspected failure by Chamberlain. Thus "public morality will be shot and he will be overthrown."[59] In its Spanish policy Britain appeared to be displaying a lack of resolve, a mixture of cynicism and weakness. In 1938 British public opinion became more favorable toward the Spanish Republic, as did anti-appeasement figures such as Winston Churchill, who had originally supported Franco but changed his allegiance in the wake of fascist intervention in Spain. Eden's resignation in February 1938, however, was a decisive victory for Chamberlain's policy of limiting the war to Spain, even if this policy meant casting a blind eye toward fascist intervention and thereby sacrificing the Spanish Republic. Chamberlain concluded that a Nationalist victory would not produce a major defeat for British interests in the Mediterranean, because Franco would require financing from London to rebuild Spain. On 12 January 1939 Halifax told the Italians that he hoped Franco "would settle the Spanish question."[60] During this period the British consistently backed international nonintervention in Spain, despite its illusory character, and aimed to draw Franco away from his fascist patrons after his perceived inevitable triumph.

In 1937 Roosevelt commented on the "ridiculous" nature of British denials that large-scale intervention was occurring in Spain.[61] He wrote to Bowers on 31 August 1938: "I do wish that our British friends would see the situation as it seems to be—but as you know, they are doing everything to stall off controversy and possible war until at least 1940. It is amazing and sad to note that so many small nations have lost their confidence in England during the past two or three years."[62] By January 1939 Roosevelt thought that Britain "had fooled herself with respect to Spain" and "cringed like a coward."[63]

Several major strands of Roosevelt's thinking in 1938 pointed toward a more interventionist stance in the Spanish Civil War. Events in Spain, Europe, and Latin America interacted to sharpen his fears about the effects of a Nationalist victory on American interests, as well as intensifying his aversion to the brutal nature of fascist aggression. Meanwhile, the Republican military stabilization made it possible for Roosevelt to consider interventionist schemes, specifically increasing the perceived efficacy of mediation. His aims were no longer focused on preventing the Spanish Civil War from engendering a wider European conflict as in 1936. Neither did he simply desire to promote nonintervention in Spain as in 1937. Instead Roosevelt sought to block a victory by Franco, if necessary through some form of American intervention.

CHAPTER 7

Covert Aid

For President Roosevelt, the worsening international security environment in 1938 coexisted with a deteriorating domestic situation. FDR's New Deal did not end the Depression; the war economy of the Second World War did. Although economic conditions eased between 1933 and 1937, a sharp contraction in 1938—the "Roosevelt Recession"—left 19 percent of Americans out of work. Furthermore, the charge that the president was a nascent dictator reemerged when FDR sought to reform the executive agencies. The House defeated the Reorganization Act with 108 Democrats defecting. A new alliance between congressional Republicans and conservative Southern Democrats blocked a range of New Deal measures on food regulation, labor standards, and housing. Roosevelt's attempt to purge conservatives from the Democratic Party largely failed. With FDR seemingly unlikely to run again in 1940, the president enjoyed limited political leverage, and was left in a weak position to demand greater control over foreign affairs.

As these domestic woes mounted, the Spanish Civil War sparked a political storm. By the spring of 1938 pressure from pro-Loyalists to repeal the Spanish embargo, and from Catholic groups to retain it, reached new heights. The British consul in New York reported in February that the city was "almost assuming the likeness of a miniature Spain."[1] FDR himself was disturbed that the country had "split up and become so emotioned [*sic*] over the Spanish issue."[2]

Caution is required in interpreting poll data on American opinions about the Spanish Civil War. Questions on the same topics were often worded differently, or even worded with a distinct bias. Poll numbers sometimes included "no opinion" answers, at other times not. In addition, it is unclear how much attention Roosevelt paid to opinion polls in this period, as he only received them directly in September 1939. But Roosevelt was at least aware of some of the poll findings. On 25 January 1939 Eleanor Roosevelt had a conversation with the president about the Gallup polls on the Spanish Civil War.[3]

With these reservations in mind, the polls in 1938–39 indicate that a considerable minority of Americans, perhaps even a majority, was still largely uninterested in Spain, or at least unwilling to take sides. When asked with which group in Spain they sympathized, those offering "no opinion" or "neither" answers represented 33 to 52 percent of respondents. This was a decline from the figure in the spring of 1937 of 66 to 79 percent. Given the options of sympathizing with the Republicans, the Nationalists, or neither side, the peak number who stated that they were pro-Republican during this period was 51 percent.[4] There were limits, therefore, to the ability of pro-Loyalists to mobilize mass sections of American society. George Orwell ended *Homage to Catalonia* by writing that everyone was "sleeping the deep, deep sleep of England, from which I sometimes fear that we shall never wake until we are jerked out of it by the roar of bombs."[5] Eleanor Roosevelt explained to Martha Gellhorn in early 1939 that Americans felt relatively safe and were unwilling to make sacrifices for other countries: "I have an idea that your younger generation is perhaps going to be willing to make some sacrifices which will really change much of today's picture."[6]

Despite the apathy of a substantial section of the public, pro-Republican groups were winning the argument for American support. The British embassy in Washington reported in January 1939 that sympathy among Americans was "very largely with the Barcelona Government," owing particularly to fears of increased German and Italian influence in Latin America.[7] Among Americans who backed one of the sides in Spain, support was 75 percent for the Spanish Republic and 25 percent for the Nationalists. The Catholic laity tended to be pro-Franco, but not overwhelmingly so: 42 percent of Catholics who sympathized with either side in December 1938 favored the Loyalists. For Protestants the figure was 83 percent. Yet despite this growing sympathy for the Loyalists, large majorities wanted to retain the embargo. Among all the polls of this period, the highest figure backing repeal of the embargo was only 34 percent. This figure did rise to over 40 percent when the question was asked only of those who claimed to be following the Spanish Civil War.[8]

What the poll numbers do not capture is the sheer intensity of feeling and emotion generated by the Spanish issue within mobilized liberal and Catholic groups. Pro-Loyalists pointed to the farce of international non-intervention and demanded a return to the traditional American policy of trading with a recognized government facing a rebellion. With the Nationalists militarily supplied by Germany and Italy, the Spanish Republic was unable to defend itself by purchasing weapons in the United States. Pro-Loyalist arguments were sometimes tinged with Anglophobia: repealing the embargo would draw the United States away from a perceived pro-British policy.

In 1938 pro-Loyalist groups shifted their efforts from promoting the extension of the embargo to Germany and Italy and argued instead for repealing the embargo against the Spanish Republic. Mail sent to the State Department in favor of extending the embargo numbered 2,004 items in March 1938, compared with 1,066 pieces of mail in favor of lifting the embargo. By May only 149 letters called for extension while 18,299 letters argued for raising the embargo.[9] The pro-Loyalist movement included a number of influential figures: the former American ambassador to Italy, Breckinridge Long; the former secretary of state Henry L. Stimson; and the former ambassador to Germany William Dodd. Ernest Hemingway wrote a series of articles in 1938 arguing for repeal of the embargo: "If the democratic nations allow Spain to be overrun by the fascists through their refusal to allow the legal Spanish government to buy and import arms to combat a military insurrection and fascist invasion then they will deserve whatever fate brings them."[10] Throughout 1938 liberals close to the president constantly reminded Roosevelt of the iniquitous effects of the embargo. Not least among these lobbyists was the president's wife Eleanor, who continued to strongly identify with the Loyalist cause.[11]

The most committed American pro-Loyalists were still fighting and dying in Spain. By 1938 some American volunteers became disillusioned, not only at the horrors of the war and the casualty rates but also at Soviet policy in Spain and the show trials taking place in Moscow. When the international brigades were disbanded in November 1938, three-quarters of the (now merged) Lincoln-Washington battalion were Spanish. Despite this, for many volunteers the experience had strengthened their belief that Spain was the first round of a larger war, and they sought to rejoin the fight in 1941.[12]

On the other side of the debate, Catholic organizations formed the backbone of efforts to retain the Spanish embargo. The publication *America* argued: "We stand unalterably opposed, as Americans who are Catholics, to the pseudo-democratic, the soured liberal, the concealed Communist forces that are applying such unholy pressure on the president and Congress to plant American guns in Spain, to fill the Spanish air with American planes and to riddle the men of Spain with American bullets." To his millions of listeners, the "radio priest" Father Coughlin depicted Franco as a "rebel for Christ, a rebel for humanity's sake," fighting a "Loyalist-Communist" regime which Coughlin claimed had killed 300,000 women and children.[13]

Despite the poll evidence that American Catholics were divided in their attitude toward Spain, politicians were impressed by the unity of the Catholic hierarchy's stance and their ability to mobilize Catholics en masse as lobbyists and voters. When the Catholic publication *Commonweal* altered its editorial position from pro-Franco to neutral in June 1938, sales dropped by a quarter in just a few months. Many American political figures were very cautious about publicly stating their pro-Loyalist views. The journalist Drew Pearson printed a list of seven anti-embargo cabinet members in 1939. One of those named, Frank Murphy, issued a public denial, despite privately telling Pearson that he did in fact favor repeal of the embargo. Bernard Baruch also privately supported aiding the "democratically elected" Spanish Republic. Yet when he contributed $11,060 in 1938 to get the American volunteers home, he faced stern criticism from Catholic publications. Baruch responded timidly that the money "was in no way an expression of sympathy for the cause for which these young men volunteered."[14]

In the spring of 1938 there was a movement in Congress to end the Spanish embargo. The repeal argument was strengthened in part by the situation in the Far East, where Roosevelt had postponed a decision on enforcing neutrality legislation in the Sino-Japanese war. Although some isolationists complained about this failure to embargo arms sales, there was little public outcry, mainly because of widespread sympathy with the Chinese. Proponents of lifting the Spanish embargo could thus argue that this action would bring both Spanish and Chinese policies into alignment.

In March 1938 Representative Jerry O'Connell introduced a House resolution to amend the existing neutrality legislation, including the Spanish embargo. Sam McReynolds, chairman of the House Foreign Relations Committee, initially agreed to hearings before finally refusing. James Roosevelt claimed that the hearings were stopped by the State Department to avoid public discussion of the Spanish embargo. On 24 March Breckinridge Long, employed as a lobbyist by pro-Loyalists, visited Roosevelt to argue in favor of repealing the embargo. FDR, sympathetic but noncommittal, suggested that Long talk to Hull. A week later Hull told Long that the embargo might be lifted if fascist intervention could be proved: "Hull said he would reconsider if he received sufficient factual information about Italo-German invasion in Spain—so sufficient to justify a change of policy so the president could revoke the Proclamation of Neutrality and embargo of war implements. The Spanish Ambassador today furnished him with substantial proof of alleged 'invasion' of Spain. Whether that is sufficient remains to be seen."[15]

Long did secure a promise that the embargo issue would be placed before the president. But on 10 April Long thought that no change of policy was likely, primarily because the Loyalists looked close to military collapse. Late March was also the height of the fight in Congress over reorganizing executive agencies, and FDR was particularly reluctant at this time to engage in a violent political quarrel to lift the embargo. On 5 April Byron Scott introduced a House resolution to repeal the Spanish embargo, but this effort also failed. Hull, who favored wider neutrality reform but not the repeal of the Spanish embargo, telegraphed the U.S. embassy in Spain in early April to state that repeal was "not in prospect." But a few weeks later Roosevelt was told that Senator Key Pittman, chairman of the Senate Foreign Relations Committee, might act on the Spanish question. On 2 May Senator Gerald Nye introduced a resolution to allow arms sales to Loyalist Spain.[16]

"Roosevelt Backs Lifting Arms Embargo on Spain; Congress Agrees It Fails; Policy Is Doomed," announced the sensational banner headline of the *New York Times* on 5 May 1938. The paper dramatically reported that the president backed repeal for both sides in Spain and that the measure would pass through Congress. Was the *New York Times* correct? Had Roosevelt decided to support lifting the arms embargo, an event with enormous potential consequences for American and European politics?

Tracing the events of the next few days is difficult. For example, the likelihood that the Nye resolution would pass through Congress was at the time, and remains, very unclear. Senator Arthur Vandenberg believed that the resolution should not be taken seriously. Pittman, however, stated that such a powerful lobby as favored repeal was rarely seen in Washington. The chief of the Division of European Affairs in the State Department, J. Pierrepont Moffat, concluded that the resolution would pass "overwhelmingly." Nye himself thought that it would be reported out of committee by a four-to-one margin. Furthermore, assessing Roosevelt's exact views of the Nye resolution is problematic because the president was away from Washington, having departed for a cruise on 30 April.[17]

Despite these difficulties, we can confidently state that the story in the

New York Times was incorrect: there is little evidence that Roosevelt sought to lift the Spanish embargo in the spring or summer of 1938. In the period before the Munich crisis, the president continued to display qualified personal support for the intrinsic aims of nonintervention in Spain. In February Roosevelt told Eleanor that it would be impossible to repeal the Neutrality Act because of public opinion, but the legislation, in any case, had some merit: "the people of this country feel that it was designed to keep us out of war, and, on the whole, it is the best instrument to accomplish that end." The existence of doubt is suggested, however, by Roosevelt's comment that Americans would require a "period of education" to change their views. Eleanor later recalled: "by trying to convince me that our course was correct, though he knew I thought we were doing the wrong thing, he was simply trying to salve his own conscience, because he himself was uncertain."[18]

Roosevelt publicly wondered whether the Loyalists would benefit from a lifting of the embargo. It was unclear, for example, if arms would be able to reach the Republic given its deteriorating military position. In the spring of 1938 the Nationalists launched a massive offensive through Aragon. By now Franco had about 20 percent superiority in men and a huge advantage in aircraft and other equipment. On 19 March Breckinridge Long wrote of Loyalist Spain, "each day becoming more hopeless in its struggle." Long commented on 1 April: "it looks as if the Loyalist government was collapsing under the pressure of big guns, tanks and aircraft superiority."[19] With the Loyalists demoralized and short of weapons, the Nationalists reached the coast on 15 April, cutting Catalonia off from the main Republican zone in southern and central Spain. By this stage the Nationalists had effectively quarantined the Spanish Republic's Mediterranean ports. Aid for Republican Spain had to follow a tortuous route, arriving first at the French Atlantic coast before being shipped across land to the Mediterranean coast.

In April 1938, when the Mexican ambassador urged Roosevelt to lift the arms embargo, the president thought that doing so would "uselessly agitate public opinion." Roosevelt told Senator William Borah that it was "too late to do any real good." The president added that the Nationalists enjoyed naval supremacy and that a third of American ships carrying arms to Spain would be sunk.[20] At press conferences during 20–23 April FDR commented that lifting the embargo would aid Franco, because only the Nationalists could purchase and transport American arms to Spain. The effect of repeal "would be that Franco, controlling the sea, could send his ships directly to the United States and load them up with bombs and airplanes."[21]

On 30 April Jay Allen recalled a conversation with Pittman. Roosevelt had "shocked" the senator by stating that he would neither oppose the Nye Resolution nor give it his blessing, "on the grounds that the material sent would be captured in the Mediterranean and used by [Franco]."[22] With the president only beginning to show uncertainty about the intrinsic merits of American nonintervention in Spain, he was unlikely to push for risky strategies that appeared doomed to fail.

These doubts were reinforced by considerable domestic and international constraints. After the hasty decision to give up presidential discretion over the Spanish embargo in January 1937, Congress rather than Roosevelt would ultimately decide the issue. Thus even if FDR backed repeal of the embargo, it could not be guaranteed to pass. Roosevelt's political capital was at a very low point in the spring of 1938, his popularity slipping as the economy waned. The chief proponent of repeal, Gerald Nye, was hardly a natural ally for the president; indeed Nye was a fierce critic of many of Roosevelt's other policies. By February 1939 the two men were barely speaking, after Nye expressed opposition to Roosevelt's rearmament plans. Furthermore, one of the key New Deal constituencies, American Catholics, was mobilized in defense of the embargo.

At the international level the president was aware of the danger that any sudden American initiatives in the Spanish Civil War could spark a European crisis. He knew that the British strongly opposed repeal of the embargo, at a time when Chamberlain was stepping up his efforts to appease Italy. Roosevelt's ambassador in London reported British attitudes toward repeal on 9 May 1938: "With all its faults non-intervention has contributed towards the preservation of peace in Europe . . . The injection of any new factor into this already overcharged and delicate situation, might have far reaching consequences."[23]

In a potentially promising development for the Spanish Republic, a group had formed in the State Department around Assistant Secretary of State George Messersmith that was critical of European appeasement efforts. Messersmith, a bitter opponent of Nazism from the start, believed that concessions to the dictators would bring European war in the end, and on less favorable terms. Hitler sought world domination and would not be satisfied with the gains made in 1938. Messersmith concluded in February that "there is no small country in South-eastern or in Northern Europe which can have any further illusions as to its security." After the Munich crisis Messersmith argued that making concessions to avoid war might actually make war inevitable and called for a more active international role for the

United States. In the State Department Stanley Hornbeck generally supported Messersmith, as did Secretary of the Interior Harold Ickes and Secretary of the Treasury Henry Morgenthau. Yet Messersmith and Hornbeck were not primarily interested in Spain: what they wanted was to stiffen wider British and French policy.[24]

Overall, in spite of Messersmith's anti-fascist stance, Roosevelt's foreign policy officials in the spring of 1938 continued overwhelmingly to back nonintervention in Spain. Self-styled realists such as Moffat, Welles, Assistant Secretary Adolf Berle, and Assistant Secretary R. Walton Moore were distrustful of Britain and skeptical about a more active international role for the United States, particularly in such a dangerous conflict as the Spanish Civil War. Berle wrote on 19 March 1938: "About half of [the State Department] is following a Wilsonian moral line which in my judgment would lead eventually to our entry into a war on the British side. The other half, headed by Sumner and myself, is still endeavoring to steer matters into an ultimate conference."[25] Berle did not see a German takeover of Czechoslovakia as a "cause for alarm." Even after the Munich crisis, Welles remained focused on Latin American relations and believed that the key to peace lay in an international economic conference between democrats and dictators.[26]

Secretary of State Cordell Hull continued to view the Spanish Civil War in terms of the need to cooperate with Britain, the potential for divisions within the western hemisphere, and the dangerous complications that could arise from any initiatives by Washington. He never wavered once in his backing for the Spanish embargo. In his conversation on 11 May with Herbert Feis, an economic advisor to the president, Hull remarked that he wished to "burn Hitler in oil." But at the same time Hull was "greatly upset" because "the present move to repeal the embargo is largely Communist-inspired. He feels and resents it, because of its possible effect on the heightening controversies in Europe."[27] Morgenthau believed that the reason Roosevelt did not lift the embargo was "less a fear of alienating organized pro-Franco groups in the country than a desire not to force the hand of his Secretary of State."[28]

Hull was perturbed over attacks on the State Department in the pro-Loyalist press, which implied that he "could not keep order in his own house." On 4 May, for example, the journalist Drew Pearson criticized R. Walton Moore for backing congressional control of the embargo in January 1937: "thus the whole map of Europe may have been changed by the ambitions of one old man." For a short while in the wake of this press censure, several State Department officials were willing to request that Congress merely repeal the arms embargo for both sides in Spain, rather than oppose repeal outright. Hull, however, wanted to delay a decision.[29] If necessary, Moore remarked, "[I am] perfectly willing to bear any odium attaching to the charge that I brought about the course taken by our Government and that it had your disapproval and represents the major blunder of the Administration and may have the effect of changing the map of Europe." Moore added that he was "trying to find an opportunity to deal face to face with Pierson [*sic*] in such manner as I desire."[30] At a press conference on 6 May, Hull "blew up" against Drew Pearson and was skeptical about repeal of the embargo. The United States had "enough to do," as Hull put it, "to look out for more immediate interests and affairs than to be watching opportunities to get into a situation fraught with danger."[31] As Breckinridge Long reported the episode, Pearson, "out of an excess of animosity and hot-headedness," published some highly critical articles about the State Department and Cordell Hull, which "got him mad," undermining Long's efforts to lift the embargo.[32]

The American ambassador to Spain, Claude Bowers, identified the Spanish war from the start as a fight between fascism and democracy. Yet for the first eighteen months of the conflict he supported nonintervention. By 1938 Bowers concluded that the embargo aided Franco, and in February he wrote that he would personally like the United States to support the Loyalists, but that American public opinion would not countenance such a move. Finally, in June 1938 Bowers wrote to Hull arguing that the U.S. government should grant the Spanish Loyalists the right to buy American aircraft: "There is but one language that [the fascists] understand—the language of force. So long as the Spanish Government is refused the right to buy anti-aircraft guns and planes for the defense of loyalist towns and cities, these bombings will continue and increase in intensity, despite the protests of the outside world. The only answer to that policy is to grant the Spanish Government the right to buy the planes and guns necessary for the protection of its people. An analogy to the present situation in Spain would be to refuse arms to the police in their war with gun-men gangsters, and to remonstrate with the gun-men against using guns against the police."[33]

The State Department had little time for Claude Bowers's fervent beliefs and colorful language, and kept him in the dark over some of the larger dimensions of Spanish policy. As Bowers privately lamented on 1 December 1938: "For a year and a half I have been hammering the State Department with the warning that were Franco to win for fascism we shall have an enemy playing the game of fascism in South America and that the triumph of the Spanish Democracy would be in our interests. I have not had any reaction whatever from the State Department."[34]

Nevertheless, Roosevelt always heeded Bowers's views. On 7 March 1938 he told Bowers that if possible he would like him to come back to Washington in the fall to help with the congressional campaign. Bowers's return would also "help in the State Department, itself."[35] There is evidence that the ambassador's information about Spain was influential in Roosevelt's later plans for mediation and humanitarian aid.

Aside from Bowers, the key European ambassadors remained strongly opposed to lifting the Spanish embargo. William C. Bullitt in Paris was so anxious about the possibility of war that in May he suggested calling a conference of the European powers to legitimize the breakup of Czechoslovakia. War would destroy western civilization to the benefit of Moscow. Bullitt did alter his views after Munich, when he argued that the United States should supply aircraft to the European democracies. In Bullitt's eyes intervention in Spain would complicate rather than simplify a resolution of the central issues of European politics.[36] Joseph Kennedy, who became ambassador to Britain in January 1938, also strongly supported the Spanish embargo. Kennedy became a close friend of Chamberlain, defended British appeasement, and highlighted the Bolshevik menace. In April, Kennedy hoped that the president would "share [the] view that [the Anglo-Italian agreement] embodies a real contribution towards world appeasement." In September 1938 Kennedy intended to remark in a speech, "I can't for the life of me understand why anyone would want to go to war to save the Czechs," but Roosevelt and the State Department insisted that the line be cut. Kennedy became a prophet of gloom about the prospects for peace and for Britain's likely survival in any future conflict, and he supported American withdrawal from European high politics.[37] With William Phillips in Rome and Hugh Wilson in Berlin both consistent in their beliefs about European affairs and the Spanish embargo, the realists now dominated the European embassies.

The president's disinclination to raise the embargo was enhanced by the nature of Nye's resolution, which would force Roosevelt into a stark choice of repudiating either the Catholics or the liberals. The proposed bill authorized the president only to lift the embargo for the Loyalists, not to reconsider wider neutrality legislation. On 30 April Long reported that he had drafted a resolution for Nye "amending the Neutrality Act by repealing the parts about 'civil strife' and providing goods shall not be shipped in American bottoms or belong to Americans." But as Long reported in May, the situation had changed: "Nye introduced his resolution last week . . . but [it] was not my resolution. He changed it the last moment and he phrased it that it applies only to Spain—not to the general neutrality law;—and proposes to authorize the President to revoke the embargo—instead of repealing the provisions of law on which the embargo rested. In other words he changed it to [his] own political partisan purpose and to place the President in the position of acting affirmatively and to take all the opposition attacks—to bear the brunt of the blame and opposition—whereas a repeal of the civil war parts of the Neutrality Act, with all political parties cooperating, would share responsibility."[38]

The story in the *New York Times* of 5 May stating Roosevelt's support for repealing the embargo was based on a leak by the administration. The journalist responsible, Arthur Krock, said in an interview in 1963 that the story had been planted.[39] The historian Leo Kanawada offers an interesting hypothesis: Roosevelt deliberately leaked the story to provoke a tidal wave of Catholic pressure on Congress and thereby defeat Nye's resolution: "a calculated political maneuver of enormous significance by a master politician."[40] In defense of this hypothesis, Roosevelt was extremely cautious about repealing the embargo at this time. In addition, the journalist Jay Allen told Harold Ickes on 7 May that the story was a deliberate plant to stir up the Catholics.[41]

Yet the evidence that Roosevelt sought to mobilize Catholic opinion against Nye is not conclusive, and there is a competing explanation: that the story was leaked as a "trial balloon," to test public opinion about repealing the embargo. Ickes was told by Drew Pearson—on the same day he heard from Jay Allen that the story was designed to inflame the Catholics—that in Pearson's opinion the "story was based on the facts." Given these different interpretations, Ickes concluded that it would be almost impossible to know Roosevelt's motives, because he was at that point sailing in the Caribbean.[42] In addition, it is not clear that leaking administration support for repeal would be a politically efficacious means of defeating Nye, since it could conceivably have emboldened the pro-repeal lobby, or focused Catholic hostility on the White House. Furthermore, newly discovered letters from Arthur Krock to Professor James Ragland between 1957 and 1962 demonstrate Krock's belief that the leaked story represented the truth. On 25 February 1957 Krock stated that his memory of events twenty years before was hazy. He recalled, however, that he did not actually write the story of 5 May but approved it as chief of the bureau: "that meant that it met a reasonable test of authenticity and my faint recollection is that the authority given me was a member of the Cabinet and some kind of confirmation on checking with the White House staff. As the situation progressed, the story seems now to have been one of those trial balloons which President Roosevelt was fond of having sent up for him, touching on policy he wanted to invoke but also wanted some advance public reaction . . . I have a feeling that Ickes, who was the sponsor of the Nye Resolution in the Cabinet was our source."[43]

Joseph Green also guessed at the time that Morgenthau or Ickes had leaked the story, believing that FDR had been won over to repeal.[44] But Ickes's own diary suggests that he was not in fact the source. On 1 May 1938, in his conversation with Ickes, Roosevelt was skeptical about lifting the embargo. Even in December 1938 Ickes wrote that he was unsure whether Roosevelt supported repeal.[45] In addition, five years after naming Ickes as the source, Krock in 1962 claimed that Cordell Hull, representing Roosevelt, had passed on the information. Krock maintained his belief that the story accurately described the wishes of the Roosevelt administration: "I assume now as I did then it represented what [Hull] wanted to have done."[46] The story clearly did not reflect Hull's views.[47] But we cannot ascertain whether the leak was an attempt to mobilize Catholics against Nye or alternatively was designed to test public opinion, with the option of later denying or even upholding the story.

If the precise motivation behind the leak is unclear, the Catholic reaction was unmistakable. Thousands of telegrams poured into Washington, and Moffat noted that "the bitterness inspired by this Spanish strife among the Left-Wingers on the one hand and the Catholic conservative elements on the other surpasses anything I have seen for years."[48] The president told Ickes on 8 May 1938: "to raise the embargo would mean the loss of every Catholic vote next fall and that the Democratic Members of Congress were jittery about it and didn't want it done." Ickes concluded that the Catholic minorities in Great Britain and America had dictated Spanish policy.[49] Roosevelt apparently told the Spanish Loyalist agent Miles Sherover: "Dammit, Sherover, if I lift the embargo, the Catholics will crucify me!"[50] Martha Gellhorn concluded that FDR "knew that there wasn't anything that could be done; the Roman Catholics had that one sewed up."[51]

Congressmen saw the Spanish embargo as political dynamite. It was learned that a Senate filibuster might be used to defeat Nye, regardless of where the president stood, because of concerns over congressional reelection in November. Pittman wrote to Ambassador Kennedy on 2 May: "The fight over the resolution—if there is a fight—will add another grief to the Democratic Congressmen who are running this year."[52] Rexford Tugwell and Thomas Corcoran, both advisors to Roosevelt, and Sumner Welles all mentioned Catholic pressure as a factor in the decision not to lift the embargo. James Roosevelt told Leo Kanawada: "although in their hearts and emotionally I am sure both my parents' sympathy was with the Republican government in Spain . . . the President most certainly was concerned with the Catholic-American community and tendency to vote en bloc during his Presidency."[53]

Yet resistance from the administration was as important as Catholic pressure in defeating Nye. Several repeal initiatives had already failed in the House in April, before the Catholic lobby had been fully mobilized. The House Foreign Affairs Committee refused to hold hearings, partly because FDR discouraged any action, and partly to avoid a public discussion of the issue. Roosevelt was still deeply cautious about the international repercussions of repealing the embargo and doubted its military value for the Loyalists. On 10 May the president gave Senator Borah three arguments against lifting the embargo: American arms would fall into the hands of the fascists; the Loyalists were probably doomed; and repeal would interfere with British and French foreign policy.[54]

But it appears that the president had considerable doubts about the merits of the Spanish embargo. Eleanor Roosevelt suggested in February 1938 that he was privately uncertain on the issue of repeal. By this stage the president clearly favored the Loyalists and recognized the danger of fascist aggression in Spain. On 22 April Jay Allen sent a telegram to Claude Bowers suggesting that Roosevelt was considering lifting the embargo on the basis that the war in Spain was no longer a civil war: "Talked [on the telephone with] my biologist friend and wonder if you know how tragically urgent situation stop white father gave intimation of concrete execution our action stop this possible legally by proclamation state civil war no longer exists implication being [that the Spanish Civil War was an] invasion [as in the case of] China stop obviously father disposed but friends say unaware urgency action stop . . . repeat that white father did make intimation." The "white father" was Roosevelt and the "biologist friend" was Juan Negrín, the Spanish Republican prime minister. We do not know the nature of the "intimation," but apparently Roosevelt was sympathetic toward bringing policy in the Spanish Civil War and the Sino-Japanese war into alignment through repeal.[55] Breckinridge Long's diary entry for 11 May stated: "[Roosevelt and Hull] had had a definite difference of opinion [over the embargo]. Tonight there are rumors Hull will resign. I doubt it." The president told his brother-in-law, G. Hall Roosevelt, that the embargo question "had not been decided."[56] Roosevelt in May 1938 was clearly wrestling with the multiple dimensions of American policy toward the Spanish Civil War.

Finally, on 11 May, Roosevelt approved Hull's letter to the Senate Foreign Relations Committee opposing the Nye resolution. Repeal that applied to both sides in Spain "would still subject us to unnecessary risks we have so far avoided. We do not know what lies ahead in the Spanish situation. The original danger still exists." The Senate Foreign Relations Committee immediately voted 17 to 1 to table the bill to repeal the embargo. With this controversial issue now defused, Pittman immediately "looked about five years younger."[57]

At this point American diplomacy toward the Spanish Civil War took an outlandish turn. Historians have found scattered references indicating the existence of a secret plot to aid the Spanish Republic by shipping American aircraft to Spain. What made this scheme noteworthy is that it stretched as far as the White House. Suggestions have been made by Frank Freidel that Roosevelt might have been personally involved, by Kenneth S. Davis that FDR was "almost certainly" not behind the plan, by Richard Traina that the president was attempting to "humor the family," by Blanche Wiesen Cook that the president's wife, Eleanor Roosevelt, was the principal organizer, and by Gerald Howson that there was little presidential involvement in this "frankly hair-brained scheme."[58] Where does the truth lie?

Newly discovered documents from Russian and American archives enable a convincing interpretation of events. In the spring of 1938 FDR supported maintenance of the Spanish embargo in part because he was privately developing an illegal scheme to circumvent Congress and the British by providing covert aid to Loyalist Spain. Roosevelt planned to send a large number of American aircraft to France, which would then be quietly shipped across the border into Spain. As a means of aiding the Loyalists, covert aid was deeply flawed. But this was also a highly significant episode, reflecting Roosevelt's changing perceptions of the Spanish Civil War as well as his ideas about creative policy making in a restricted political environment. We first need to set out the evidence for the covert aid episode. Much of the evidence is indirect or circumstantial, so we also need to see whether Roosevelt's involvement in the scheme is compatible with what we know about his beliefs in 1938.

The embargo introduced in January 1937 made it unlawful to ship arms directly to Spain "or to any other foreign country for transshipment to Spain," with penalties including a fine of as much as $10,000 and up to five years in prison.[59] Despite this legal prohibition on arms sales, rumors reached Spain of an impending large shipment of planes from the United States. In April 1938 Ernest Hemingway and Herbert Mathews of the *New York Times* told American volunteers that FDR planned to send two hundred planes to France if the French would send two hundred planes to Spain.[60] Although the details were incorrect, this rumor was apparently based on fact.

On 23 February 1938 the Spanish Republican ambassador Fernando de los Rios visited Assistant Secretary of State Sumner Welles to request an "urgent" audience with President Roosevelt. The ambassador was particularly worried by Hitler's recent speech indicating the German intention to secure a Nationalist victory in Spain, adding that "the Franco aviation forces had been very greatly augmented through the addition of German planes of the most modern type and that the confidential agents of the Loyalist government had verified the fact that these planes had gone directly to Nationalist Spain from Germany, flying over France during the night hours . . . Germany today was taking a more active participation in the Spanish war than at any previous time." Such reports clearly had an impact on the president. On 28 February he personally forwarded information to the secretary of war explaining how German-Italian air supremacy in Spain would imperil the Republican position.[61]

The newly opened Russian archives indicate that Roosevelt met de los Rios a few days later, "in early March." This conversation was repeated by de los Rios to the Soviet ambassador to the United States, who in turn forwarded details to Moscow. In the meeting de los Rios complained bitterly to FDR about the effects of the embargo on the Loyalist war effort: "Roosevelt replied to the Ambassador that one could not count on a lifting of the embargo but that he promised to give directives not to hinder the export of any weapons to France and not to enquire about the further destination of the cargo." In addition, as de los Rios reported, the president held a conversation on this same topic with the Mexican ambassador to the United States: "Roosevelt announced to the Mexican that he had taken steps to bring about the unimpeded export of arms to France 'to any company without verification' and that he would take steps toward the same unimpeded export via Mexico."[62]

This was important: the State Department had blocked several shipments of American weapons to France, Mexico, Latvia, Greece, and Turkey because of concerns that their final destination could be Spain. According to an earlier State Department ruling, countries receiving American arms had to provide assurances through the use of "end-user certificates" that the arms would remain within their borders for two years.[63] "I do not know what the practical effect of these statements [will be]," the Soviet ambassador reported, but de los Rios "trusts them."[64]

A window of opportunity for American arms supplies to the Loyalists existed in the spring and summer of 1938, after the French decided to open the frontier with Spain to military shipments from 17 March. The perception in the United States was that considerable supplies were getting through. Eleanor Roosevelt wrote to Martha Gellhorn on 23 May: "They insist in this country that, through France, as much material is going to the Loyalists as is going to Franco through Germany and Italy. Of course it is very hard to gauge."[65] Bullitt told Hull in May—almost certainly an exaggeration—that three hundred Soviet planes had crossed the frontier into Loyalist Spain. The French "had to cut down many miles of trees along the sides of the roads in order that the large bombers might pass." According to Bullitt, the French had told the British that they would ship across the frontier anything that any country wished to send to Spain.[66]

We are able to trace the unfolding of the American plot to circumvent neutrality legislation because a series of informants in the aircraft industry kept the State Department aware of developments. On 19 May 1938 Joseph Hartson of the Glenn L. Martin Company visited Joseph Green, head of the Office of Arms and Munitions Control. Hartson told Green that Miles Sherover had approached him with a proposal to purchase $50 million of bombing aircraft. Sherover, who had engaged in business deals involving the Russian government since the 1920s and was now the purchasing agent for the Loyalists in the United States, sent dozens of legal shipments of trucks, tires, machine tools, and other strategic materials from the United States to Loyalist Spain via France. He was, according to Adolf Berle, "one of the few men . . . who has made money out of the left wing."[67]

Sherover wanted the planes exported to France, consigned to a French company, with an obvious intention to transship them illegally to Spain. Sherover had added intriguingly: "matters could be so arranged that no difficulty would arise in connection with the exportation from the United States." If Sherover expected this proposal to remain confidential he was mistaken. Joseph Green found Hartson to be "an unusually reliant informant." Several weeks later, on 8 June, Green received another visit, this time from Major Victor Bertandias of the Douglas Aircraft Company, who reported attempts by an "unnamed businessman" to purchase several hundred used DC-2s and DC-3s for France, Sweden, and Greece—all clearly intended for Spain. Green noted on 13 June that a "large, well-organized plan is now afoot to buy used planes of any description in large numbers and export them to Spain by indirect shipment."[68]

One difficulty for the Loyalists, given the perilous state of their finances, was how they were going to pay for these aircraft. In 1936 most of the Spanish Republic's gold supply had famously been sent to Moscow to purchase Soviet arms. Less well known is that much of the Spanish silver supply ended up in the United States, and may have been intended to pay for American weapons. Roosevelt's support for Secretary of the Treasury Henry Morgenthau in his efforts to purchase Loyalist silver represents both the least important and most successful of the president's Spanish policies in 1938–39.[69]

The Neutrality Act of 1937 did not prevent Morgenthau from purchasing Republican silver coins, even though the Treasury usually only bought silver bars. On 20 January 1938 Ambassador de los Rios approached Sumner Welles about a possible American purchase of Spanish silver. Offered 55 million ounces, Morgenthau accepted 5 million as a trial shipment. Franco's lawyers in America immediately made a claim on the proceeds, arguing that the silver had been stolen from the Bank of Spain by communist agents, and that the U.S. government had thus connived with the Loyalists in illegal acts.[70]

The Treasury could have refused to pay for the silver until the Loyalists had cleared their legal title to it, but that course would fail to aid the Spanish government. Despite legal summons, Morgenthau planned to purchase ten million ounces of silver a month from Spain as well as twenty million from China, distributing the purchases "on the basis of direct hits by bombs." In court Henry L. Stimson represented the Treasury, remarking that he always preferred to advocate for the side with which he sympathized. John Foster Dulles represented Franco. It was the former secretary of state versus the future secretary of state.

Two facts about the case, eventually won by the Treasury, are pertinent.[71] First, the State Department refused to cooperate, rebuffing the Treasury's request for diplomatic immunity for a Loyalist officer of the Bank of Spain. Second, "in the face of Franco's legal opposition and the clear disapproval of the Department of State, Roosevelt from first to last supported [Morgenthau's] efforts to sustain the Loyalists."[72] In particular, Roosevelt backed the decision to ask Stimson to act as a legal representative. Although he may have known nothing about the covert aid scheme, Morgenthau explained to Ambassador de los Rios in June 1938, "We can give you cash . . . And you could do whatever you wanted with the cash."[73] During 1938 the U.S. Treasury paid $14 million to the Spanish government for 35 million ounces of silver. This was a considerable sum, given that a successful Loyalist fund-raising effort in the United States produced about $2 million for the Republican cause.

On 21 June 1938 the covert aid plot shifted to the Paris office of the American ambassador to France, William C. Bullitt. So surprised was Bullitt by the day's developments that he immediately fired off a detailed account to FDR in a "very private letter which requires no answer." Events began with the morning arrival of the French foreign secretary Georges Bonnet. The Spanish government had berated Bonnet for agreeing on 13 June to close the French frontier to military shipments, because they were suddenly able to "buy more than one hundred planes in the United States at once for immediate delivery to Spain via France." Bullitt relayed to President Roosevelt surprising news: "the Spanish Ambassador [to France] had asserted that you personally had approved the sale of these planes to the Spanish Government and that you were arranging for the evasion of the Neutrality Act involved in their shipment to France, knowing fully that their destination would be Spain." Bullitt was skeptical about this extraordinary claim and contacted the State Department for instructions, avoiding any mention of the charge that FDR was personally involved.[74]

Before he could get a reply from Washington, Bullitt suddenly received a telephone call from Gracie Hall Roosevelt. Hall was the brother of FDR's wife, Eleanor. Hall had been educated at Groton and Harvard and was a man of great charisma and physical vitality. After pursuing a career as an electrical engineer, Hall served in the Army Air Service in the First World War. In the decades to follow, Hall became well known in the French aviation world and later developed many contacts among pro-Loyalists. He first helped to provide arms for Spain toward the end of 1936, when he personally vouched at the State Department that France was the ultimate destination for a shipment of nineteen aircraft, which nevertheless ended up in Loyalist Spain.[75]

Eleanor Roosevelt had already contacted Ambassador Bullitt about the imminent arrival of her brother in Paris, asking the ambassador to do anything he could for him. Bullitt therefore invited Hall and his son Daniel to a ball. Hall, however, wanted to see Bullitt at once and went immediately to his office. Hall's claims upon arrival added to Bullitt's day of surprises. As the ambassador repeated the conversation to the president:

[Hall] acting through Harold Talbot of Cleveland,[76] had managed to gather for the Spanish Government approximately 150 new and second-hand planes of various makes—all of which he specified. He said that he had discussed this transaction with you and that it had your entire approval. He stated that you and he and Jimmy [James Roosevelt] had discussed all the details and that you had agreed to wink at the evasion of the Neutrality Act involved, because of your interest in maintaining the resistance of the Spanish Government against Franco, and on Monday, June 13th, had sent for Joseph Green,[77] who is in charge of such matters in the Department of State, and had ordered him to permit the export of these planes and to accept such falsified papers as might be presented and not scrutinize the entire matter too carefully.

When Bullitt told Hall that the embassy had heard nothing about this, Hall said that the president "had thought of writing" to Bullitt, but that since Hall "would arrive in Paris as quickly as a letter," the president "had preferred to have him explain the matter" to Bullitt "by word of mouth." When Bullitt informed Hall that the French government had closed the frontier to arms shipments on 13 June, Hall replied that he would contact James Roosevelt "with great discretion," because "the situation seemed to have changed since he left America." Bullitt added in his letter to FDR that he "could not imagine a moment more unpropitious" to organize covert arms sales. Not only would such an action violate the laws of the United States, it could also derail French and British attempts to withdraw foreign troops from Spain and attempt mediation.[78]

After Hall left, the State Department answered Bullitt's earlier enquiries by denying that its policy had altered. Joseph Green telephoned to say that the State Department was "fully aware of the attempt that certain people were making to ship a large number of second-hand planes to Spain, and had definitely decided to refuse export licenses for the shipment of such planes."[79] Recognizing the sensitivity of the episode, Bullitt finished his letter to Roosevelt by remarking that he had "not the slightest desire to know what lies behind this expedition of Hall's," adding that he would reveal these facts only to the president himself.[80]

But the details did leak out. Harold Ickes on 16 July recorded in his diary a story that Drew Pearson claimed was "absolutely straight" but that he had promised not to print: "When the Administration refused to lift the embargo against the shipment of arms to Spain, the President sent assurances to Drew Pearson through Tom Corcoran[81] that arms would be allowed to

clear for France whence they could be transshipped to Spain. This was satisfactory to the Spanish Loyalists and they proceeded to set up a French
corporation to handle the prospective shipments. When Bill Bullitt learned
of this, he sent a query to Washington. Not having been told of the President's interest, the State Department promptly clamped down so that this
plan of getting arms into Spain failed." FDR had personally given the orders
because "Mrs Roosevelt later told Bob Allen that she knew this had been
done." Ickes blamed the State Department for the failure of the scheme,
believing that it was "firmly resolved to further the foreign policy of Chamberlain."[82]

With the scheme disintegrating because of the State Department's
knowledge and the closure of the French frontier, Hall and his son Daniel
traveled from Paris to Spain. Daniel stayed in Spain for six weeks to interview members of the international brigades.[83] On 23 July Hall telephoned
FDR concerning the progress of the covert aid scheme. This time, because
Roosevelt was aboard ship, the message was written down and then given
to the president—thus allowing for its survival in the archives: "Impossible
to proceed with plain program [*sic*]. Welles advises last instructions from
you are not to change any Departmental regulations even if law allows.
Previous Mexican situation resulted in ruling requiring nation to assure
State Department that shipments would not leave country destined in less
than two years. This ruling now extended to all other countries. Present
conditions might well warrant changing regulations. No change in law or
proclamation involved. Shall follow instructions."[84] Hall reported that the
collapse of the aircraft "program" was due to the State Department's continued requirement for strict "end-user" guarantees, and requested further
directions from Roosevelt.

With the president soon occupied by the Munich crisis of September
1938, the covert aid scheme slipped into the background. But the story had
another twist. On 13 October Hall, Miles Sherover, and General R. C. Marshall visited the State Department to discuss the export of twenty-two Bel-
lanca aircraft as well as a number of DC-3 aircraft to France. In the official
account, Hall and Sherover were reminded of repeated efforts to export
the Bellancas indirectly to Spain, as well as Hall's earlier role in the transshipment of American aircraft in 1936. Hall then argued that no objection
should be made against the export of arms destined for the Loyalist government and apparently ended the conversation by stating that he would
visit Ambassador Bullitt in Paris.[85]

In a letter about the episode in March 1944, Joseph Green added significant details. Hall had claimed to be "an emissary from the White House and that his plans had the approval and support of the President." This claim was never included in the official memorandum of the meeting, "for reasons you can readily imagine." Green also revealed that after the meeting in 1938, Sumner Welles discussed the situation with FDR. The White House then stated that it "did not desire exceptional treatment of any kind for Mr. Hall Roosevelt." The president "spoke to me personally about this matter," Green added, but was unwilling to record this conversation on paper, even six years after the event, presumably because it incriminated the president, Hall Roosevelt, or both.[86]

Two days after the State Department meeting, on 15 October 1938, Hall was back at the White House. Just before FDR went to the theater to see *Knickerbocker Holiday*, Hall and Miles Sherover joined him for dinner. We do not know whether they discussed the covert aid program, but Sherover did agree to provide the president with captured German and Italian aircraft from Spain. At the end of December the president secretly ordered a ship to pick up some of the latest models at Marseilles. In February 1939 Sherover contacted the president, wishing "to make a complete report" of what he had accomplished. FDR sent a memo to his secretary: "Suggest that he send the report via Hall."[87] Thus the only tangible result from a plot to send planes from the United States to Spain was that aircraft from Spain were shipped to the United States.

How convincing is the evidence that Roosevelt encouraged the illegal covert aid scheme? We should be skeptical about the president's involvement, because the risks of sending covert aid were considerable and, at the same time, the scheme was seriously flawed. Furthermore, many historians have noted the difficulties in understanding Roosevelt's beliefs and motivations, given his enigmatic personality and his disinclination to write down his innermost thoughts.[88]

Is it possible therefore that the documents simply reflect the dissembling style of FDR, and the wishful thinking of his pro-Loyalist friends and family? There is some indirect evidence to support the interpretation that Roosevelt in March 1938 was deliberately misleading the Loyalist ambassador about his intentions. On occasion the president exaggerated his willingness and capacity to act in foreign policy, in order to boost the morale of the European democracies. For example, the British repeatedly expressed their frustration at FDR's private assurances of Washington's support during 1938–41 because of his perceived failure to follow through with these pledges.[89] The Soviet ambassador to the United States, describing Roose-

velt's covert aid plan in April 1938, noted that the president's many antifascist pronouncements were "in such striking contrast to [his] actions that it
has become nauseating."[90]

Alternatively, one could argue that Hall Roosevelt, not FDR, was the
initiator of the scheme, deliberately misrepresenting the president's wishes
to Ambassador Bullitt in Paris. Hall was strongly pro-Loyalist and on other
occasions helped facilitate the transfer of aircraft to Spain in defiance of
administration policy. Hall was also an alcoholic, and thus represented an
unusual choice of emissary for such a delicate operation.[91] There is some
evidence that Hall used White House connections for personal projects that
occasionally embarrassed the president. In 1935, when Hall was involved
in a plan for an aluminum plant, Roosevelt wrote to Senator Joe Robinson
of Arkansas to make clear that Hall "should have nothing to do with this,"
despite his family connections.[92]

But neither of these interpretations is persuasive. The evidence strongly
suggests that in March 1938 Roosevelt outlined a covert aid scheme to
the Spanish and Mexican ambassadors, the first stages of which were cautiously implemented when the president encouraged Hall to travel to Paris
in June. Harold Ickes, Thomas Corcoran, Drew Pearson, the Loyalist ambassador to France, the Soviet, Mexican, and Spanish ambassadors to the
United States, apparently both Eleanor and James Roosevelt, and of course
Hall himself all provide evidence that the president played a role in the
covert aid scheme. When Roosevelt told the Mexican ambassador in March
that he had taken steps to bring about the unimpeded export of arms to
France "to any company without verification," he was probably exaggerating what he had in fact already done. But the events surrounding Hall's
arrival in Paris strongly support the conclusion that Roosevelt's statements
in March were not simply vacuous promises.

Despite his alcoholism, Hall did have relevant qualities as an emissary,
principally his Loyalist, aircraft, and family connections. In this regard, the
newly discovered telephone message from Hall to the president in July is
a crucial document—the closest thing we have to a smoking gun. It was
recorded because by chance the president was at sea. It establishes that
Hall visited Paris either with the encouragement or under the instructions
of the president. This conclusion is supported by the behavior of Roosevelt
and Hall after October 1938, with the brothers-in-law continuing very ami-
cable relations for three years until Hall's death from liver disease in 1941.[93]
Indeed, Roosevelt engaged Hall and Miles Sherover in another top-secret
scheme in October 1938, this time to procure German and Italian aircraft

from Spain. None of this behavior can be easily reconciled with the theory that Hall traveled unilaterally to Paris, where he embarked on a series of extraordinary lies that could easily have landed FDR in an international and domestic political crisis.

We can strengthen the case by showing the consistency between FDR's role in the covert aid scheme and his wider beliefs in 1938. By the spring of 1938 Roosevelt's support for the Loyalists was becoming increasingly trenchant, because of wider fascist aggression, evidence of German preparations for war, and fears that the Spanish Civil War could become a model for the German penetration of Latin America. FDR was certainly aware at the time of the desperate need for aircraft in the Spanish Republic. In March 1938 Herbert Mathews contacted the president through Ernest Hemingway, arguing that for the Loyalists the "shows [*sic*] over unless have two hundred pursuit planes immediately."[94] With the French frontier open for the passage of arms, and the Loyalist financial position in the United States eased by the sale of silver, a clear opportunity existed for the shipment of aircraft.

In early 1938, despite his pro-Loyalism and his awareness of the Republican need for planes, Roosevelt was reluctant to attempt to lift the congressional embargo on arms sales to Spain. Neutrality legislation, including the Spanish embargo, had some merit in keeping the United States out of foreign wars. In addition, if the embargo were raised Roosevelt might feel pressured into allowing arms sales to both the Nationalists and the Loyalists, so that the United States would not seem to be choosing sides. But in that case Franco might benefit more than the Spanish Republic. Furthermore, any attempt at lifting the embargo faced substantial domestic and international constraints. The attraction of covert aid was therefore obvious: American aircraft could reach Loyalist Spain while avoiding a clash with the British, American Catholics, or the foreign policy bureaucracy. Breckinridge Long, who was working as a Loyalist agent at the time, realized the considerable political costs of embargo repeal, but suggested in March 1938 that the State Department might find "some way by indirection to wink at transshipments of military equipment."[95]

If the purposes of covert aid are congruent with Roosevelt's beliefs at this time, the tactics used also bear the stamp of FDR. The president considered air power the key to modern warfare, and after the Munich crisis he enacted a determined policy of supplying Britain and France with aircraft. Covert aid is consistent with Roosevelt's general proclivity toward devious or secret schemes and plots, often using unofficial emissaries—

his "fascination with covert operations."[96] For example, in January 1938 the president told a French emissary, Senator Amaury de La Grange, that France could expect a "broad interpretation of the embargo" in time of war, which the senator believed meant "surreptitious delivery [of arms] via Canada." FDR made clear at the end of February in a meeting with Jean Monnet and William C. Bullitt that in the event of war, "If worse came to worst and he failed [to repeal the neutrality legislation] . . . he would have the planes pushed across the border into Canada. He told Bullitt to search for areas where planes could land on the American side, and he sketched a map indicating likely places."[97] Only a few days later, in early March, Roosevelt told the Mexican and Spanish ambassadors that the United States would circumvent the embargo by providing aircraft to Spain via France and Mexico.

If the evidence is persuasive that Roosevelt outlined a covert aid scheme in March and encouraged Hall's initiative in June, there are problems that still require explanation. For example, why did Hall visit Ambassador Bullitt, a man who greatly distrusted the Soviet Union, sought to avoid another European war at all costs, and consistently opposed American intervention in Spain? Perhaps Roosevelt thought that the support of the ambassador to France was an essential prerequisite for the success of the scheme. Bullitt enjoyed very intimate relations with Roosevelt, as well as with foreign diplomats, and had joined FDR in the meeting with Jean Monnet in February 1938, at which a similar covert aid scheme with France had been discussed.

More fundamentally, we have to reconcile Roosevelt the cautious politician with his apparent willingness to put his career on the line for a deeply flawed scheme. The most likely answer is that Roosevelt supported the covert aid plan in theory, but acted very conservatively once it had been set in motion. Covert aid was one of Roosevelt's classic trial balloons, to be denied if it became public or encountered opposition within the administration. Of course, this cautious attitude meant that the initiative was virtually doomed from the start. In June 1938 covert aid received a series of fatal blows, including the opposition of the State Department and William C. Bullitt, the closure of the French frontier, and the possibility that arms shipments could undermine European efforts at mediating the Spanish conflict.

Despite its ultimate failure, the initiative is important in several respects. At a time of personal political difficulty, if it was discovered that the president was planning to illegally break neutrality legislation to aid Republican

Spain, his capacity in foreign affairs could easily have been crippled. In addition, the 150 planes to be provided, while insufficient to win the war for the Republic, could have had an impact on Loyalist battlefield success given that the Spanish Republic had in the region of one thousand effective aircraft during the entire war.[98]

In 1938 Roosevelt had to overcome an impressive coalition to intervene in the Spanish Civil War. The British continued to promote the American embargo. The majority of State Department notables, including Hull, Welles, Berle, and Moore, were strongly opposed to allowing arms sales to Spain. The most prominent European ambassadors, Kennedy, Bullitt, Phillips, and Wilson, were all committed to the embargo and readily expounded the dangers of its repeal. In addition, Roosevelt had to search for greater influence in Spain at a time when his domestic support had never been lower, on an issue that was one of the greatest foreign policy controversies in America since the First World War.

Despite this, Roosevelt's attempt to provide covert arms to Spain represented a deviation from the administration's nonintervention policy. In explaining this change, we find a close correlation with FDR's beliefs. By 1938 Roosevelt was increasingly worried by the impact of a victory by Franco on European and Latin American security, and shipping planes to Spain would be a tangible means of preventing or at least delaying this outcome. During the episode the president never allowed his bureaucracy to control policy; indeed Roosevelt sent Hall to Paris as a personal envoy, without the State Department's knowledge. If Hull had known about the plot, he might have revised his later comment: "The President and I were in complete agreement on our policy of nonintervention in Spain throughout the war. At no time did any difference of opinion arise between us."[99]

Ickes believed that the fear of a Catholic backlash prevented Roosevelt from lifting the Spanish embargo in May 1938, a view echoed by many contemporaries and historians.[100] This argument has some truth, but there were powerful reasons independent of the Catholic lobby for retaining the embargo, particularly the effects that repeal would have on wider European politics and the collapsing military position of the Loyalists. Furthermore, Catholic pressure did not immobilize the president. Instead he sought to outflank domestic and international constraints by pursuing an extraordinary scheme to secretly ship American aircraft to the Spanish Republic. Covert aid thus fits into the wider pattern of Roosevelt's diplomacy in the months before the Munich crisis. The president was doubtful about the merits of appeasement, but not yet certain that British conciliation efforts would fail. His response was to experiment, by searching for effective means of reinforcing European democracy without sacrificing his shrinking domestic support. After the Munich crisis, and Roosevelt's clarification of the fascist threat, the president increasingly identified the Spanish Republican cause and American national interests as one and the same.

CHAPTER 8

Mediation, Humanitarian Relief, and Repealing the Arms Embargo

On 30 September 1938 Prime Minister Neville Chamberlain returned to England from Munich, having negotiated the dismemberment of the Czechoslovakian state. Stepping out of his aircraft, and waving a piece of paper that Hitler had signed committing Germany and England never again to go to war, Chamberlain declared to the cheering crowds: "I believe it is peace for our time." The picture powerfully captures essential elements of the British appeasement policy: the widespread antiwar feeling in Britain, Chamberlain's misplaced trust in the reasonable goals of Hitler, and British willingness to sacrifice European states to avoid another conflict. A few weeks later, after midterm elections in the United States in November had almost doubled the number of Republican seats in the House (which increased from 88 to 169), one newly elected congressman, Stephen Bolles of Wisconsin, explained his victory: "I had the guts enough to protest publicly . . . the Red Spain attitude of our congressional delegation." According to Bolles, this was the reason why he received 90 percent of the Irish Catholic vote in his district.[1]

Both images are important in explaining why in late 1938 the political environment in which to pursue American diplomacy in the Spanish Civil War had, if anything, become even more problematic. With the international climate rapidly worsening and a general war apparently imminent, the British perceived any attempt to lift the American embargo as a dangerous intervention in European affairs. At the domestic level, Roosevelt had never been weaker politically, and American Catholics were mobilized against lifting the arms embargo. In addition, many of FDR's foreign policy bureaucrats, notably Secretary of State Cordell Hull, remained deeply concerned about the potential repercussions for Europe and Latin America of an interventionist Spanish policy.

At the same time, the Munich crisis had a major effect on Roosevelt's thinking about international affairs and the Spanish Civil War. FDR re-evaluated the crisis in October and November as a serious defeat for national interests. Munich heightened his existing fears about the impact that a victory by Franco would have on European and Latin American security. The crisis illustrated the necessity of acting to strengthen European democracy—in Britain, in France, and also in Spain. Roosevelt found himself moving much closer to the "last great cause" analysis of Ambassador Claude Bowers, who in 1938 aligned American interests with the fate of the Spanish Republic. By the end of the war FDR was a partisan, albeit a belated one, for the Loyalists.

These changing beliefs explain why, after rebuffing mediation proposals for over two years, FDR in November 1938 constructed an ambitious plan for pan-American mediation in the Spanish Civil War. In addition, in early 1938 the British thought it extremely unlikely that the U.S. government would provide humanitarian relief to Spain, but by the end of the year Roosevelt had devised a scheme for sending 100,000 barrels of wheat every month, which would go overwhelmingly to the Spanish Republic. Finally, after the collapse of the covert aid initiative in June 1938, and the Munich crisis, Roosevelt between November 1938 and January 1939 attempted to lift the congressional embargo on arms sales to Spain.

From the start of the Spanish Civil War there were widespread hopes that America's relative distance from the conflict and European great power politics would enable it to play a conciliatory role. But for two years after 1936 the United States turned down participation in every mediation proposal. Such efforts, it was believed, would interfere with American non-intervention and most likely fail. In December 1936 the State Department offered only moral support for British efforts to remove foreigners from Spain.[2] When William Phillips described a request from Uruguay for joint pan-American mediation in the Spanish Civil War as "of course, a fantastic idea," he was referring to its implausibility, not to its merit. The Cubans were assured in 1937 that the United States was not in a position to act. In the same year Roosevelt personally refused a Mexican proposal for American mediation "because of the certainty that it would be rejected." In January 1938 Moffat opposed a proposal for Washington to mediate "on the basis that this would constitute intervention in the domestic affairs of a foreign country."[3]

After two years of outright rejection, Roosevelt reversed his opinion in 1938, not only agreeing to take part in conciliation proposals but personally devising a mediation plan. Roosevelt's reassessment of the Spanish Civil War increased his perceptions of the cost of a Nationalist victory and thereby enhanced the desirability of a compromise solution. There is a close correlation between Roosevelt's policy reversal on Spanish mediation and his evaluation of the Munich Crisis in October–November 1938 as a defeat for American interests. In addition, in November 1938 mediation was believed to have a high chance of working. There were considerable hopes that both sides in Spain would accept a negotiated solution, in light of reports that the military position was deadlocked, as well as exaggerated estimates of the internal difficulties within the Nationalist coalition.

On 31 August 1938 Roosevelt offered the first hints of a change in American policy. He was particularly interested in Bowers's report that military events favored the Loyalists and that the Nationalists were divided. A Nationalist attack on Catalonia in April 1938, after Franco's offensive through Aragon, might have ended the war by the summer. But Franco wanted to physically destroy the Republican military rather than provoke a sudden collapse of the Loyalist position, and he thus turned Nationalist forces toward Valencia. Taking advantage of this decision, and of arms arriving through the open frontier with France, the Spanish Republic then stabilized its position and counterattacked on the river Ebro in July and August, advancing forty kilometers. FDR remarked that positive information from Bowers about the Spanish Republican position was consistent with his other sources: "Perhaps a little later on—if the Czech situation does not end disastrously—I can make some kind of a move for the purpose of at least aiding in ending the Spanish War."[4]

Two months later, on 31 October, with the Munich Crisis settled, FDR explained his plan to Adolf Berle: "The President is thinking in large lines. If the Vatican would propose it, he would be prepared to name a three-man commission to govern Spain for a period of months, then gradually to associate Spaniards and so ultimately to bring back a Spanish government."[5] Typically aware of the potential for domestic political repercussions, Roosevelt placed great weight on co-opting Catholic support. A week later Berle was in New York to inquire whether the Catholic Church would ask the president to mediate in Spain. On 10 November Berle tackled the mediation issue with Cordell Hull, who was "not at all shocked by the idea and suggested that we try to put it in form."[6] In the coming weeks the scheme evolved: the United States would seek a unanimous proposal for mediation at the pan-American conference in Lima in December.[7]

Berle and the State Department official James Dunn wrote a draft message to be proposed by FDR and then submitted by the Lima Conference to Franco and the Loyalists. The document stated that a million Spaniards had died since 1936 and that the world had been deprived of Spanish culture. All foreign powers were to be withdrawn from Spain: "outside influences cannot be permitted to determine the fate of a free people." FDR's message would conclude: "I now suggest the declaration of an armistice between the contending forces which shall last for the period of one year, to be declared by both sides, with the understanding that during that year an attempt shall be made to reconstitute a unified Spanish nation." Roosevelt would then offer to nominate members for a governing commission made up of Loyalists and Nationalists, "although in a private capacity and not representing the Government of the United States." This commission would lay down general rules for freedom of worship and limited regional autonomy. The United States would, in addition, pledge economic assistance to Spain.

Berle and Dunn struggled to describe what united rather than divided the participants in this bloody civil war: "Both sides have given heroic devotion to an ideal which both sides in different manner profess: a renascent, resurgent Spain; a Spain conscious of herself, proud to make her ancient and independent contribution to the world; a Spain maintaining inviolate her greatest traditions, yet bringing to the service of each of her people the best of modern thought."[8] This mediation document was eventually shortened and redrafted as a direct appeal from the Lima Conference: "acting in the right which its constituent nations have to claim recognition for the interests of humanity and of civilization."[9]

Berle was certainly hopeful about mediation. The "career people," he remarked, regarded Roosevelt's plan as having "at least an even chance of its being successful." Berle added: "I think that Loyalist Spain would accept; there is a possibility that Franco might, but that if he did not, the knowledge that he had declined would liberate political forces which might force peace within a few months. Further if he did refuse it would clear the way for changing our position in the matter of the Spanish embargo."[10] American hopes of mediating in the Spanish Civil War were overly optimistic. The Loyalists would almost certainly agree to negotiate. From the summer of 1938 the Republican Prime Minister Juan Negrín engaged in a personal diplomatic mission to persuade the great powers to mediate in Spain. In August, Bowers reported a unanimous vote by the Republican government to accept a commission appointed by Roosevelt to govern Spain.[11]

But Franco was unlikely to accept. On 12 October 1938 the Nationalist press denounced conciliation efforts.[12] Ironically, the events of Munich, which helped impress upon Roosevelt the need for mediation in Spain, also undermined the chances that Roosevelt's proposal would be successful. Germany subsequently realized that Britain and France would never fight over Spain and sent new military aid to Franco, which left the Nationalists rightly confident of victory. The Loyalist attack on the river Ebro ground to a halt, and Franco recaptured all the lost territory by November, building up his forces for a final assault on Catalonia. Meanwhile, Stalin's disillusionment with British and French actions at Munich led him to consider aligning with Germany, and his interest in the fate of the Spanish Republic declined.[13]

It would have been awkward, however, for Franco to refuse a unanimous proposal for pan-American mediation. Furthermore, a wider context was evident in Roosevelt's thinking. Berle noted to Roosevelt that the idea "worked along with" Roosevelt's policies, "whether successful or unsuccessful." Mediation efforts might buttress the broader resistance of the British and French, and if Franco proved intransigent, could facilitate ending the American embargo.[14]

Such contingencies were never tested, because the mediation scheme collapsed at Lima. Charles A. Thomson of the Foreign Policy Association reported that the conference "refused to take action on mediation in the Spanish Civil War and avoided discussion of the refugee questions."[15] To generate pan-American unity for mediation, it was paramount that papal support be generated and secrecy maintained. We do not know the extent of Washington's contacts with the Vatican, but one difficulty was the pope's recognition of the Nationalists, de facto in August 1937 and de jure in May 1938.[16] There was also a lack of secrecy, with the London press aware of the American initiative on day one of the Lima conference. On 1 December the British ambassador told Hull that London would look favorably on any mediation attempt. Yet Sumner Welles believed that the British might have leaked the mediation plan, suggesting hostility to the American initiative. Further indiscretion occurred when the French unwisely announced their support for pan-American mediation. On 15 December the French ambassador visited Welles and argued in favor of an appeal from the Lima conference. Welles replied that this step would only be useful if "taken unanimously by all of the twenty-one republics." Furthermore, if it became publicly known that France supported mediation then it would be impossible to proceed, because Franco would reject such a proposal in advance.[17] Welles told Moffat that the French were "trying to 'horn in' on the efforts of the Lima Conference to offer mediation in Spain." Welles thought: "if anything was calculated to destroy the possibility of such a resolution going through at Lima it was the possibility that European nations might try to make use of it for their own purposes."[18]

Without papal support or secrecy, it was very difficult to get twenty-one governments to act as a single entity. Latin American disagreements over mediation had been demonstrated a year earlier in December 1937, when Cuba requested joint conciliation efforts. The Bolivians were doubtful; Mexico refused outright because equal treatment would legitimize the rebels; and Paraguay upheld its policy of nonintervention in Europe.[19] The divisive nature of the Spanish Civil War was especially pertinent, because the primary foreign policy aim of the United States at the Lima conference was to establish wider pan-American solidarity in the face of international aggression. This was problematic enough. Argentina, for example, refused to show alarm at the Nazi menace. For Hull the ten days at Lima were "among the most difficult" of his career, because of the Argentinean refusal to agree to a substantive and binding conference statement on pan-American security. The final "Declaration of Lima" did little more than provide grounds for future consultation. If the peace, security, or territorial integrity of any American state were threatened then all states would "make effective their solidarity."[20]

If Roosevelt sought bold American leadership at Lima for the mediation proposal, then Cordell Hull was not the man to provide it. For the secretary of state, Spanish mediation was very much a secondary objective compared to hemispheric unity, and it may not have been an objective at all. On 17 December Hull wrote that two projects for mediation had been presented by Cuba and Argentina: "The committee on initiatives met this morning to discuss this matter but failed to reach an agreement although the definite disposition to take some action exists on the part of several delegations." The Cuban draft focused on the spiritual and material impact of the Spanish Civil War on the American states and suggested that a special group be set up to organize an appeal to both sides in Spain.[21]

Two days later Hull "made the suggestion that it might be better to postpone taking any definite vote [on Spanish mediation] until toward the end of the Conference. He said that such postponement would avoid any public impression that the Conference would take a stand one way or another on the Spanish question and would give an opportunity for more informal discussion of the matter." In the end only Cuba, Mexico, and Haiti voted for the Cuban proposal. Hull then reported back to Washington: "The consensus of the committee was that nothing could be done as matters now stood though the matter was held open pending possible developments during the week. It was definitely determined not to open the matter for debate at least for the time being. Since such debate would probably emphasize the differences this seems wholly desirable."[22]

"In the only truly courageous speech yet made here," the *Herald Tribune* reported on 21 December, the Cuban ambassador to the United States denounced the "innocuous and timid" efforts of the conference to mediate in Spain. The ambassador spoke with passion and to the obvious discomfort of most delegates. "For its transcendent universality and for its American significance, the grave tragedy of Spain cannot be ignored by the New World, nor considered removed from its vital interests and therefore outside the scope of this assembly . . . the great sorrows of Spain are the sorrows of America, and the fundamental interests of Spain are also the interests of America." The conference "gave him the tribute of applause" but would not support any bold proposals to mediate.[23] Berle concluded: "As it turned out we got nowhere. The plan was for the president to ask for an armistice in Spain. Mr. Welles proposed that we have many American nations associate themselves with us in the project. Secretary Hull at Lima took up a Cuban project in somewhat the same sense; but he was unable to secure agreement. By consequence the matter died before it was born."[24]

Far from taking up the Cuban project, Hull delayed and thereby undermined mediation efforts, sensitive to any issue that divided the American states. The Cuban delegation felt "profoundly and sincerely proud of having been left almost alone, with Mexico and Haiti, in this enterprise of love and mercy."[25] Roosevelt left the trial balloon of Spanish mediation in the hands of Hull, but as soon as the secretary of state arrived at Lima, he simply let go.

In the winter of 1938–39 Roosevelt tried to prevent the Spanish Republic from succumbing to starvation. He was in this instance able to build on efforts by the State Department to tackle the problem, and cooperate with the American Red Cross and the American Friends Service Committee, which had provided funds for relief efforts in Spain since 1936. The crux of the problem was that "impartial" American relief, distributed to Spaniards on the basis of need, would go disproportionately to the Spanish Loyalists, thus inciting Catholic hostility to American "intervention." While Nationalist Spain had a wheat surplus in 1938, the Loyalist zone had over three million refugees, and a critical food situation was developing in Madrid and Barcelona.

From an early point in the Spanish Civil War, outside actors encouraged the U.S. government to offer humanitarian relief to Spain. For example, in the spring of 1938 the British tried and failed to involve the Roosevelt administration in an international scheme to provide food and other goods for refugee children in Spain. The British ambassador to the United States, Ronald Lindsay, noted in February 1938 that "it is extremely unlikely that the United States Government will be able to take any practical interest in the cause of relief in Spain."[26] Despite this, on 22 July 1938 the Spanish Republican ambassador de los Rios visited Sumner Welles, stating that the Loyalist refugee situation "was becoming desperate" and reminding the administration of American relief efforts in Belgium, Germany, and Russia after the First World War.[27] In response, Roosevelt, the State Department, and the American Red Cross developed a plan in the summer of 1938 to send 250,000 barrels of government-held surplus flour to Spain.[28] Clearly the president was personally interested: when he had lunch with Norman Davis of the Red Cross in September, Roosevelt "had various ideas for expanding the flow of relief money, plus the possibility of obtaining and sending other commodities."[29]

But in the coming months the scheme foundered. The Republic hovered on the brink of starvation, with the whole population on minimal rations. The Spanish government appealed to Roosevelt again for aid through the German author Ernst Toller and Claude Bowers. The administration was able to provide 100,000 barrels of flour each month for six months. Legally it could not make a gift of the wheat; nor was the Red Cross able to afford the transportation costs involved. Only 60,000 barrels were eventually sent. Furthermore, efforts to recruit an American fund-raising committee had stalled owing to widespread fears of being identified with either the fascists or the communists in Spain.[30]

At this point Roosevelt intervened directly. He personally nominated a Committee for Impartial Civilian Relief in Spain, comprising fourteen wealthy and prominent people, which would work with the Red Cross and the American Friends Service Committee to raise $500,000 to send the wheat.[31] The British were cautiously supportive of American efforts, "conveying to President Roosevelt the fact that H. M. Government would not regard the supplying of food in some form to Spain, as unhelpful."[32] The key to success lay in maintaining the appearance of impartiality in a fiercely divided domestic environment. To appease pro-Franco Catholics, on 19 December Roosevelt asked a Catholic, George MacDonald, to become chairman of the committee. Within a few days the committee was established in New York City. However, when the press release outlining the scheme was distributed on 21 December, Moffat already envisaged difficulties: "Sumner Welles and the rest of us are particularly anxious that the humanitarian and the political aspects of feeding are kept entirely separate."[33]

Given the fractured nature of opinion toward the Spanish Civil War in the United States, humanitarian relief efforts were bound to be controversial. On the basis of need, most of the wheat would go to the Loyalists. Moffat wrote in September that the United States intended to "distribute [food] according to need which means in effect about 4 to 1 on the Loyalist side." The journalists Drew Pearson and Bob Allen were convinced that the scheme had been conceived by FDR "to keep the Loyalists alive and fighting during the winter." Such relief would certainly indirectly aid the Spanish government's war effort. For example, Bowers wrote on 1 October that the gravest military threat to the Loyalists came from the "food problem." The British, the State Department learned in mid-November, "were convinced that Franco could not win the war unless he were able to starve out the Loyalists."[34] A British Member of Parliament who had recently visited Spain told Ickes that "the first shipment of American flour had had a wonderful effect on the morale of the Loyalists."[35]

Catholic protests against Roosevelt's humanitarian aid plan began almost immediately. Bitter editorials were legion in the Catholic press, often linking the relief proposal to concurrent efforts to lift the embargo. Moffat wrote on 13 January that the Knights of Columbus were protesting against Spanish relief.[36] This was predictable, but the relief committee was also hamstrung by the choice of MacDonald as chairman. Apparently Catholic pressure had "driven MacDonald crazy, and he, in turn," was "about to make the Friends crazy." The chairman's relationship with the committee was one of friction. By February he refused to cooperate, or even sanction a replacement for himself. MacDonald thus destroyed the committee's fund-raising capacity: only one-tenth of the $500,000 hoped for was ever collected. On 17 January Norman Davis visited Roosevelt to state that he would "never again function through an independent committee." For the first time accusations had been leveled against the Red Cross "that its Spanish feeding program is in effect a political maneuver."[37]

This outcome was a great disappointment to Roosevelt. His decision to set up a fund-raising committee was not an easy one, because it meant that he had to share responsibility for the committee's success or failure. Furthermore, given the trenchant Catholic opposition in 1937 to a proposal to bring Basque refugee children to the United States, he must have expected a negative Catholic reaction to his scheme, however impartial he claimed it to be. Catholic pressure against Spanish relief did indeed prove significant. The evidence also suggests that a committee of substantial stature and enthusiasm was immobilized by the actions of a disgruntled chairman.

During the spring of 1938 Roosevelt attempted to aid the Republic while circumventing domestic and international constraints by sending covert aid to Loyalist Spain. After this scheme collapsed, Roosevelt's attention was focused on the developing crisis over Czechoslovakia. In the wake of the Munich settlement, the president realized that to substantially aid the Loyalists he would have to lift the Spanish embargo. There are indications that Roosevelt supported repeal as early as 7 November.[38] He certainly did so by 19 November, when Moffat noted in his diary: "Long meeting in the Secretary's office with regard to the possibility of an announcement by the President that he would ask Congress to repeal the Spanish embargo measure in January. The President is clearly anxious to do so . . . The Secretary absorbed all the pros and cons and put them before the President with his own recommendation to think them through more carefully before a public commitment. Later he told Jimmy Dunn and myself that he thought that the President would move on this very shortly; if so he hoped he would tie his recommendation up with his entire neutrality policy rather than isolating the Spanish phase for separate treatment."[39] On 25 November FDR wrote to Ickes, who was lobbying for repeal: "I agree absolutely with the desirability of making a change."[40] The State Department was now split on the issue: Berle backed FDR; Moffat favored allowing cash-and-carry arms sales to Spain; while Hull continued to oppose lifting the embargo.

The events of May 1938 demonstrated that Congress was wary about the embargo issue. To make the situation worse, in November 1938 a large cohort of leftist (and pro–Spanish Republic) Democrats were swept from office in the midterm elections.[41] Roosevelt was deeply sensitive to these events. On 18 December 1938 the attorney general wrote in his diary: "In all my conferences with the President I think I can say that I have never seen him more deeply concerned over the future, or the outcome of the Party or the prospects. No one from the outside can ever know or appreciate the tremendous burden that rests on the President."[42]

How could Roosevelt raise the Spanish embargo without initiating a violent fight in Congress? There was one potential solution. If the Neutrality Act of 1 May 1937, which gave the president discretion over arms embargoes in foreign civil wars, was deemed to have canceled the resolution of 8 January 1937, which created a mandatory embargo on Spain, FDR could end the embargo simply by presidential proclamation. He informed Ickes on 25 November 1938 that "the difficulty is the legal one"—whether the second resolution replaced the first.[43] On the same day FDR sent a memo to the State Department asking which resolution the embargo was applied under. Hull and Welles stated that the embargo existed under both the January and May resolutions. The alternative belief, that the May resolution had canceled that of January, was in their opinion "entirely without foundation." Joseph Green suggested that there was "so little merit" to the argument that "the point scarcely merits extensive discussion."[44] The British were also privately convinced that the resolution of 8 January was still in effect.[45]

Despite the unanimous opposition of the State Department to the legality of repeal by presidential proclamation, FDR wrote to Attorney General Homer Cummings on 28 November to ask his opinion of the issue, noting that there was "some merit" to the case that he could proclaim the end of the embargo.[46] In his report, the assistant solicitor general, Golden W. Bell, wrote that although it would be difficult to guess what a court might decide, it was his "intuition" that the second act was designed to substitute for the first.[47] As the historian Richard Traina has pointed out, this interpretation does not take into account the explicit declaration by McReynolds in 1937 that the January law was still in effect.[48] According to Cummings's diary, on 18 December FDR and Cummings "took up the question of the Spanish Embargo and what course the President could pursue. We went over this at great length." Cummings's supporting brief was apparently enough to dissuade Roosevelt from acting.[49]

Yet the president continued to try to establish his legal right to lift the embargo. On 21 December Roosevelt sent to Welles a petition from members of the American Bar arguing for the right to repeal by proclamation. Again on 24 January 1939, the president requested Welles's views on similar arguments. On 6 February FDR wanted to speak to the attorney general once more about the legality of lifting the embargo by proclamation.[50] It should be noted that Congress apparently took the view that the resolution of 8 January remained in force, because it specifically repealed this resolution as part of the later Neutrality Act of 4 November 1939.

If Roosevelt was never convinced about his legal right to proclaim the end of the embargo, the only alternative was congressional action. Given the political climate, the president would need influential allies. Ickes reported in late December that Roosevelt "wants the initiative to be taken by Congress, one reason being the Catholic Church is deeply interested in the Spanish situation and he prefers to share the responsibility with Congress."[51] On 15 December Roosevelt conferred with Senator Key Pittman about altering the neutrality legislation and tried to persuade him to take the lead. Pittman, while claiming to oppose "isolationism," was skeptical about foreigners and felt no particular attachment to either side fighting in Spain. He was more concerned about defending the autonomy of his Senate Foreign Relations Committee from encroachment by the president or State Department. Sensitive to what he called political realities and seeking to avoid involvement in a bitter public debate, Pittman was extremely cautious about Spanish policy. He delayed the president, wanting to talk first with other senators.[52]

However, a new factor arose on 17 December, when Welles passed accurate information to Roosevelt that Franco was about to begin his final offensive, which would probably "decide the issue." Supplied with new German arms, Franco launched an assault on 23 December that caused a rapid collapse of the Spanish Republican position in Catalonia and led to the capture of Barcelona at the end of January.[53] Roosevelt on 4 January 1939 used his annual message to Congress to link the Spanish Civil War with national interests. Without being explicitly mentioned, the Spanish Civil War is one of the major underlying subjects of the speech. Roosevelt stated that although the Munich crisis had temporarily averted conflict: "All about us rage undeclared wars."[54] The United States must oppose acts of aggression, albeit through "practical, peaceful lines." Democracies "cannot forever let pass, without effective protest, acts of aggression against sister nations—acts which automatically undermine all of us." There followed a clear reference to the failed Spanish embargo: "At the very least, we can and should avoid any action, or any lack of action, which will encourage, assist or build up an aggressor. We have learned that when we deliberately try to legislate neutrality, our neutrality laws may operate unevenly and unfairly—may actually give aid to an aggressor and deny it to the victim. The instinct of self-preservation should warn us that we ought not to let that happen anymore."

Even though Spain was never mentioned by name, the language used closely parallels FDR's interpretation of the Spanish Civil War. In 1941, for example, the president defined the Spanish conflict in terms of "the aggressor forces" and "the victims of aggression."[55] Welles and Moffat both believed that Roosevelt was referring to the Spanish Civil War in his annual message, and that the president had made clear his recommendations for

Congress to follow. Moffat wrote on 4 January that "rightly or wrongly he is leading the crusade against dictatorships."[56] Claude Bowers even claimed that his letters about the Spanish Civil War had been quoted almost exactly in Roosevelt's speech.[57]

Roosevelt's cautious approach to the Spanish embargo in the speech was very similar to his later efforts to alter neutrality legislation after the Second World War broke out. Rather than state outright that Washington's arms embargo hurt the British, and thereby incur isolationist wrath, FDR claimed that neutrality legislation should be amended because it gave "a definite advantage to one belligerent as against another." He avoided naming any names, but people got the message.[58]

The Spanish Republican paper *Vanguardia* wrote in an editorial about Roosevelt's message of 4 January: "Can anyone doubt that on saying this, Roosevelt has fastened in his mind, the shameful and demoralizing example of the London [nonintervention] Committee?"[59] In contrast, the Franco press in Spain thought that Roosevelt's condemnation of "aggressors" aided by American neutrality legislation could not possibly have referred to them. "The shoe does not fit [the Nationalists]," one paper claimed, adding that Roosevelt's hostility toward the totalitarian powers in Europe was "inexplicable." At the same time, the Spanish Nationalists recognized the shift in FDR's thinking, and the Franco press began a fierce campaign against the United States and President Roosevelt.[60]

On 11 January Pittman announced that the Senate Foreign Relations Committee would begin hearings at the end of January on neutrality revision. He added a warning to Roosevelt: because Congress was unreceptive, pushing any specific measures would produce a political backlash. William Bullitt argued that the administration could request repeal of the embargo, and if it were passed the British and French would quickly follow suit. But three questions remained: Would this save the Loyalists? Would the United States go through with things if a wider war broke out? Would Congress support the president? Bullitt's implied answer on all three counts was no.[61]

At this point the Senate Foreign Relations Committee was clearly influenced by the domestic controversy over the Spanish Civil War in the United States, which peaked in early 1939. Roosevelt wrote to Bowers on 26 January 1939: "You can have little idea of the intensity of public opinion in this country on the Spanish issue."[62] The *Washington Post* in February remarked that no other modern conflict, including the war of 1914–18, had "so aroused bitterness and divided communities far removed from the actual fighting."[63] In 1939 pro-Loyalists became much better organized and formed the Coordinating Committee to Lift the Embargo. With substantial funds, they arranged nationwide public meetings and rallies. In early 1939 250,000 telegrams urging that the embargo be lifted were sent to Washington in just one week.[64]

At the same time, Catholic bishops were using the pulpit to defend the embargo. Some 1.75 million pro-embargo messages had reached the capital by 5 February. "Lift the Embargo Week," starting on 9 January 1939, was soon rivaled by "Keep the Embargo Week." On 15 January the Knights of Columbus declared that lifting the embargo would serve to aid a "vicious and despotic government," one whose acts of oppression had been so vile that they had forced the people into a rebellion to escape "annihilation or slavery."[65]

Sumner Welles telephoned Pittman on 19 January and discovered that the Senate Committee had "unanimously voted to drop any consideration of the neutrality or Spanish embargo for the present." Pittman stated: "The conflicting avalanche of telegrams from both sides [of the Spanish embargo debate] had convinced individual Senators that they were on too hot a spot to sit with ease and that the sooner that they could get off it by avoiding the issue the happier they would be." Senator Robert Taft, for example, received fifteen thousand telegrams in one weekend arguing for retention of the embargo. On 23 January Moffat reported Pittman's view: "Inasmuch as he believed that the Loyalist cause was doomed anyway, by reason of the failure of Britain and France to move, he doubted whether any group of Senators would want to risk the political danger for a pure theory. He said that thus far only two Bills had been offered. The real reason was that most Senators wanted to force the President to make a recommendation and then snipe at it, rather than declare their own positions in advance."[66]

Eleanor talked to FDR on the evening of 25 January about what Congress would do "particularly in view of the Gallup poll," which indicated that three-quarters of respondents with a view on the Spanish Civil War supported the Loyalists: "[Roosevelt] said he felt that the majority of the Congressmen, because they were not sure that the people really understood what they were voting about, would try to delay any vote on changing the neutrality law or lifting the Spanish embargo, because they did not want to take the responsibility of the stand. He still feels that it cannot be done by executive order."[67]

The Munich crisis played an important role in both Roosevelt's clarification of wider European security and his changing views of the Spanish

Civil War. There existed a potential conflict between these two strands of thinking, because a bitter Spanish embargo fight in Congress could reduce support for Roosevelt's broader policies. The State Department saw the difficulties of having the Spanish embargo tied up with the question of revising wider neutrality legislation. Pittman stated that no neutrality revision would be possible while Spain was so dominant in people's minds. Hull thought it a "mistake to risk the transfer of the venom existing between Catholics and Left Wingers on the embargo to the broader subject of revising our neutrality legislation." On 25 January Moffat noted that "while people's thoughts were entirely centered on Spain . . . any discussion of the Neutrality Act would be considered by both Congress and the public in relation to that particular struggle." Breckinridge Long agreed: the end of the war in Spain would "permit this government to consider what it should do about a new neutrality bill without the fear of complications because of the Spanish situation. Up to now to have considered neutrality would have been simply to consider the Spanish situation, because there has been a good deal of feeling both pro and con in this country."[68]

In January 1939 neutrality revision played a relatively insignificant role in the president's thinking about how to aid the democracies. Roosevelt focused instead on finding ways to circumvent existing neutrality legislation by providing aircraft to Britain and France. On 16 January 1939 he expressed his intention that "every effort be made to expedite the procurement of any type of plane desired by the French government."[69] Indeed, FDR only acted to reform the wider neutrality laws after Hitler occupied the remaining parts of Czechoslovakia in March 1939, although his efforts were defeated in Congress in the summer.

Nevertheless, Roosevelt's plan for large-scale aircraft purchases in January 1939 would also require congressional support, which could be undermined by a fight over the embargo. The president was well aware of Catholic views on the Spanish Civil War. He kept in contact with Catholic groups through Cardinal Mundelein, who he said in November 1936 had "been perfectly magnificent all through the campaign and is a grand person in every way."[70] Mundelein apparently advised caution on the embargo, partly because he may have wanted the United States to mediate in Spain.[71]

On 11 January 1939 Michael Francis Doyle, an influential Catholic layman and Roosevelt supporter, visited the administration to obtain the facts about the Spanish embargo. Doyle wrote to FDR on 15 January 1939, describing how Catholics going to Sunday Mass had been directed to send letters to Washington protesting the repeal of the embargo. Doyle stated that he had "promised to keep the President informed in this matter."[72] To push for repeal would risk losing the support of Catholic figures such as Senator David Walsh, who was firmly pro-embargo, but also a consistent defender of Roosevelt's military program.[73] Meanwhile Gerald Nye, the major Senate voice behind repeal of the Spanish embargo, declared that Roosevelt's rearmament plans were "shocking" and bound to envelop the United States in a European war: "Get the uniforms ready for the boys."[74]

Yet more important than domestic pressure in Roosevelt's failure to press Pittman over the Spanish embargo was the Loyalist military collapse in January 1939, which made repeal a virtual irrelevance. On 16 January the fall of Barcelona looked imminent.[75] Ickes remarked on 22 January that it was "too late" to help the Republic.[76] The next day Breckinridge Long reported: "The Spanish Civil War seems about over." A week later Long described how "the impression made on the official mind as well as the popular mind of this country that Franco had practically succeeded in vanquishing the regular government would prohibit the United States from taking any action at this time."[77]

A further difficulty for the administration occurred on 18 January, when Henry L. Stimson, former Republican secretary of state and Roosevelt's future secretary of war, wrote to Cordell Hull advising that the president had the power and the duty to lift the Spanish embargo by proclamation. In Stimson's mind the embargo's disastrous nature had become increasingly evident: "We do not see the end of the evil yet by a long shot."[78] The letter was leaked to the press, so Stimson sent a revised version to the *New York Times*, where it was published on 24 January and caused considerable debate. Stimson argued that the Spanish Republic was the recognized government of Spain, and regardless of its domestic political system had the legal right to buy arms to defend itself against internal rebellion. The United States had vigorously claimed this right in its own civil war. By refusing this right, Washington was now implicated in the Loyalist defeat. Introduced to protect the peace, the embargo itself threatened the peace of the United States: "Any danger that may come to the people of the United States from the situation in Spain would arise not from any lawful sale of munitions in our markets to the Government of Spain, but from the assistance which our embargo has given to the enemies of Spain. It is the success of the lawless precedents created by those enemies which would constitute our real danger . . . The prestige and safety of our country will not be promoted by abandoning its self-respecting traditions, in order to avoid the hostility of reckless violators of international law in Europe."

Martin Conboy, a lawyer in New York, replied to the *New York Times*, arguing that the embargo conformed to America's neutrality policy and that Congress rather than the president had the legal right to lift or maintain the embargo. The analogy drawn by Conboy was with the First World War, when arms sales by the United States to one side led inexorably to its involvement in the Great War, at disastrous cost.[79]

State Department officials were unsure how to reply to Stimson. If they opposed his arguments then they might offend a foreign policy ally and would not be giving a true picture of their beliefs. But if they agreed with Stimson they would be "admitting" that their "course during the last two years has been wrong." With Barcelona about to fall, Roosevelt considered using Stimson's letter as the basis for a last-minute effort to save the Spanish Republic. On 20 January Hull met with FDR to discuss Spain: "Tentatively, the President is considering a reply to Mr. Stimson's letter in which he reviews the whole course of our policy with respect to Spain and urges a negotiated rather than a military peace." Moffat was instructed to prepare a draft.[80] But the president wrote on 24 January: "At this moment things look like a victory for one side . . . What a pity it could not have been a negotiated peace." In the end, Hull offered Stimson a polite but noncommittal response.[81]

With Congress unwilling to act and the Spanish Republic collapsing, Roosevelt appeared before his Cabinet and "very frankly stated, and this for the first time, that the embargo had been a grave mistake . . . The president said we would never do such a thing again." Roosevelt suggested that the United States should have allowed arms sales as long as the weapons were transported to Spain in non-American ships, a policy similar to that proposed by Breckinridge Long to Senator Nye in the spring of 1938.[82] This notion reflected the president's mind of 1939, not his beliefs in 1936. During the first weeks of the war Roosevelt considered leading the international efforts to limit the war to Spain, and looked very favorably upon nonintervention.

With the final collapse of the Loyalists in January and February, over 400,000 Republicans went into exile. On 24 February 1939 the French Chambre voted to recognize Franco, and Marshal Philippe Pétain became the French ambassador to Spain. Three days later the British recognized the Nationalist regime. On 1 April 1939 Franco issued a handwritten pronouncement: "today, with the Red Army captive and disarmed, our victorious troops have achieved their final military objectives. The war is over."[83]

For the United States, this left only the question of recognizing the

Nationalists. Despite the swift British and French recognition, as well as pressure from business interests and the State Department, Roosevelt was reluctant to act more quickly than absolutely necessary. The president remarked on 23 February that there should be "no haste" in following the British and French. He wanted it leaked that the United States was waiting to see if Franco would treat the defeated Spaniards with "Christian magnanimity."[84] In March Roosevelt told Bowers that there should be no hurry in recognizing Franco. But by 29 March almost everyone in Hull's office supported recognition. Moffat reported that only the United States and the USSR had not recognized the inevitable, "an embarrassing partnership." To Moffat's obvious annoyance, Roosevelt was "in no hurry at all" and wanted "to see if there are any large scale persecutions and massacres." On 3 April FDR finally approved recognition.[85]

Roosevelt's transition—first perceiving the Spanish Civil War as a potential spark for wider war; then recognizing the threat of fascist intervention; and finally reassessing the conflict as one in which clear-cut American interests were at stake—was reflected in policy decisions on mediation, humanitarian aid, and the Spanish embargo. On all these issues the president had previously resisted pressure to act. But after the Munich crisis Roosevelt sought politically efficacious means of intervening in Spain because his beliefs had changed.

International pressures did not force Roosevelt's hand. London offered some encouragement for humanitarian relief, but may have tried to undermine mediation efforts. In early 1939 concern about British opinion was noticeably absent in the debate about repeal of the Spanish embargo. By this stage, some officials in London saw repeal as a potentially positive step in the alteration of wider American neutrality legislation. As the *New York Times* reported it, even though ending the embargo ran counter to the British and French policy of nonintervention in Spain: "British officials . . . expressed the belief that such action might be of immense practical value to the democracies if a major war came."[86]

By 1939 the influence of the State Department was declining in the Spanish embargo debate. Officials pleaded an inability to act, and attempted to maneuver interested parties toward Congress.[87] With regard to domestic political constraints, Roosevelt first searched for ways to bypass Congress altogether, through covert aid and ending the embargo by proclamation. In February 1939 he explained his lack of action to Ickes as being due not to Catholic pressure but to the legal opinion of Cummings.[88] Furthermore, the president also attempted to manipulate public opinion. On 15 November 1938, for example, Welles forwarded a memorandum from de los Rios highlighting the number of Italians in Spain. Roosevelt wrote back: "S.W. Why not leak this to the press? FDR."[89] After the covert aid and presidential proclamation strategies had failed, Roosevelt examined ways of sharing the responsibility of embargo repeal with Congress. At this point Catholic pressure clearly influenced the actions of a number of congressmen. FDR was himself sensitive to Catholic opinion, particularly because he needed domestic support for his rearmament plans.

Catholic pressure at a time of domestic weakness showed the limits under which FDR operated. The failure of the mediation plan also illustrates FDR's restricted capacity to enforce his will. He was not personally present at Lima, and would have found it very difficult in any case to gain unanimity from twenty-one governments so divided over Spain, and so cautious in their attitude toward hemispheric solidarity. The irony is that Roosevelt sought pan-American unity in part because of his fears that a conflict inspired by the Spanish Civil War might break out in South and Central America. Yet as Hull was well aware, the Latin American concord necessary to avert this scenario would be threatened by proposing mediation in Spain. Roosevelt's ultimate constraint, however, lay in battlefield events in Spain itself. The primary reason why he did not push the embargo issue in 1939 may well have been the collapse of the Spanish Republic, which markedly altered the cost-benefit analysis: risking wider support would not produce any tangible gain.

CHAPTER 9

The Aftermath

The tragedy of the Spanish Civil War continued in 1939 for the hundreds of thousands of Loyalist refugees who fled from Spain. Initially kept in atrocious conditions in camps in southern France, thousands fought or labored for the French government in 1940. After the fall of France many Spanish refugees were captured and sent to concentration camps in Germany, where ten thousand died. Other Spanish Civil War veterans joined the French resistance. One veteran, Tito, went on to play a major role in the war in Yugoslavia. Spaniards fighting with the French army were among the first troops to liberate Paris in August 1944, their tanks bearing the names "Madrid" and "Guernica." Some seven hundred Republicans fought for the Soviet Union against the Nazi invader.[1]

After the American Civil War Abraham Lincoln had advocated a reconciliatory policy with regard to the South of "Malice towards none, charity for all." Franco's approach to postwar governance was the exact opposite. He maintained the civil war divisions through a systematic program of brutal repression. Using a card index of suspected liberals and leftists carefully compiled during the war, the Nationalists killed 150,000–200,000 Republicans and imprisoned between one and two million in a penal archipelago of prisons, camps, and forced labor battalions. This was the covenant of blood, bonding the victors in the repression of leftist and reformist Spain.[2]

In September 1939 the Second World War broke out, five months after the Spanish Civil War ended. The relationship between the two conflicts was complex, and the Spanish Civil War was not a straightforward prelude to the larger battle. After all, fascists fought against communists in Spain, but Germany and the USSR started the Second World War as allies. Furthermore, the violence in Spain was limited to the Iberian Peninsula and did not provide a direct spark for European war. Cordell Hull later defended American nonintervention, suggesting that it had aligned the United States with Britain and France and prevented the worsening of an explosive situation.[3]

But the Spanish Civil War not only made a second world war more likely; it also contributed negatively to the strategic environment in which Britain and France would fight. The conflict in Spain fused the Italian-German alliance. During the course of the war Hitler signed the Axis agreement with Italy and the anti-Comintern pacts with Italy and Japan. As a result of the Spanish Civil War there emerged a new potential fascist ally in General Franco. Spain quickly signed the anti-Comintern agreement, as well as a bilateral treaty of friendship with Germany.[4]

As well as consolidating the relationship between Berlin and Rome, the Spanish Civil War played a significant role in preventing the emergence of a grand alliance of Britain, France, and the Soviet Union. The Spanish Civil War repeatedly divided Britain and France, and isolated both countries from Moscow. Hitler cleverly played on British fears of Stalin's revolutionary designs in Spain. Furthermore, Britain's desire to maintain relations with Franco in 1939 became an argument against an alliance with the Soviet Union. In May 1939 the chief of staff in London had to decide on "the balance of strategic value in war as between Spain as an enemy and Russia as an ally." Chamberlain had already made up his mind: "if an alliance which is incapable of giving much effective aid were to alienate Spain or drive her into the Axis camp we should lose far more in the west than we could ever hope to gain in the East."[5] The Soviet Union saw little fruit from its attempt to align with the western democracies, and turned instead toward a rapprochement with Germany. Of those who intervened in Spain, the real winner was Hitler rather than Mussolini. For Rome the war produced a hollow victory at significant material cost relative to its limited military capacity.[6]

Within the United States the Spanish Civil War had a complex effect on domestic attitudes toward foreign affairs. For many Americans on the left, the experience of the Spanish Civil War called into question their isolationist views. Neutrality in Spain had brought the United States into league with the aggressor fascist states and undermined the cause of democracy in Europe. The historian James Martin writes that the anti-embargo drive entrenched pro-Russian and antifascist views among America's liberal population: "In view of the lengthy course of disillusionment over the First World War, it is unlikely that so many of those who were involved in this would have adjusted to the Second with so little friction, had it not been for the conditioning of the Spanish Civil War."[7] Although many intellectuals were left disheartened by the lies and hypocrisy of the conflict, John Diggins has argued: "Ultimately, of course, it was the Spanish Civil War that brought the overwhelming majority of literary intellectuals into an unequivocal anti-Fascist front."[8]

By contrast, the British embassy had suggested in January 1939 that the embargo controversy would "give ammo to isolationists."[9] For many Catholics, events in Spain reinforced their desire to keep out of European affairs. The Catholic journal *Commonweal* adamantly opposed lifting the embargo, and extended this position to all American warlike policies: "There is no enemy at the gate. Any attack on our shores is inconceivable."[10] Indeed, the Spanish embargo controversy of January 1939 may have played a role in frustrating revision of the wider neutrality laws, which did not occur until after war had broken out in Europe. Overall, the effects of the conflict in Spain were rarely simple. Norman Thomas wrote of its impact on him personally: "I had to moderate my religious beliefs and my pacifism to the degree that I thought of war as an enormous evil—but in some cases a lesser evil than submission." But Thomas opposed direct intervention in the Second World War. Although he would later regret this decision, the Spanish Civil War had made Thomas "pretty cynical about the possibility of anything good coming out of the slaughter that was to come."[11]

Many communist American veterans of the international brigades engaged in Orwellian doublethink after the Nazi-Soviet Pact, following the official Moscow line by abandoning antifascism and campaigning against American entry into the war against Germany. But in the wake of the German invasion of the USSR and the Japanese attack on Pearl Harbor in 1941, volunteers from the Spanish Civil War served in the armed forces. The Office of Strategic Services, precursor to the CIA, recruited several veterans for undercover operations in Europe. But on the whole the U.S. military was hostile to the veterans, often confining them to base.[12]

Roosevelt preferred for historians to believe that everything was clear in his mind and that he consistently pursued coherent policies. In relation to the Spanish Civil War, however, FDR was quite often uncertain, learned from events, and displayed markedly changing views. There is truth in Bowers's statement that "the president 'squirmed' a great deal over the American policy."[13] In contrast to his sentiments about other American foreign policies in the 1930s, Roosevelt felt genuinely guilty about Washington's role in the Spanish Civil War, recognizing that his own decisions had contributed to the failure of a cause in which he had come to believe.

One difficulty in understanding how the president perceived the Spanish Civil War after 1939 is that Roosevelt's public testimony is deeply misleading. During a press conference in June 1940 Roosevelt rewrote history by stating that the congressional arms embargo of 1937 had represented neither "the desire [nor] policy of the administration." He claimed that the nonintervention policy had resulted from a fear of war by the European powers.[14] The closest we have to an official version of events is Roosevelt's explanatory note of 1943 on Spanish policy in the series *The Public Papers and Addresses of Franklin D. Roosevelt*. FDR's piece is an apologia both for the formation of the Spanish embargo and for its retention. First, Roosevelt stated that in 1936–37 the American people were "unalterably committed to the policy of refusing to contribute to foreign conflict by the furnishing of arms." Second, according to his note the European democracies urged a policy of nonintervention to prevent escalation of the Spanish Civil War. The embargo was retained because the congressional resolution of 8 January 1937 was still in effect, and public opinion demanded "complete isolation" from arms sales to belligerents. Finally, "If American war material had been allowed to be sold to the participants in the Spanish conflict, the overwhelming probability was that the Rebel forces would have received greater assistance through American implements of war than would have the Loyalists of Spain. Of course, this is exactly the opposite result from the one desired by those who were urging that the embargo be lifted."[15]

Noticeably absent from this account is Roosevelt's personal desire that the embargo be lifted, and overall the piece substantially misrepresents the president's thinking about the Spanish Civil War. One reason is that the final version was altered. In FDR's first draft he justified continuing the embargo by stating that "the aggressors" in Spain had control over more shipping than the Loyalists, and thus if the embargo had been lifted "the aggressor forces would have received greater assistance through American implements of war than would the victims of aggression." Reviewing this version before publication, Sumner Welles pointed out to Roosevelt the inadvisability of such language: "I do not recall that the President or the Department ever publicly branded as aggressors the Rebels in the Spanish civil conflict."[16]

A conflict between aggressor and victim reflected Roosevelt's true beliefs about the Spanish Civil War after 1939. Roosevelt was far from satisfied at a wise or inevitable policy choice, as the piece that he wrote in 1943 implied. In Elliott Roosevelt's words: "Hindsight convinced Father that neutrality [in Spain] was a gigantic error."[17] Roosevelt told his Cabinet on 27 January 1939 about the "grave mistake" that had been made, a mistake he promised on several occasions never to repeat.[18] When the first ambassador to Nationalist Spain, Alexander Weddell, was appointed, he asked FDR for a message to deliver to Franco. Weddell was told to remind Franco that Roosevelt "did not like dictators."[19]

More than regret, we find evidence of clear remorse. The economist Leon Henderson heard Eleanor rebuke the president for not acting: "You and I, Mr. Henderson, will some day learn a lesson from this tragic error over Spain. We were morally right, but too weak. We should have pushed *him* harder." Henderson interpreted Roosevelt's silence as an admission that the charge was deserved.[20] The German defeat of France in June 1940 provided additional reasons for Roosevelt to look back apologetically: "The President apparently was in a mood for confession because, without any lead from either Tom [Corcoran] or Ben [Cohen], he volunteered the statement that he had made a great mistake in the matter of the Spanish embargo, that he was sorry he had done this, and that he would not do it again in similar circumstances."[21]

When Claude Bowers returned in 1939 and met FDR, he was informed: "we have made a mistake; you have been right all along." The president "spoke bitterly about Franco."[22] The historian Richard Traina has argued that "Bowers was being deceived": Roosevelt was afraid of the ambassador's trenchant pen and sought to appease him by exaggerating his own regret.[23] Bowers was certainly unpopular with key State Department officials, and his own later account of events would contain a number of inaccuracies, including the suggestion that as ambassador to Spain he had always opposed the embargo.[24] But in truth, there was little deception in the president's comments to Bowers. Roosevelt's interpretation of the Spanish Civil War had grown steadily closer to that of his ambassador. FDR told Senator Joseph Guffey that Bowers had been "exactly right throughout the war." Bowers was offered the ambassadorship to Chile, which in Roosevelt's words was "a post of great importance to us in the fight against fascism."[25]

Roosevelt was not alone in feeling regret at American policy in the Spanish Civil War. His ambassador to Mexico, Josephus Daniels, wrote that "for the Spanish crimes the three great democracies [Britain, France, and the United States] must take full responsibility in history."[26] The American socialist leader Norman Thomas, according to his biographer, "regarded Roosevelt's Spanish policy as one of his greatest errors, one that made World War II inevitable and brought decades of tragic oppression to Spain herself."[27] Senator Claude Pepper similarly argued in 1939 that Roosevelt's failure to back the Spanish Republic was his biggest mistake.[28] Harry Truman also regretted his support in the 1930s for the Spanish embargo, a policy that undermined the "democratic forces in Spain" and lost a potential ally in the Second World War.[29]

Eleanor Roosevelt visited London during the Second World War and went to a dinner party with Prime Minister Winston Churchill, at which, as Eleanor recalled, they had "a slight difference of opinion." Churchill asked if the United States was now sending sufficient supplies to Spain. Eleanor interrupted to remark that "it was a little too late": supplies should have been sent "to help the Loyalists during their civil war." Churchill said that he had been pro-Franco until Germany and Italy intervened: he and Eleanor "would have been the first to lose" their "heads if the Loyalists had won." Eleanor retorted that losing her head was unimportant, whereupon Churchill said: "I don't want you to lose your head and neither do I want to lose mine." When Clementine Churchill suggested that Eleanor was right, Churchill was extremely annoyed: "I have held certain beliefs for sixty years and I'm not going to change now." Clementine then got up as a signal that dinner was over.[30]

As we have seen, the Spanish Civil War shaped Roosevelt's perceptions of the fascist threat in Europe and Latin America, and the weaknesses of British appeasement policy. The Spanish embargo also encouraged Roosevelt to rethink his belief in wider neutrality legislation. After war broke out in Europe, Roosevelt spoke before a joint session of Congress on 21 September 1939 to recommend revision of the neutrality laws. The president recalled his State of the Union address of 4 January 1939, which had implicitly criticized the Spanish embargo. "In the same message, I also said: 'We have learned that when we deliberately try to legislate neutrality, our neutrality laws may operate unevenly and unfairly—may actually give aid to an aggressor and deny it to the victim. The instinct of self-preservation should warn us that we ought not to let that happen any more.' It was because of what I foresaw last January from watching the trend of foreign affairs and their probable effect upon us that I recommended to the Congress in July of this year that changes be enacted in our neutrality law."[31]

Roosevelt's covert aid policy may also have been influential beyond 1939. Among the papers of Ernest Cuneo, a lawyer, writer, and intelligence officer close to the Roosevelt administration, is an undated account of American policy and the Spanish Civil War that includes the following passage:

> There was a trace of a pattern in the Spanish Civil War which later
> became very important. Under the Neutrality Act, arms shipments to
> Spain were prohibited. It was a criminal statute, and it had incor-

porated under it a provision that no arms would be shipped to any place if the ultimate destination was Spain. This inadvertently created a loophole. The loophole was that they would be shipped to an ultimate destination which was not at war. It was thus arranged that some arms would go to people in France, who would lend them to the Loyalists on condition that they be returned to their ultimate destination, France. This was part of the genesis of the lend-lease pattern later employed to assist the Allies. The Administration was swinging towards acceptance of this view, when it became obvious that it was too little and too late.[32]

Having become a belated partisan for the Loyalists, Roosevelt after 1939 was the western Allied leader most hostile to Franco. Relations between the United States and Spain during the Second World War were frequently antagonistic, over matters of Spanish aid to the Axis powers and fascist propaganda in Latin America, as well as economic disputes. Large elements of the American public were deeply opposed to Franco Spain. Political figures close to the president who had backed the Loyalists during the Spanish Civil War, including Harold Ickes and Henry Wallace, supported an American invasion of Spain before the North African landings in 1942. Even Secretary of State Cordell Hull found the abrasive style of Franco's diplomacy almost too much to bear. On 13 September 1941 he told the Spanish ambassador that "in all the relations of the [U.S.] Government with the most backward and ignorant governments in the world," the United States had never received such "a lack of ordinary courtesy or consideration." Spanish diplomacy had represented "aggravated discourtesy and contempt."[33]

Despite his own views, and a domestic public hostile to the Spanish regime, Roosevelt always stressed in his wartime Spanish policy the necessity for a rapid victory over Nazi Germany. Britain generally took the lead on Spanish policy until 1945 because of its proximity to Spain. Churchill saw continuing Spanish neutrality in the war as critical to British survival, given the strategic importance of Gibraltar, and he generally argued for a policy of engagement toward Franco. As Churchill later recalled: "Spain held the key to all British enterprises in the Mediterranean."[34] American diplomats in Spain also tended to argue that American trade with Franco was the best means of drawing him away from the fascist states.

Alexander W. Weddell replaced Bowers as ambassador to Spain in 1939, and was in turn replaced by Carlton J. H. Hayes in May 1942. Hayes, who was Catholic, regarded Franco's victory as preferable to that of the Spanish Republic, and ended up defending the Nationalist regime. The anti-Franco left in the United States was a constant source of irritation for Hayes, who maintained regretfully that they were not "as intent upon winning the present war against the Axis as they are upon continuing the seven-year-old Spanish Civil War."[35]

Hayes's argument that the United States should improve relations with Madrid was based on Spain's formal neutrality throughout the Second World War. Yet Franco was very close to the fascist dictators, especially Mussolini, and the fall of France presented him with a clear opportunity for territorial gain. In the summer and fall of 1940 Franco offered to join the Axis war effort under certain conditions, before Hitler had applied any meaningful pressure. Franco was committed to entering the war, and would have done so if Germany had not refused his demands for material aid and colonies held by Vichy France. Hitler was confident of victory, and instead of satisfying Franco's appetite for territory he wanted Spain to cede one of its Canary Islands to Germany, probably as a base for the prototype long-range Messerschmitt 264 or *Amerika-Bomber*.[36]

After 1940 Spain's ostensible neutrality became increasingly benevolent toward Germany. Franco provided bases for German and Italian submarines and planes, refueled German destroyers, allowed German reconnaissance planes to fly with Spanish markings, and after September 1941 sent the volunteer Blue Division of eighteen thousand Spanish troops to fight the USSR on the Eastern Front. In the early stages of the war the Spanish press virulently attacked the United States, and the Nationalist regime attempted to spread propaganda throughout Latin America. Relations with the United States worsened still further once the pro-Axis Serrano Suner became foreign minister. To the American ambassador, Weddell, Suner declared Spanish "solidarity" with the fascist states.[37]

But in December 1940 and on several subsequent occasions Franco resisted Berlin's calls to enter the war, because of his growing doubts about the certainty of German victory. Ribbentrop complained about "that ungrateful coward Franco who owes us everything and now won't join us."[38] Despite the ties between the two regimes, Hitler thought that Franco was "an inferior character," and described the Spanish government in 1945 as one of "plutocratic exploiters led by the nose by priests."[39] By 1943 relations between Franco and the fascist states had weakened, and with the changing balance of military fortunes in 1944–45, Franco shifted opportunistically toward the Allies.

The United States tried to leverage its economic power to ensure Spanish neutrality. Roosevelt agreed in October 1940 to send humanitarian supplies to Spain through the Red Cross, an action that he claimed was "of the utmost importance to make every practical effort to keep Spain out of the war or from aiding the Axis powers."[40] With Spanish wheat and oil supplies controlled, Franco would be unable to stockpile for entry into the war, and would in addition see the benefits arising from cooperation with the democracies. FDR also had genuine humanitarian concerns given the devastated Spanish economy. In November 1940 he called Spain "the most destitute of all the poor countries."[41] Once the United States entered the war the core aim was to limit German influence over Franco. For example, the Allies offered high prices for Spanish wolfram that the Germans had to match. The United States cooperated with a British scheme to bribe moderate and pro-neutrality Spanish generals with millions of pounds to keep Spain out of the war.[42]

Although Churchill was consistently opposed to any policy which antagonized Franco, his fears that Spain was about to join the Axis meant that Britain on a number of occasions came close to a unilateral seizure of Spanish territory, which could easily have sparked war. In 1940–41 Britain planned to capture Spanish bases in the Azores, the Cape Verde Islands, and the Canary Islands in a preemptive strike if it seemed likely that Portugal or Spain would enter the war. This invasion plan was almost enacted in 1940 when Franco imposed Spanish control over Tangier, previously an internationally ruled zone. In August 1941 FDR encouraged Churchill to risk a conflict against Spain by seizing the Canary Islands. On the brink of war, Churchill suddenly reassessed events and decided that Franco was not about to declare for the Axis. During the Torch landings in Northwest Africa in 1942, the Americans were fearful that Franco could wreak massive damage on vulnerable forces passing through Gibraltar and insisted that part of the landing occur on the Atlantic coast at Morocco. Roosevelt sent a letter to Franco assuring him that the North African attack was not directed at Spain.[43]

From early 1943 the United States began to demand Spanish concessions in return for oil shipments. Roosevelt was by now anxious for a hard line against Franco, indicated by his refusal to meet the Spanish ambassador or even acknowledge Franco's New Year greetings. The United States made the unilateral decision in January 1944 to introduce an oil embargo until Spain agreed to a series of requests, including relinquishing Italian ships in Spanish ports and reducing wolfram exports to Germany. The American public included a vocal lobby hostile to any accommodation with Franco given the talismanic memory of the Spanish Civil War.[44] Because of this, in

the presidential election year of 1944 Churchill was willing to take responsibility for the deal eventually reached over oil shipments to Spain, in order
to protect the president. Churchill described the United States in January
1945 as "very anti-Franco and also anti-Spanish."[45]

In early 1945, after his resignation as ambassador, Carlton Hayes made
a considered and lengthy report to FDR in favor of friendly postwar relations between the United States and Spain. Arguing that Franco's regime
was stable and that he had made a number of recent efforts to aid the Allied
cause, Hayes believed that decision makers should look beyond those sections of American public opinion hostile to Franco, as well as the propaganda of those who had lost the Spanish Civil War: "General Franco represents that part of the Spanish nation which finally won a three years' civil
war; and it would indeed be quite a novelty in human history if the victors
in such a war should say to the vanquished only five or six years afterwards:
'We are sorry; we shouldn't have won; we have made a mess of things; we
will now restore you to power and welcome back your former leaders and
let them do to us what they will.' Imagine General Grant saying anything
like that to the leaders of the Southern Confederacy in the midst of our
own post-Civil-War Reconstruction!"

According to Hayes, if the aim of American policy was to remove all
dictators, then Franco would have to go, but so would dictators in Russia,
Portugal, and Latin America. Hayes argued that democracy was unlikely in
Spain, and that Franco would slowly liberalize the country, a process that
could be encouraged by a friendly United States. American interests would
also benefit from a policy of engagement.[46]

However, in sharp contrast to Hayes, Roosevelt saw Nationalist Spain
through the lens of the Spanish Civil War, and signaled that one of his
postwar aims was removal of the Franco regime. FDR could thus remedy a
situation that had arisen partly because of his own decisions in the 1930s.
He replied to Hayes on 14 March: "at the present time [American policy]
must inevitably take account of the fact that the present regime in Spain is
one which is repugnant to American ideas of democracy and good government."[47] Stating his views to the new ambassador, Norman Armour, FDR
argued that Franco Spain was to be treated as an enemy state, isolated, and
potentially removed. The American people "distrust" the Spanish regime,
because it was helped to power by the fascist states in 1939, had a totalitarian system, and assisted the Axis in the Second World War:

> The fact that our Government maintains formal diplomatic relations
> with the present Spanish regime should not be interpreted by anyone

to imply approval of that regime and its sole party, the Falange, which has been openly hostile to the United States and which has tried to spread its fascist party ideas in the Western Hemisphere. Our victory over Germany will carry with it the extermination of Nazi and similar ideologies.

As you know, it is not our practice in normal circumstances, to interfere in the internal affairs of other countries unless there exists a threat to international peace. The form of government in Spain and the policies pursued by that Government are quite properly the concern of the Spanish people. I should be lacking in candor, however, if I did not tell you that I can see no place in the community of nations for governments founded on fascist principles.[48]

Victory over Hitler removed the strategic necessity for caution toward Spain and created the possibility of reversing the result of the Spanish Civil War. For many Spanish Republicans in exile the spring of 1945 appeared to be the decisive moment. Allied armies in Europe would complete the victory over European fascism by moving into Spain. One month later, on 12 April, Franklin D. Roosevelt died. The Spanish Falange celebrated and the Spanish Republicans fell into despair.[49] It is tempting to speculate on how American policy toward Franco might have changed if Roosevelt had lived, but this counterfactual is submerged within the larger question of whether the cold war would have developed as it did. It was this cold war context that led Truman and Eisenhower to embark on the road to reconciliation with Franco.

There was a tension in American policy toward Spain after 1945 between the argument that Franco Spain was inadmissible to the international community because of its origins, its war record, and its domestic system—Roosevelt's view in 1945—and the cold war strategic argument that Spain was a crucial partner in the western alliance. In the months after FDR's death, the movement to take action against Franco remained strong. The Soviets were hostile to the Nationalist regime, not only because of the Russian role in the Spanish Civil War but also because Franco had provided troops for Germany on the Eastern Front. At the Potsdam Conference in July 1945 Stalin wanted the regime removed from power. The French government was also sympathetic to the Spanish Republicans, many of whom after escaping to France had fought heroically against the Vichy government and the Germans. Charles de Gaulle spoke of his desire to see Spain embark on the road to democracy. French socialists and communists lobbied for sanctions against Franco. After the election defeat of

Winston Churchill in 1945, there were high hopes that the new socialist Labour government would support intervention in Spain. Prime Minister Clement Attlee had earlier argued for economic sanctions against Spain to destabilize the regime, and promised in 1945 to resolve the Spanish question as soon as possible.[50] In July 1945 Cordell Hull worried that the Labour government would initiate a Spanish policy "sharply divergent from that followed by the Churchill Government and by the United States Government." Hull stated that during the war Churchill had argued for "more liberal treatment of the Franco regime than the American Government would have been disposed to accord." Hull suggested "tightening up" American policy on Spain to preempt more radical change from Britain.[51]

In the United States, President Harry Truman continued Roosevelt's policy of isolating the Franco regime. Truman, like Roosevelt, regretted his support for the Spanish embargo in the 1930s, and he was dismayed by Franco's attacks on Freemasonry in Spain. Truman seemed amenable to Stalin's demand for direct action against the Spanish regime at Potsdam, but Britain was hostile and the plans were abandoned.[52] The Potsdam Declaration did oppose Spanish entry into the United Nations because of "its origins, its nature, its record, and its close association with the aggressor States."[53] Anglo-American opposition to the Spanish regime was restated in 1946, although both countries rejected the option of direct intervention. The United States published German documents illustrating Spanish collaboration with the Axis in the Second World War and backed a United Nations resolution in December 1946 calling on member states to recall their ambassadors from Spain. A time limit of one year was established for political change in Spain before new sanctions would be applied. Many Americans who had been mobilized during the Spanish Civil War lobbied their government to act against Franco after 1945. The American Federation of Labor, for example, urged recognition of the Spanish Republican government in exile.[54]

But the coalition of forces ranged against Franco was fragile, and with the onset of the cold war it began to disintegrate. The British Labour government never followed a forceful anti-Franco policy: indeed, to the great regret of Spanish Republicans there was substantial continuity with the policy of Churchill. The Labour government continued to see the issue as an internal matter for the Spanish people to decide. Concerned that a communist Spain could threaten Gibraltar and aware of the benefits from increased trade links with Spain at a time of national recovery, the Labour government would go no further than condemnation of Franco and mild encouragement for a constitutional monarchy in Spain.[55]

By 1949 a complete reversal was occurring in United States policy toward Spain. In an environment shaped by the cold war, the Marshall Plan, and the Truman Doctrine, there was a global reassessment of right-wing dictatorships as potential bastions of anticommunism. In a future third world war the Pyrenees could provide a natural barrier to Soviet advancement on the continent. Spain might be the foothold from which the United States would proceed to liberate Europe. Between 1946 and 1949 the British and the Americans supported monarchist forces fighting against communist insurgents in the Greek Civil War, a situation that might be replicated in Spain if the two countries attempted to remove Franco. By 1950 Secretary of State Dean Acheson viewed the policy of isolating Spain as a mistake, a result of organized propaganda efforts keeping the Spanish Civil War controversy "alive here and abroad." Instead, he believed, the United States should normalize relations with Spain and seek an alliance with Franco. It was the argument of Carlton Hayes in 1945, but now it had the backing of the president. Under the impetus of the Korean War and Washington's increasingly urgent view of the communist threat, the United States enacted a series of economic agreements with Spain in the early 1950s. Finally, in 1953 the United States signed the Pact of Madrid, which formally allied the two countries and granted the United States a number of bases in Spain, in exchange for military and economic aid that totaled $1.4 billion over the next decade. In 1955 Spain was admitted to the United Nations and Franco's period in isolation was at an end.[56]

During the Second World War many Americans such as Harry Truman and Sumner Welles reassessed the Spanish Civil War as the first stage of a wider conflict between democracy and fascism, and as a result viewed the Spanish Republican cause more favorably. The onset of the cold war produced further reevaluations. As the United States rebuilt relations with Franco in the 1950s and 1960s, Julius W. Pratt commented: "In the long pull of the Cold War, better a Franco Spain than a Communist Spain."[57] J. Edgar Hoover claimed that American volunteers in the international brigades had furthered Bolshevism's international greed.[58] The Veterans of the Abraham Lincoln Brigade was placed on the Department of Justice's subversive list in 1947 as a communist front organization. In the era of McCarthyism, association with the Spanish Republican cause in the 1930s was often viewed as a sign of disloyalty. Events in Spain between 1936 and 1939 had not changed, but the lenses through which these events were perceived had altered dramatically once again.

CHAPTER 10

From a Vicarious Sacrifice to a Grave Mistake

The outcome of the Spanish Civil War was determined to a large extent by decisions made in London, Paris, Berlin, Rome, Moscow, and Washington. The balance sheet of foreign aid is difficult to assess, because timing mattered almost as much as the quantity of material or troops. The provision of relatively few German and Italian aircraft in July and August 1936 had a dramatic impact: the first major military airlift in history transformed the prospects of the Nationalist rebellion. The latest research indicates that overall, foreign intervention was strongly balanced against the Spanish Republic.[1] Franco could rely on two great powers, neither of which was willing to see him lose, as well as the support of Portugal. Soviet material aid to the Loyalists, while considerable, never matched the extent of fascist support and was often accompanied by ruthless control and cynical self-interest. American nonintervention was also significant in the defeat of the Spanish Republic, because the United States was a major source of aircraft, the lack of which would hamstring Loyalist battlefield performance throughout the war. The importance of the American embargo for the Nationalist victory helps to explain why the Spanish Civil War caused such a bitter controversy in the United States.

Religion, class, and ideology, as well as perceptions of international security and national interests, all shaped American views of the Spanish Civil War. Anyone who read Catholic writings likening General Franco to George Washington and describing the conflict in Spain as one between Christianity and communism, then turned to pro-Loyalist writings depicting a historic battle between democracy and fascism, might wonder if they were describing the same war. In the context of the Second World War, many Americans looked back on the embargo policy as a disastrous error and saw the Spanish Civil War as the first round of a global conflict to which the United States was now belatedly committed. However, viewed through the cold war lens, events in Spain in 1936–39 assumed a new form as a classic Soviet attempt to spread international communism, a model for later behavior in Eastern Europe, Korea, Cuba, and elsewhere. Franco became, in some people's eyes, the "sentinel of the West"—a bulwark against communism.

Given this diversity of perception, both across different groups and individuals and across time, how did Roosevelt view the Spanish Civil War? At the start of the conflict, the president's core beliefs led him to avoid American entry into foreign wars, and predisposed him to pursue cooperation with Britain and downplay the Soviet threat. Although Roosevelt sought to slow the drift to war, the wider international security environment was ambiguous, and the president was uncertain about the relative efficacy of appeasement versus deterrence. After the generals rose in Spain, Roosevelt maintained his cautiously supportive attitude toward the Spanish Republic, evident since 1931, by sympathizing with the Loyalists even as he doubted their democratic credentials. In 1936 Roosevelt did not see the outcome of the Spanish Civil War as having major consequences for national interests. Rather, his great fear was that the conflict in Spain might spark a general war, in much the same way that a local dispute in the Balkans had escalated in 1914. As a result, the president displayed a strong preference from the start for international nonintervention in Spain. The president's Republican sympathies translated into a tendency to take the Loyalist side on borderline or relatively minor issues such as prosecuting recruiters for the international brigades, or allowing passports for medical personnel.

In 1937 Roosevelt began to worry less about the possibility that Spain would spark a broader international conflict, and more about the extent of fascist intervention. FDR was attracted to the idea of extending the arms embargo to Germany and Italy for a number of reasons: his pro-Republicanism; his tolerant attitude toward Soviet involvement in Spain; and perhaps most importantly, his belief that this initiative might serve to reduce international intervention in Spain. Roosevelt abandoned the idea after hearing that it would interfere with British efforts to remove foreign forces from the peninsula. Both Roosevelt's sympathy for the Loyalists and his unwillingness to intervene and aid the Republican cause were captured in a comment to Martha Gellhorn in July 1937: "Spain is a vicarious sacrifice for all of us."[2]

In 1938–39 Roosevelt's perceptions of the Spanish Civil War were transformed. The president reassessed a Nationalist victory in 1938 as clearly harmful for American interests. This shift partly reflected a wider re-appraisal of European events after the Anschluss, the rise of German air power, and especially the Munich crisis. In October–November 1938 Roosevelt concluded that Hitler was incapable of negotiation and henceforth followed a determined policy of aiding Britain and France with American aircraft. Given Spain's strategic position, a victory by Franco could undermine the security of France and Britain. In addition, FDR linked a Nationalist triumph with worsening Latin American security, perceiving the Spanish Civil War as a potential model for German intervention in civil wars in the western hemisphere. The president was also repulsed by the brutality of the Nationalist campaign and Franco's conservative-fascist ideology. The Spanish Civil War split American opinion into those who wanted to isolate the United States from a dangerous European conflict and those who sought to aid the antifascist cause. Roosevelt's thinking included elements from both positions, but over time he gravitated toward the second.

By 1939 Roosevelt believed that the Spanish embargo was a "grave mistake," and he suggested that the war in Spain could be the first round of a European civil war.[3] Roosevelt promised never to make this disastrous error again. Although he was consistently opposed to the Franco regime in Spain, his beliefs were trumped by wider strategic concerns in Europe. In the weeks before his death, with Germany almost defeated, Roosevelt signaled the postwar aim of regime change in Spain.

The major alignments in the Spanish Civil War had been established by the end of 1936 and did not significantly change by 1939. Spaniard fought Spaniard for reasons rooted in indigenous social, economic, and political divisions. The Loyalists maintained an ambiguous commitment to democracy, and the Nationalists were more traditionalists than fascists. Germany, Italy, and the Soviet Union internationalized the war by providing massive military support in the search for strategic and ideological goals. If these factors were broadly constant, what altered by 1938 was the European and Latin American context in which the Spanish Civil War was being fought. It was this changing context that made the American president look at similar events from a radically different perspective.

Roosevelt's beliefs about the Spanish Civil War were shaped by his wider international views, but the influence was reciprocal. In the period before the Anschluss, fascist intervention in Spain provided the clearest evidence of German and Italian aggression in Europe. The Spanish Civil War contributed to FDR's concerns about Latin American security. Roosevelt's disillusionment with British policy in Spain is also striking. Furthermore, his increasing awareness of the iniquitous role of the American embargo led the president to question his broader attachment to neutrality legislation. The Spanish Civil War demonstrated quite clearly to Roosevelt that inaction, neutrality, and appeasement did not protect American interests.

This analysis of Roosevelt's beliefs undermines the view, expressed most strongly by the historian George Flynn, that Spain was an issue FDR "always considered incidental" and "tried to avoid."[4] The president thought the Spanish Civil War significant from the start, and by late 1938 Spain was one of his most important policy areas. Flynn concluded that for Roosevelt "non-involvement in Spain represented all that seemed best in historic American diplomacy." Yet FDR stated in January 1939 that "this embargo controverted old American principles and invalidated international law," and in 1940 he referred to Spanish policy as being "in complete violation of our normal, usual practice."[5]

Roosevelt's perceptions influenced his assessment of incoming information about Spain and his evaluation of options, as well as his choice of a course of action. FDR's support for international nonintervention was gradually replaced with partisan backing for the Loyalists and the desire to impede Franco's march to victory. Roosevelt opposed Senator Nye's proposal to repeal the embargo in May 1938 in part because he was instigating a plan for covert aid to Loyalist Spain. The president consistently backed purchases of Spanish Republican silver in the face of opposition from the State Department. In November 1938 Roosevelt radically altered administration policy by supporting repeal of the embargo and devising a scheme for pan-American mediation. Finally, in December he intervened to revive a flagging humanitarian aid policy. Given the international, domestic, and bureaucratic constraints, the president's changing beliefs are the only satisfactory explanation for these policy choices.

Roosevelt had no grand plan, but these measures still represented a fairly coherent set of linked proposals. For example, it was made clear in November 1938 that if Franco rejected pan-American mediation, this would clear the way for repeal of the embargo. However, the interrelationship between the different policies also complicated matters. The reliance on Catholic backing for mediation in Spain was one reason for Roosevelt's caution on the embargo issue in the winter of 1938–39. Similarly, Catholic hostility to the humanitarian aid plan was partly the result of a perceived linkage with concurrent efforts to lift the embargo.

What was the role of the battlefield situation in Spain in shaping Roosevelt's views and policy preferences? In 1936–37, when FDR sought to limit the war to Spain and restrict international intervention, there is no evidence that the initial Nationalist successes, the defense of Madrid, the Loyalist victory at Guadalajara, or the Nationalist conquest of the Basque region had any significant impact on the president's thinking. At this stage, FDR was not primarily concerned with which side in Spain won.

During 1938–39, when the president displayed increasing support for the Loyalists, the battlefield situation had a complex effect on his views. The two Republican military collapses, in the spring of 1938 and then decisively in January 1939, mobilized American pro-Loyalist sentiment for immediate intervention. But the Loyalist defeats could also be used to argue that intervention would be ineffective or irrelevant. Roosevelt tended toward the second analysis. When he received his initial information about the Loyalist reverses, in February–March 1938 and in December 1938, the president's interest in Spanish events heightened, his sympathies for the Republic were strengthened, and he appears to have stepped up his search for effective action. In the first case, he developed his covert aid scheme. In the second he used the State of the Union address to link the Spanish Civil War with American national interests. But as the military position worsened still further, it became less likely that Roosevelt would decisively intervene. In April and May 1938 FDR repeatedly stated that lifting the embargo would not help the Loyalists, and might even aid Franco. In contrast, the belief in the summer of 1938 that military stalemate existed in Spain increased FDR's desire to act, in particular to mediate. Finally, the sudden collapse of the Republican position in January 1939 was critical in Roosevelt's decision not to press the embargo issue. FDR was too practical a politician to expend political capital on lost causes, even when that cause was his own, as it was with Spain.

For many historians the Spanish Civil War was the archetypal case demonstrating Roosevelt's incapacity in foreign policy in the 1930s. In substantive aid from the United States, the Spanish Republic only ended up with $14 million and a few thousand barrels of grain. Neither did much to impede Franco's advance. Roosevelt ultimately failed in his Spanish policy, in part because of his own mistakes. For example, FDR generally sought flexibility, refusing to bind his future options in Spain by making firm pledges. But there was one crucial exception—the legal embargo in January 1937. Roosevelt accepted mandatory legislation in order to immediately stop American arms dealers from sending weapons to Spain. At the time, Roosevelt did not envisage that he might later want to lift the embargo. FDR thus denied himself flexibility—a cardinal error for a creative policy maker.

One only needs to read Roosevelt's repeated enquiries in 1938–39 about the possibility of repeal by proclamation to see that the president deeply regretted this self-imposed constraint. If Roosevelt had fought in January 1937 for presidential discretion over arms sales in the Spanish Civil War—a discretionary power that was granted by Congress in May 1937 for other internal conflicts—there is a strong likelihood that he would ultimately have lifted the Spanish embargo.

Together with this failure to maintain flexibility, we can also discern in Spanish policy some of the wider weaknesses of Roosevelt's competitive and chaotic model of decision making: his "adhocracy." There was almost no detailed analysis, as the basis for a reasoned policy, of exactly what American aims and interests in the Spanish Civil War were. This unsystematic policy making would come as no surprise to the British, who regularly thought that Roosevelt's foreign policy was contradictory and confusing, his suggestions half-baked and unreliable. The covert aid episode illustrates a number of FDR's less impressive decision-making characteristics: his dissembling style, his naïveté, and the credibility gap between the president's words and his actions.

What Roosevelt did not do until the last minute is educate the public or Congress about what he believed was at stake in Spain. This charge is significant because FDR considered one of his principal roles to be that of a public educator. In a number of other cases he explained complex international problems in comprehensible terms, for example by invoking the notion of a "quarantine" or a "good neighbor."[6] On the issue of the Spanish Civil War, there was an evident need for education. Public opinion polls showed a positive relationship between knowledge about the war and support for ending the embargo. The polls in 1939 revealed that although a majority opposed repeal, this majority was made up primarily of those who claimed not to be following the Spanish Civil War. In contrast, most of those who favored repeal claimed to be following the events in Spain. Only in the president's address of 4 January 1939 do we see signs of his trying to educate the public and Congress, when he commented that American neutrality policies had aided aggression, but even here FDR did not specifically refer to the Spanish Civil War.

While these criticisms are valid, they do not represent the full picture. The tangible impact of Roosevelt's Spanish policies in 1938 was limited, but in a broader context they were very significant. The policies represented a key stage in the development of FDR's overall strategy from 1935 to 1941: aiding the democracies and the victims of aggression by methods short of war. As Roosevelt remarked in his State of the Union address in 1939: "There are many methods short of war, but stronger and more effective than mere words, of bringing home to aggressor governments the aggregate sentiments of our own people."[7] Many historians have depicted the Spanish Civil War as one of Roosevelt's most isolationist episodes, but it was actually the occasion for FDR's first interventionist European policies.

From 1935 to 1938 Roosevelt contemplated various schemes to deter or contain Italy, Germany, and Japan, but these were invariably negative schemes to selectively deny American products. Roosevelt chose not to enforce the American embargo in Japan's war with China, believing that doing so would undermine the Chinese war effort. In 1937 FDR outlined a possible "quarantine" of aggressors through the multilateral application of sanctions. The proposal to extend the arms embargo to the fascist states in 1937 because of their intervention in Spain also fits into this pattern. Despite considering these various negative schemes, very little action occurred.

In contrast, in 1938 FDR initiated or supported plans for shipping arms and food to Spain, providing cash for silver and mediating a compromise solution. All these policies were designed to challenge the aggressor states, while crucially avoiding the risk of American entry into war. However unsuccessful the Spanish initiatives proved to be, these policies nevertheless signified a new willingness by Roosevelt to intervene and aid European democracy, and would be accompanied after the Munich crisis with a plan to support Britain and France with American aircraft. After 1939, Axis victories increased the domestic acceptability of support for Britain and its allies. Roosevelt became increasingly bold in his proposals for aid short of war, with the destroyers-for-bases deal, Lend Lease, and an undeclared naval war against Germany in the Atlantic. The Spanish Civil War thus represented a clear juncture in the evolution of this overall strategy, which lasted from the Ethiopian war until Pearl Harbor.

Roosevelt's decision making in the Spanish Civil War also revealed some important positive aspects. FDR's changing beliefs in 1938 demonstrated his capacity to learn from events, challenge existing interpretations, and comprehend what was really at stake in international affairs. Donald Cameron Watt writes: "It is in fact in [Roosevelt's] ability to rise above his own generational, social, political and nationalist prejudices and react to the real issues that this maddening yet admirable figure differs so strikingly from those who served him, the Berles, Sumner Welleses and Moffats, the petty-minded self-styled 'realists' of the State Department."[8]

The Spanish Civil War was in many respects a worst-case scenario for purposeful leadership, but Roosevelt was active, adapted his thinking to new information, and proved flexible in his tactics. He once described his desire for "bold, persistent experimentation . . . It is common sense to take a method and try it: If it fails, admit it frankly and try another. But above all, try something."[9] As Roosevelt's interest in Spain rose, he sought new, informal sources of information. He employed channels of policy making outside the State Department, supporting the Treasury's stance on Spanish silver purchases and using an informal envoy, Hall Roosevelt, in the covert aid plan. When uncertain, FDR typically tested the domestic acceptability of his proposals, for example by leaking the story of his support for repealing the embargo to the *New York Times* in May 1938. If the domestic acceptability of proposals was in doubt, Roosevelt sought to circumvent or bypass these constraints. All these strategies can be contrasted with a policy of genuine drift, which is how many historians characterize the episode.

Our understanding of Roosevelt's policy making is deepened when we consider the relationship between the president and the international and domestic policy constraints. The Spanish Civil War did not directly threaten the United States; therefore there was no objective international pressure to compel presidential action. Instead, Richard Traina argues that the United States complied with British and French policy in 1936–38: "the most important fact was American inability to reject British leadership."[10] The German ambassador in Washington also told Berlin in May 1938 that the British influence was decisive in American policy making.[11] But Roosevelt's and Hull's personal wish to cooperate with Britain takes us back to the issue of individual perception. Not everyone believed in 1936–39 that greater cooperation with Britain was necessary or desirable. Senator Nye, for example, opposed Washington's tendency of "coming to heel like a well-trained dog every time England whistled."[12] Senator Borah stated: "I am no more desirous of cooperating with Great Britain than I am with Italy."[13] Furthermore, the evidence shows that Roosevelt independently supported international nonintervention in Spain from the start, before any meaningful British pressure had been applied. As the conflict progressed, Roosevelt became increasingly disillusioned with British weakness. Consideration of British opinion was a declining factor, noticeably absent at the end of 1938 with regard to the questions of repeal, mediation, and humanitarian aid.

Roosevelt was undeniably sensitive to Catholic pressure, reflecting the crucial position held by Catholics in the New Deal coalition. The Catholic constraint partly explains Roosevelt's refusal to publicly state his views on the Spanish Civil War. But did Catholics "dictate" American foreign policy on Spain, as some have suggested?[14] The most significant example of incongruence between Roosevelt's preferences and Spanish policy is the failure to lift the embargo in 1939, an outcome that the president clearly regretted. Catholic pressure on Congress is an important part of the explanation for this. Overall, Catholics demonstrated a greater capacity to defend the status quo than to initiate policy. The structure of the American political system creates many opportunities to obstruct change, particularly when, as with the embargo, that change is to an established policy. Roosevelt's political standing was also at an all-time low in 1937–39. The court-packing debacle, the "Roosevelt recession," and the failed party purge of 1938 largely removed the prestige and political capital generated by the landslide election victory of 1936, limiting both FDR's desire and his capacity to engage in a public fight with pro-Franco Catholics.

But domestic political constraints did not shape Roosevelt's basic beliefs about the Spanish Civil War, or his major policy goals. In 1938 the political incentives pointed in favor of continued strict nonintervention and presidential passivity, but Roosevelt instead chose to aid the Spanish Republic. When determined to act, he tried outflanking or co-opting Catholic opposition. Covert aid and ending the embargo by proclamation were attractive because they circumvented congressional resistance. When Roosevelt's thoughts turned to mediation and humanitarian aid he immediately sought to involve Catholic elements.[15]

Contemporaries who thought that Catholics had forced Roosevelt's hand tended to be left-wing pro-Loyalists like Norman Thomas, Miles Sherover, Louis Fischer, Claude Bowers, Eleanor Roosevelt, and Martha Gellhorn. For these figures the Catholics became a scapegoat for a much more complex reality. Knowing his audience, Roosevelt played on these perceptions. FDR gave the Loyalist agent Miles Sherover the impression that the Catholic vote had indeed affected him.[16] Similarly, in 1937 FDR implied that Catholic pressure had played a role when he discussed with Norman Thomas the possibility of extending the embargo to Germany and Italy. But as we have seen, the president immediately ignored this consideration in a letter to Hull.

One illustration of the difficulties involved in pinning down Roosevelt's beliefs is that he offered varying rationales for policy decisions in the Spanish Civil War depending on his audience. In 1940, with the United States drawing closer to Britain, Roosevelt emphasized that he had followed a European lead back in 1936.[17] Then in 1943, in his published justification for the embargo, Roosevelt stressed the role of wider American public opinion.[18] In contrast, FDR told his internationalist wife Eleanor, "the League of Nations had asked us to remain neutral."[19] Talking to Bowers in 1939, he blamed Spanish Civil War decisions on the foreign policy bureaucracy: "I have been imposed upon by false information sent me from across the street," nodding his head toward the State Department. Bowers was receptive to this excuse, as he had long argued that a strategically placed pro-Franco element in the State Department misled the president.[20]

But was Roosevelt telling Bowers the whole truth? To what extent did the foreign policy bureaucracy distort FDR's preferences? Howard Jablon has suggested that "Hull determined the government's attitude toward the Spanish Civil War."[21] But Roosevelt was prepared to overrule Cordell Hull, for example over passports for Loyalist medical personnel in 1937. Hull always recognized the ultimate authority of the president in decision making regarding the Spanish Civil War. On 19 November 1938 Hull thought that Roosevelt would "move on [embargo repeal] very shortly; if so he hoped he would tie his recommendation up with his entire neutrality policy rather than isolating the Spanish phase for separate treatment."[22] Reacting to Roosevelt's tendency to include a range of officials and departments in foreign policy making, Hull told Herbert Feis in May 1938 that it was "virtually intolerable to have other members of the Cabinet making leading utterances regarding foreign affairs which vitally affected his ability, as secretary of state, to manage those affairs well. The secretary stated the President would not give orders to stop."[23] Indeed, even when the State Department was united in opposition, FDR still pursued issues that offered potential results, for example with the idea of extending the embargo in 1937, and the notion of ending the embargo by proclamation in 1938.

Which bureaucrat gave advice to Roosevelt or performed a particular function often depended less on organizational position than on the personal predilections of the president. Arthur Krock recalled that when maneuvering on the "great chessboard of diplomacy," FDR would "never let Hull have much to do with it at all," instead preferring to use Sumner Welles in an informal capacity.[24] Harold Ickes was greatly dissatisfied with American policy in the Spanish Civil War, but he did not think that bureaucrats had subverted the decision-making process. Rather, he disliked the president's style of making decisions by dividing his advisors and working with them as individuals. "What I cannot understand is why such an important policy [as the Spanish Civil War] should have been decided upon without a full and frank discussion in the Cabinet. The president is altogether too prone to decide important questions either alone or with the particular

Cabinet officer who is interested."[25] The relationship between the president and his bureaucracy provides one of the major flaws in the argument that anticommunist American officials deliberately undermined the Spanish Republic by denying it arms.[26] Although Bullitt, Moore, and others were concerned by the prospect of a Bolshevik Spain, they were not making the decisions between 1936 and 1939.

The bureaucracy was more important in implementing key decisions than in making them. The enforcement of the embargo, for example, was a State Department responsibility, and as Ickes noted, "the State Department literally shut down on all efforts to allow planes to be exported to Spain."[27] Similarly, it was not Roosevelt but Hull who was responsible for implementing the mediation proposal at the Lima Conference. Hull saw Spanish mediation as a secondary aim to hemispheric unity, and sacrificed the scheme when divisions became apparent.

Roosevelt was not the only person who mattered in making Spanish policy. Hull helped to shape the moral embargo in 1936, when his analysis of events was similar to that of the president. Morgenthau was the driving force behind the Spanish silver purchases. Adolf Berle played a significant role in formulating the mediation plan. A wide cast of other characters also played a part—Eleanor, Hall Roosevelt, Harold Ickes, R. Walton Moore, William Bullitt, Sumner Welles, Gerald Nye, and Ernest Hemingway. But any understanding of the complex and shifting Spanish policy needs to give a major role to President Roosevelt and his changing perceptions of Spain and the wider domestic and international policy environment. As many scholars have accurately noted, the Spanish Civil War provided one of the most constraining policy settings of FDR's presidency. It is Roosevelt's reaction to these constraints that has caused confusion. Perhaps this is not surprising given that the president's response was marked variously by creativity, inconsistency, activity, incoherence, experimentation, as well as both flexibility and inflexibility.

Psychological theory predicts that when decision makers are faced with a conflict between values, rather than engage in a tradeoff between those values they will seek a solution that sacrifices neither one, even if that solution is inadequate in many respects. Barbara Farnham has argued that Roosevelt in 1938 displayed a value conflict between checking Hitler's aggression and avoiding American entry into war. The president sought to transcend this value conflict by providing American aircraft to Britain and France, which would aid the democracies without risking war. A similar dynamic was evident with Spain. Once Roosevelt had clarified the meaning of the Spanish Civil War in 1938, he was attracted to a range of strategies including covert aid, repeal of the embargo by proclamation, and Catholic involvement in mediation and humanitarian aid, which promised to help the Loyalists while retaining domestic support. The president was reluctant to either abandon the Loyalists, or make political choices that were domestically unacceptable.[28]

Seeking politically tolerable means of supporting the Spanish Republic, Roosevelt was active, experimental, and creative. The president's instinct was to pursue strategies from behind the scenes, partly because he considered himself a lightning rod for critics of the administration, and partly to enable the pursuit of multiple policy options at the same time. In his State of the Union address of 1939, for example, Roosevelt preferred to claim that impartial embargoes by the United States aided aggression, and leave his audience to make the obvious connection with Spanish policy, rather than wade into a fierce domestic controversy with a specific indictment of the Spanish embargo. FDR therefore shied away from the kind of decisive, public, and politically hazardous intervention that might ultimately have been necessary to save the Spanish Republic.

Despite the hopes of the Spanish Republican Ambassador Fernando de los Rios, the United States never became the arsenal of Spanish democracy. Roosevelt was all too well aware that almost all his policies ultimately failed. By the time he perceived the conflict as one involving clear-cut American interests, the war was already in its final stages. The president's attempts to aid the Spanish Republic were defeated by Latin American divisions, Catholic opposition, and the Loyalist military collapse of January 1939. The Munich crisis helped to focus Roosevelt's mind on helping the Loyalists, but it also made the success of his initiatives less likely. Hitler's certainty that he could now act with impunity in Spain led Germany to offer decisive aid to Franco, breaking the military stalemate and undermining the possibility of mediation. Roosevelt expressed regret and guilt for American policy on numerous occasions after 1939. Finally, in the spring of 1945, with the Nazis on the verge of defeat, Roosevelt revealed his wish to see the Franco regime removed from power. For the Spanish Republicans, expecting a rapid return to Madrid, it was a false dawn. Within eight years, the United States and Franco Spain would be allies in the cold war.

Notes

Chapter 1: The American Sphinx and the Spanish War

1 Interview with Claude G. Bowers, Columbia University Oral History Project (1954), 125–26.
2 For the argument that Roosevelt was the greatest figure of his century see Black, *Franklin Delano Roosevelt*.
3 Puzzo, *Spain and the Great Powers*, v; Weintrub, *The Last Great Cause*.
4 Mathews, *Half of Spain Died*, 173.
5 Carr, *The Spanish Tragedy*, 203.
6 Truman, *Memoirs*, 155; Ickes, *The Secret Diary of Harold L. Ickes*, vol. 3, 217; Mathews, *Half of Spain Died*, 177. See also Roosevelt, *Complete Presidential Press Conferences of Franklin D. Roosevelt*, 5 June 1940.
7 Welles, *The Time for Decision*, 306.
8 Dallek, *Franklin D. Roosevelt and American Foreign Policy*, 143, 529.
9 Guttmann, ed., *American Neutrality and the Spanish Civil War*, 100.
10 Carroll, *The Odyssey of the Abraham Lincoln Brigade*, 374–75.
11 Alfred Kazin, "The Wound That Will Not Heal," 39–41.
12 Brown, "Idealism, Realpolitik or Domestic Politics."
13 Tierney, "Irrelevant or Malevolent?"
14 Loewenheim and Feis, *The Historian and the Diplomat*, 95.
15 Flynn, *Roosevelt and Romanism*, 44–55; Brendon, *The Dark Valley*, 330.
16 Kanawada, *Franklin D. Roosevelt's Diplomacy and American Catholics, Italians, and Jews*; Taylor, *The United States and the Spanish Civil War*.
17 Cole, *Roosevelt and the Isolationists*.
18 Traina, *American Diplomacy and the Spanish Civil War*.
19 Little, *Malevolent Neutrality*.
20 Freidel, *Franklin D. Roosevelt*, 272; Kinsella, *Leadership in Isolation*, 216.
21 Waltz, *Theory of International Politics*.
22 Cole, *Roosevelt and the Isolationists*, 234–37.
23 Halperin and Allison, "Bureaucratic Politics."

24   Reynolds, *The Creation of the Anglo-American Alliance.*
25   Kimball, *The Juggler,* 7; Heinrichs, *Threshold of War,* vii.
26   Reynolds, *The Creation of the Anglo-American Alliance,* 26–27.
27   Dallek, *Hail to the Chief,* 141–44.
28   Divine, *The Reluctant Belligerent;* Divine, *The Illusion of Neutrality;* Offner, *American Appeasement.* For the internationalist view see Dallek, *Franklin D. Roosevelt and American Foreign Policy.* Wayne S. Cole argues that Roosevelt was an internationalist who aligned himself with isolationist senators in order to pass domestic legislation, an alliance that weakened and then collapsed in the late 1930s. Cole, *Roosevelt and the Isolationists.*
29   Burns, *Roosevelt;* Marks, *Wind over Sand.*
30   Morgan, *FDR,* 39; Marks, *Wind over Sand,* 1; Heinrichs, *Threshold of War,* vii; Harper, *American Visions of Europe,* 13.
31   Tugwell, *The Democratic Roosevelt,* 15.
32   Stimson diary, 18 December 1940.
33   Marks, *Wind over Sand,* 5. For details of Roosevelt's disinclination toward keeping written accounts of policy deliberations see Kimball, *The Juggler,* 203 n. 2.
34   Furet, *The Passing of an Illusion,* 261.
35   Orwell, "Looking Back on the Spanish War," available in *The Penguin Complete Longer Non-fiction of George Orwell.*
36   Puzzo, *Spain and the Great Powers.*
37   Kimball, *The Juggler,* 4; Heinrichs, *Threshold of War.*
38   George, "The Causal Nexus between Cognitive Beliefs and Decision-making Behaviour," 105–13.
39   Freidel, *Franklin D. Roosevelt,* 268–69.
40   Eckstein, "Case Study and Theory in Political Science"; George, "Case Studies and Theory Development."

Chapter 2: International Intervention and Nonintervention

1   Morgan, *FDR,* 438.
2   Dallek, *Franklin D. Roosevelt and American Foreign Policy,* 122.
3   Mary Habeck, "The Spanish Civil War and the Origins of the Second World War," *The Origins of the Second World War Reconsidered,* ed. Martel, 205.
4   Jackson, *The Spanish Republic and the Civil War,* 5–6; Carr, *Modern Spain,* 98–116.
5   Preston, *The Coming of the Spanish Civil War,* chapters 1–4; Jackson, *The Spanish Republic and the Civil War,* chapters 2–10; Carr, *Modern Spain,* 117–35.
6   Preston, *The Coming of the Spanish Civil War,* 200; Alpert, *A New International History of the Spanish Civil War,* 19; Jackson, *The Spanish Republic and the Civil War,* chapters 11–13; Preston, *The Spanish Civil War,* 48.
7   Carroll, *The Odyssey of the Abraham Lincoln Brigade,* 55–59.
8   Preston, *The Spanish Civil War,* 5.

9   Alpert, *A New International History of the Spanish Civil War*, 14.

10 Little, *Malevolent Neutrality*, 232–33; Edwards, *The British Government and the Spanish Civil War*.

11 The exact nature of British pressure is unclear. Blum later recalled that from the British "counsels of prudence were dispensed and sharp fears expressed." Alpert, *A New International History of the Spanish Civil War*, 12, 21; Traina, *American Diplomacy and the Spanish Civil War*, 34, 253; Weber, *The Hollow Years*, 167; Warner, "France and Non-intervention in Spain," 203–20; Young, *In Command of France*; Adamthwaite, *France and the Coming of the Second World War*; Ambassador Strauss to Cordell Hull, 27 July 1936, *Foreign Relations of the United States* [hereinafter *FRUS*], 1936, vol. 2, 447; Enrique Moradiellos, "The Allies and the Spanish Civil War," *Spain and the Great Powers in the Twentieth Century*, ed. Balfour and Preston, 102; Thomas, *Britain, France and Appeasement*, 92–96.

12 Butler and Woodward, eds., *Documents on British Foreign Policy*; Edwards, *The British Government and the Spanish Civil War*, chapter 3; Buchanan, *Britain and the Spanish Civil War*, 37–47; Cooper, *Old Men Forget*, 205; Moradiellos, "The Allies and the Spanish Civil War," *Spain and the Great Powers in the Twentieth Century*, ed. Balfour and Preston, 103; McKercher, *Transition of Power*, 233; Thomas, *The Spanish Civil War*, 337; Alpert, *A New International History of the Spanish Civil War*, 17; Payne, *The Spanish Revolution*, 266; Watt, *Succeeding John Bull*, 75; Thomas, *Britain, France and Appeasement*, 92–93; Barnett, *The Collapse of British Power*; Schmidt, *The Politics and Economics of Appeasement*.

13 Padelford, *International Law and Diplomacy in the Spanish Civil Strife*, 53–120; Alpert, *A New International History of the Spanish Civil War*, 59.

14 Veatch, "The League of Nations and the Spanish Civil War"; Esenwein and Shubert, *Spain at War*, 190.

15 Thomas, *The Spanish Civil War*, 264; van der Esch, *Prelude to War*, 72–85; Alpert, *A New International History of the Spanish Civil War*, 115.

16 Christian Leitz, "Nazi Germany and Francoist Spain, 1936–1945," *Spain and the Great Powers in the Twentieth Century*, ed. Balfour and Preston, 128–29. The German ambassador to Italy explained in December 1936: "The struggle for dominant political influence in Spain lays bare the natural opposition between Italy and France; at the same time the position of Italy as a power in the western Mediterranean comes into competition with that of Britain. All the more clearly will Italy recognise the advisability of confronting the Western powers shoulder to shoulder with Germany." *Documents on German Foreign Policy*; Alpert, *A New International History of the Spanish Civil War*, 26–34, 171; Preston, *Franco*, 159–60; Whealey, *Hitler and Spain*, 138; Moradiellos, "The Allies and the Spanish Civil War," *Spain and the Great Powers in the Twentieth Century*, ed. Balfour and Preston, 104; Weinberg, *The Foreign Policy of Hitler's Germany*; Jackson, *The Spanish Republic and the Civil War*, 248–49; Carr, *The Spanish Tragedy*, 137–39.

17 Alpert, *A New International History of the Spanish Civil War*, 36–37, 92–94; Paul Preston, "Italy and Spain in Civil War and World War, 1936–1943," *Spain and the*

Great Powers in the Twentieth Century, ed. Balfour and Preston, 151–76; Coverdale, *Italian Intervention in the Spanish Civil War*; Carr, *The Spanish Tragedy*, 136; Preston, *Franco*, 156; Whealey, *Hitler and Spain*, 131–36.

18 Payne, *The Spanish Civil War, the Soviet Union and Communism*, 144–55, 295; Jonathan Haslam, "Soviet Russia and the Spanish Problem," *The Origins of World War Two*, ed. Boyce and Maiolo, 70–85; Denis Smyth, "We Are with You: Solidarity and Self-Interest in Soviet Policy towards Republican Spain, 1936–1939," *The Republic Besieged*, ed. Preston and Mackenzie; Haslam, *The USSR and the Struggle for Collective Security in Europe*; Roberts, *Unholy Alliance*; Alpert, *A New International History of the Spanish Civil War*, 72–76, 103.

19 Aleksandr Orlov, the head of Soviet intelligence in Spain, received the Order of Lenin in 1937, in part because he coordinated the shipment of the Spanish gold to the Soviet Union. In 1938, Orlov, fearing that he would be next to die in Stalin's purges, suddenly disappeared and took his family to live incognito in the United States. In a letter, Orlov told the Soviet authorities that he would not reveal any secrets, pointedly mentioning his knowledge of Moscow's spies in Britain, Donald Maclean and Kim Philby. Orlov added that documents damaging to Moscow had been placed in a safety deposit box with instructions that they be opened and publicized if he or his family suffered any harm. Orlov was left alone, and eventually worked as a consultant at the University of Michigan Law School. Payne, *The Spanish Civil War, the Soviet Union and Communism*, 150, 261–62.

20 Radosh, Habeck, and Sevostianov, eds., *Spain Betrayed*; Enrique Moradiellos, "The Allies and the Spanish Civil War," *Spain and the Great Powers in the Twentieth Century*, ed. Balfour and Preston, 108–9; Howson, *Arms for Spain*; Traina, *American Diplomacy and the Spanish Civil War*, 37; Haslam, *The USSR and the Struggle for Collective Security in Europe*, 124–25.

21 Preston, *Franco*, 167; Alpert, *A New International History of the Spanish Civil War*, 53–54.

22 Alpert, *A New International History of the Spanish Civil War*, 130–35.

23 On 30 September 1936 the U.S. ambassador to Mexico, Josephus Daniels, described the major interest among Mexicans in the Spanish Civil War. The Mexicans were, he said, "intensely partisan" in their support for the Republic. Josephus Daniels to Roosevelt, 30 September 1936, Josephus Daniels papers, microfilm copy, Franklin D. Roosevelt Library. See also Josephus Daniels to Cordell Hull, 28, 31 July 1938, Department of State Records [hereinafter DSR] 852.00/2365, 852.00/2366; Josephus Daniels to Claude G. Bowers, 13 November 1936, 2 March 1937, 31 May 1938, Bowers papers II; Alpert, *A New International History of the Spanish Civil War*, 108, 162; Powell, *Mexico and the Spanish Civil War*, chapter 3; Esenwein and Shubert, *Spain at War*, 190.

Chapter 3: Roosevelt's Perceptions, 1936–1937

1 Used as the title for Warren Kimball's recent study *The Juggler*, 7.
2 Brendon, *The Dark Valley*, 234.
3 Burns, *Roosevelt*, 472–78.
4 Speech by Roosevelt, Chautauqua, N.Y., 14 August 1936, *Franklin D. Roosevelt and Foreign Affairs* [hereinafter *FDR and FA*], vol. 3, 377–84.
5 Gordenker, "The Legacy of Franklin D. Roosevelt's Internationalism," 200–210.
6 Roosevelt told British Prime Minister Ramsay MacDonald in 1933, "I am concerned by events in Germany because I feel that an insane rush to further armaments in Continental Europe is infinitely more dangerous than any number of squabbles over gold or stabilization of tariffs." Roosevelt to Ramsay MacDonald, 30 August 1933, *FRUS*, 1933, vol. 1, 210.
7 Reynolds, *From Munich to Pearl Harbor*, 34–35; Dallek, *Franklin D. Roosevelt and American Foreign Policy*, 10–19.
8 Connally, *My Name Is Tom Connally*, 218; Dallek, *Franklin D. Roosevelt and American Foreign Policy*, 54; Divine, *The Reluctant Belligerent*, 4; Burns, *Roosevelt*, 262–63.
9 Dallek, *Franklin D. Roosevelt and American Foreign Policy*, 66–71; Davis, *FDR: Into the Storm*, 552–62; Divine, *The Reluctant Belligerent*, 19–24.
10 Leuchtenberg, *Franklin D. Roosevelt and the New Deal*, 210–21; Dallek, *Franklin D. Roosevelt and American Foreign Policy*, 78; Cole, *Roosevelt and the Isolationists*, 6–7; Farnham, *Roosevelt and the Munich Crisis*, 53–55; Schlesinger, *The Age of Roosevelt*, vol. 1, 192.
11 Kinsella, *Leadership in Isolation*, 210; Farnham, *Roosevelt and the Munich Crisis*, 53; Reynolds, *The Creation of the Anglo-American Alliance*, 32; Ickes, *The Secret Diary of Harold L. Ickes*, vol. 2, 89–90, 187.
12 Dallek, *Franklin D. Roosevelt and American Foreign Policy*, 110, 137; Farnham, *Roosevelt and the Munich Crisis*, 57–58.
13 Haglund, *Latin America and the Transformation of American Strategic Thought*, 1–80; Hull, *The Memoirs of Cordell Hull*, vol. 1, 496; Farnham, *Roosevelt and the Munich Crisis*, 60; Wood, *The Making of the Good Neighbor Policy*; Gellman, *Good Neighbor Diplomacy*; Kimball, *The Juggler*, 107–25.
14 Casey, *Cautious Crusade*, 6–7; Roosevelt, ed., *F.D.R.: His Personal Letters*, vol. 1, 379–80.
15 For Roosevelt and Mussolini see Doenecke and Stoler, *Debating Franklin D. Roosevelt's Foreign Policies*, 14; Dallek, *Franklin D. Roosevelt and American Foreign Policy*, 145; Freidel, *Franklin D. Roosevelt*, 270; Welles, *Sumner Welles*, 213; Schmitz, *Thank God They're on Our Side*, chapter 3.
16 Traina, *American Diplomacy and the Spanish Civil War*, 108.
17 McKercher, *Transition of Power*, 220; Harris, *The United States and the Italo-Ethiopian Crisis*; Farnham, *Roosevelt and the Munich Crisis*, 61–62; Casey, *Cautious Crusade*, 8–9. In October 1937, for example, Roosevelt supported Sumner

Welles's suggestion that the dictators be included in an international peace initiative. Roosevelt returned to the idea in January 1938, communicating to Prime Minister Neville Chamberlain of Britain his support for an international conference on arms reduction, international law, and economic issues. Farnham, *Roosevelt and the Munich Crisis*, 64–72; Welles, *The Time for Decision*, 64–66; Schmitz, *Thank God They're on Our Side*, chapter 3.

18   Draft State Department Report, 15 January 1937, *FDR and FA,* vol. 4, 65–74; Harper, *American Visions of Europe*, 62.

19   Dobson, *U.S. Economic Statecraft for Survival*; Dallek, *Franklin D. Roosevelt and American Foreign Policy*, 102–26; Farnham, *Roosevelt and the Munich Crisis*, 55–57.

20   Dallek, *Franklin D. Roosevelt and American Foreign Policy*, 76.

21   Divine, *The Reluctant Belligerent*, 46.

22   Sherwood, *Roosevelt and Hopkins*, 79.

23   Reynolds, *From Munich to Pearl Harbor*, 38; Borg, "Notes on Roosevelt's Quarantine Speech"; Dallek, *Franklin D. Roosevelt and American Foreign Policy*, 148–49; Farnham, *Roosevelt and the Munich Crisis*, 69; Haight, "Franklin D. Roosevelt and a Naval Quarantine of Japan."

24   In 1932 Roosevelt told a British journalist that if Britain and the United States could achieve "a complete identity of political and economic interests," they would "acquire the true leadership of the world." Dallek, *Franklin D. Roosevelt and American Foreign Policy*, 23. See also Harrison, "A Presidential Demarche"; Harrison, "Testing the Water." For the view that Roosevelt was ham-handed in his relations with Britain see Watt, *Succeeding John Bull*, 82–97; Reynolds, *The Creation of the Anglo-American Alliance*, 25; Morgan, *FDR,* 505–6. For Roosevelt's anti-colonialism see Louis, *Imperialism at Bay*; Watt, *Succeeding John Bull*, 80–82; Kimball, *The Juggler*, 47.

25   Watt, *Succeeding John Bull*, 72–73.

26   Doenecke and Stoler, *Debating Franklin D. Roosevelt's Foreign Policies*, 32; McKercher, *Transition of Power*, 148. British officials regularly referred to Roosevelt as an "amateur," a pusillanimous figure without convictions. Watt, *Succeeding John Bull*, 84.

27   Doenecke and Stoler, *Debating Franklin D. Roosevelt's Foreign Policies*, 32.

28   Reynolds, *The Creation of the Anglo-American Alliance*, chapter 1.

29   Reynolds, *The Creation of the Anglo-American Alliance*; McKercher, *Transition of Power*; Baram, "Undermining the British"; Thorne, *Allies of a Kind*; Watt, *Succeeding John Bull*, 76–84.

30   Dallek, *Franklin D. Roosevelt and American Foreign Policy*, 145.

31   Gaddis, *Strategies of Containment*, 9–10; Nisbet, *Roosevelt and Stalin*, 4–11; William E. Kinsella Jr., "Franklin D. Roosevelt and the Soviet Union, 1933–1941," *Franklin D. Roosevelt and the Formation of the Modern World*, ed. Howard and Pederson; Glantz, *FDR and the Soviet Union*.

32   Harper, *American Visions of Europe*, 26; Ward, *Before the Trumpet*, 200.

33 Roosevelt to Claude G. Bowers, 5 February 1934, Bowers papers II; Sehlinger and Hamilton, *Spokesman for Democracy*, 273–74; Jones, ed., *U.S. Diplomats in Europe*, 132. Irwin Laughlin would later campaign against lifting the American embargo, arguing that only a Nationalist victory could rescue Spain from communism. Valaik, "Catholics, Neutrality, and the Spanish Embargo," 78.

34 Roosevelt to Claude G. Bowers, 22 August 1933, 6 October 1934, Bowers papers II; *FDR and FA*, vol. 1, 586–87, 609; Little, *Malevolent Neutrality*, 133, 153, 160; Sehlinger and Hamilton, *Spokesman for Democracy*, 166–67, 172–75.

35 Claude G. Bowers to Cordell Hull, 23 September 1936, Claude G. Bowers to Roosevelt, 29 October 1936, *FDR and FA*, vol. 3, 435, 465. For further evidence of Soviet intervention see DSR 852.00/2395, 852.00/3726, 852.00/3739. William Phillips to Roosevelt, 14 January 1937, *FDR and FA*, vol. 4, 52–58; Bullitt, ed., *For the President, Personal and Secret*, 210; Morgan-Green report, 52–54. The Morgan-Green report, prepared by John Morgan and Joseph C. Green, is a State Department analysis of American diplomacy and the Spanish Civil War, completed in 1944–45. It is located in carton 13 of the Joseph C. Green papers at Princeton University.

36 Roosevelt, ed., *F.D.R.: His Personal Letters*, 614. In the *Examiner* on 24 July 1936 Hearst wrote: "Spain today is prey to the same forces of national disintegration that are working in France and Belgium. This force is Communism . . . And what has happened in France and Spain can happen here . . . To be conscious of this danger is to tighten up our Americanism."

37 Claude G. Bowers to Roosevelt, 31 March 1937, Roosevelt to Stephen T. Early, 14 April 1937, Michael J. McDermott to Stephen T. Early, 15 April 1937, *FDR and FA*, vol. 4, 439, vol. 5, 62–63, 72.

38 William C. Bullitt to Cordell Hull, 20 February 1937, 30 April 1937, *FRUS*, 1937, vol. 1, 46–54, 291–92.

39 Memorandum, Joseph C. Green to Mr. Savage, November 1944, 15–20, Materials for Morgan-Green Report, Green papers, carton 13.

40 Norman Thomas to Roosevelt, 31 August 1936, *FDR and FA*, vol. 3, 408–9, 412–13; Arthur Krock papers, Princeton University, box 1, book 1, 1928–48, 75; Dallek, *Franklin D. Roosevelt and American Foreign Policy*, 131; Morgan, *FDR*, 438. "Scarcely a day passed," Hull recorded, "but that I was called upon to give consideration to the Spanish situation." Hull, *The Memoirs of Cordell Hull*, vol. 1, 504.

41 Connally, *My Name Is Tom Connally*, 222–23.

42 Memorandum, 8 July 1937, Roosevelt papers, OF 422-a; Moorehead, *Gellhorn*, 132; Ivens, *The Camera and I*, 130–32; Martha Gellhorn to Eleanor Roosevelt, 1938, Eleanor Roosevelt papers box 1459; Eleanor Roosevelt Oral History Project, box 2, "Martha Gellhorn," 20, Franklin D. Roosevelt Presidential Library.

43 Ickes, *The Secret Diary of Harold L. Ickes*, vol. 2, 277–78.

44 As FDR explained in 1939: "there were many, including myself, who hoped that having restored order and morale in Italy, [Mussolini] would, of his own ac-

cord, work toward a restoration of democratic processes." Roosevelt to Stephen Early, 10 January 1939, Roosevelt papers, PPF 5763.

45 Roosevelt, ed., *F.D.R.: His Personal Letters*, 614.
46 Connally, *My Name Is Tom Connally*, 222–23; José Camprubi to Roosevelt, 30 January 1937, *FDR and FA*, vol. 4, 129–30.
47 Arthur Krock papers, box 1, book 1, 1928–48, 82a. William Bullitt wrote from Paris on 24 November 1936, arguing that although the Spanish Civil War might "bring Europe to the very edge of war," war would "not spring directly out of it." Bullitt, ed., *For the President, Personal and Secret*, 186; Ickes, *The Secret Diary of Harold L. Ickes*, vol. 2, 73, 90–91; Welles, *Seven Decisions That Shaped History*, 14.
48 Farnham, *Roosevelt and the Munich Crisis*, 65.
49 Dallek, *Franklin D. Roosevelt and American Foreign Policy*, 145.
50 Eden papers, Public Records Office, London, FO 954.
51 Robert W. Bingham to R. Walton Moore, 20 November 1936, *FRUS,* 1936, vol. 2, 562; Ickes, *The Secret Diary of Harold L. Ickes*, vol. 2, 5. The administration was aware of the arrival of substantial Soviet weaponry. See for example the Morgan-Green report, 50–51.

Chapter 4: The Arms Embargo

1 *New York American*, 1 February 1937.
2 For efforts to rescue citizens see Cordell Hull to Roosevelt, 28 July 1936, *FDR and FA,* vol. 3, 356; *FRUS,* 1936, vol. 2, 626–784; DSR 852.00/2408–24.
3 Pratt, *Cordell Hull*; Traina, *American Diplomacy and the Spanish Civil War*, 18.
4 Hull, *The Memoirs of Cordell Hull*, vol. 1, 476–77; *FRUS,* 1936, vol. 2, 454–55, 457–58.
5 Ambassador Strauss to Cordell Hull, 27 July 1936, Cordell Hull memorandum, 4 August 1936, *FRUS,* 1936, vol. 2, 447, 457–58, 462–67; DSR 852.00/2434, 852.00/2545. According to the U.S. embassy in Rome, Italy considered a prospective nonintervention agreement by Britain, France, and Italy ineffective, "in that other countries which were not bound by the agreement might furnish aid to either side in the Spanish conflict." Kirk to Cordell Hull, 4 August 1936, DSR 852.00/2394. On 11 August Hull was told that the French would be "pleased" if the United States introduced an arms embargo on Spain, but Paris would not invite such a move. Wilson to Cordell Hull, 11 August 1936, DSR 852.00/2517.
6 Hull, *The Memoirs of Cordell Hull*, vol. 1, 481–85, 500–501; *FRUS,* 1936, vol. 2, 509, 512, 519–23, 536–38, 553–76.
7 Traina, *American Diplomacy and the Spanish Civil War*, 145–50.
8 Speech by Roosevelt, Chautauqua, 14 August 1936, *FDR and FA*, vol. 3, 377–84. FDR remarked that Hull was "the only member of the cabinet who brings me any political strength that I don't have in my own right." Harper, *American Visions of Europe*, 49; Taylor, *The United States and the Spanish Civil War*, 40–47; Cortada, *Two Nations over Time*, 190–200.

9 Traina, *American Diplomacy and the Spanish Civil War*, 19–21.

10 Welles, *Sumner Welles*, 209–10; Morgan, *FDR*, 678.

11 For details of Moore's views see the Moore papers; R. Walton Moore to Roosevelt, 11 November 1936, Roosevelt papers, PPF 1043; Roosevelt papers, PSF, R. Walton Moore. For Phillips see Phillips, *Ventures in Diplomacy*; William Phillips to Roosevelt, 14 January, 22 April, 1937, *FDR and FA*, vol. 4, 52–58, vol. 5, 91–95.

12 Little, "Antibolshevism and American Foreign Policy," 387.

13 The American vice-consul at Seville wrote a paper in September 1936 entitled "The Future of Liberty in Spain," in which he argued that Spanish universal suffrage would lead to anarchism or communism. "When liberty makes its reappearance the approach will be different than in Anglo-Saxon countries. Whereas we began with liberty and successfully imposed discipline to restrain its free use to the injury of others, Spain will have to start with discipline and gradually relax it to permit free expression." The report was graded "excellent." DSR 852.00/3330.

14 "Barcelona in Grip of Left Terror; Nuns, Priests and Fascists Slain," *New York Times*, 1 August 1936.

15 William Phillips journal, William Phillips papers, Harvard University, 3, 4 August 1936; Wendelin to Cordell Hull, 1, 25 August 1936, DSR 852.00/2349, 852.00/2434, 852.00/2817; Strauss to Cordell Hull, 4 August 1936, Henderson to Cordell Hull, 4 August 1936, Wendelin to Cordell Hull, 22 August 1936, Perkins to Cordell Hull, 19 September 1936, *FRUS*, 1936, vol. 2, 459, 461, 679–80, 723–24; Traina, *American Diplomacy and the Spanish Civil War*, 61–62.

16 Claude G. Bowers to Cordell Hull, 25 August 1937, Bowers papers II. The chief of the Division of European Affairs, Jay Pierrepont Moffat, thought that the use of the phrase "Reds" was "inadvertent." Jay Pierrepont Moffat to Claude G. Bowers, 4 October 1937, Bowers papers II.

17 Craig and Gilbert, *The Diplomats*, 655.

18 Claude G. Bowers to Roosevelt, 26 August 1936, 16 September 1936, *FDR and FA*, vol. 3, 395–400, 435–39; Claude G. Bowers to Cordell Hull, 30 December 1936, Roosevelt papers, PSF, Spain, box 50.

19 Claude G. Bowers to Cordell Hull, 20 July 1937, *FDR and FA*, vol. 6, 187; Falcoff and Pike, *The Spanish Civil War*, 26.

20 Claude G. Bowers to Roosevelt, 9 September 1936, Claude G. Bowers to Cordell Hull, 23 September 1936, *FDR and FA*, vol. 3, 415, 436–39; Bowers diary, 24 June 1937; R. Walton Moore to Roosevelt, 27 November 1936, *FDR and FA*, vol. 3, 512–13.

21 Harper, *American Visions of Europe*, 43–44; Jones, ed., *U.S. Diplomats in Europe*, 133.

22 Jones, ed., *U.S. Diplomats in Europe*, 133.

23 Roosevelt to Claude G. Bowers, 15 January 1937, *FDR and FA*, vol. 4, 76–77.

24 Roosevelt to Cordell Hull, 17 June 1937, *FDR and FA*, vol. 5, 391.

25 William C. Bullitt to R. Walton Moore, 25, 28 November 1936, *FRUS,* 1936, vol. 2, 575–80; William C. Bullitt to Roosevelt, 24 November 1936, *FDR and FA,* vol. 3, 502; Craig and Gilbert, *The Diplomats,* 649–81; Traina, *American Diplomacy and the Spanish Civil War,* 24–25; Bullitt, ed., *For the President, Personal and Secret,* 180–81, 245; Little, *Malevolent Neutrality,* 201.

26 Stanley K. Hornbeck memorandum, DSR 852.00/2552; Harper, *American Visions of Europe,* 50–53; Reynolds, *The Creation of the Anglo-American Alliance,* 28–29; Jablon, *Crossroads of Decision,* 127–29; Heinrichs, *Diplomacy and Force,* 70–71; Little, *Malevolent Neutrality,* 237.

27 Major isolationist constituents included those with faith in the geostrategic impregnability of the United States, those who stressed the threat to domestic politics from foreign adventures, pacifists, unilateralists, and the indifferent. Jonas, *Isolationism in America,* 5–6, 15–23, 32–69, 111–33; Cole, *Senator Gerald P. Nye and American Foreign Relations,* 90–104; Doenecke, "Non-interventionism of the Left"; Dallek, *The American Style of Foreign Policy,* 111–13; Reynolds, *From Munich to Pearl Harbor,* 6.

28 Farnham, *Roosevelt and the Munich Crisis,* 50–52; Cole, *Roosevelt and the Isolationists,* 6–7; Millis, *Road to War*; Dallek, *The American Style of Foreign Policy,* 115; Divine, *The Reluctant Belligerent,* 12; Doenecke, *Storm on the Horizon.* As a measure of isolationist sentiment, 73 percent of Americans according to one poll favored a national referendum before war could be declared. FDR did defeat a congressional resolution to this effect, in early 1938, but by a vote of only 209 to 188. Bolt Jr., *Ballots before Bullets.*

29 Speech by Roosevelt at Chautauqua, 14 August 1936, *FDR and FA,* vol. 3, 377–84; Dallek, *Franklin D. Roosevelt and American Foreign Policy,* 129–31; Burns, *The Three Roosevelts,* 352; Cole, *Senator Gerald P. Nye and American Foreign Relations,* 136–38; Roosevelt papers, OF 1561.

30 Roosevelt and Brough, *A Rendezvous with Destiny,* 137–39.

31 Freidel, *Franklin D. Roosevelt,* 205.

32 Roosevelt and Brough, *A Rendezvous with Destiny,* 137–39.

33 Connally, *My Name Is Tom Connally,* 222–23.

34 Hull, *The Memoirs of Cordell Hull,* vol. 1, 477; Morgan-Green report, 31–32; Haglund, *Latin America and the Transformation of American Strategic Thought,* 46–47. Cordell Hull wanted to avoid repeating the experience of failed interventions in Latin America. He explained in October 1936 that "the Government of the United States had at times in the past occasionally taken entirely innocent steps when difficulties occurred in Latin American countries and that these innocent steps had often led to other complications which had in effect caused interference and even intervention by the United States. Frequently regrettable situations had arisen out of such beginnings." *FRUS,* 1936, vol. 2, 537.

35 Press release, 11 August 1936, R. Walton Moore papers, box 19, "Spanish Revolution"; William Phillips memorandum, 7 August 1936, *FRUS,* 1936, vol. 2, 469–71; Padelford, *International Law and Diplomacy in the Spanish Civil Strife,* 51–52.

36 Burns, *Roosevelt*, 257; Jablon, *Crossroads of Decision*, 120–22; Divine, *The Reluctant Belligerent*, chapter 2; Offner, *American Appeasement*, 127–28; Dallek, *Franklin D. Roosevelt and American Foreign Policy*, 111.

37 In Berlin the British ambassador was told that an American embargo on arms sales to Spain was "essential to make [nonintervention] effective." Robert W. Bingham to Cordell Hull, 11 August 1936, DSR 852.00/2520; William Phillips journal, 11 August 1936; William Phillips memorandum, 7 August 1936, *FRUS*, 1936, vol. 2, 467; Traina, *American Diplomacy and the Spanish Civil War*, 53.

38 William Phillips to Roosevelt, 10 August 1936, Green papers, Correspondence, carton 13; Joseph Green to Mr. Savage, November 1944 memorandum, Material for the Morgan-Green Report, Green papers, carton 13; William Phillips journal, 10 August 1936; Traina, *American Diplomacy and the Spanish Civil War*, 55; William Phillips to the Glenn Martin Company, 10 August 1936, *FRUS*, 1936, vol. 2, 475–76.

39 Press conference, 21 August 1936, *FDR and FA*, vol. 3, 394.

40 Fleischman, *Norman Thomas*, 176. In a letter drafted by the assistant secretary of state R. Walton Moore to Norman Thomas, sent on 25 January 1937, Moore argued that the moral embargo had been introduced weeks before the European nonintervention agreement was arranged "while the policy of those nations towards the Spanish conflict was still uncertain and undetermined. No suggestion was made to us by any European country in regard to the attitude which we should adopt at that time nor has there been any subsequent suggestions of such a nature." *FDR and FA*, vol. 3, 592. The European states did, however, make the United States aware of developments, with a clear implied desire for American cooperation. The French *chargé d'affaires* visited Hull on 4 August 1936 to outline the French government's nonintervention plan. Hull then "remarked casually in closing that of course the Chargé was aware of the general attitude of this Government towards the doctrine of non-intervention." Cordell Hull memorandum, 4 August 1936, *FRUS*, 1936, vol. 2, 457–58. On 11 August Hull was told that the French would be "pleased" if the United States introduced an arms embargo on Spain, but Paris would not invite such a move. Wilson to Cordell Hull, 11 August 1936, DSR 852.00/2517.

41 Howson, *Arms for Spain*, 164–78; Traina, *American Diplomacy and the Spanish Civil War*, 79; West European Division memorandum, 27 August 1936, DSR 852.24/95; Reed memorandum, 14 September 1936, *FRUS*, 1936, vol. 2, 530–31; Josephus Daniels to Roosevelt, 20 September 1936, Daniels papers, box 16; Morgan-Green Report, 65–70; Traina, *American Diplomacy and the Spanish Civil War*, 78–79; Jablon, *Crossroads of Decision*, 127–30; Alpert, *A New International History of the Spanish Civil War*, chapter 14.

42 For the emerging evidence of British intentions see *FRUS*, 1936, vol. 2, 506–7, 535.

43 Memorandum, 24 December 1936, Green papers, carton 13; Public Records Office, FO 115:3412.

44 Memorandum, 24 December 1936, Green papers, carton 13; *New York Times,* 30 December 1936; *Washington Post,* 30, 31 December 1936.

45 Memoranda, 4, 5 January 1937, Material for the Morgan-Green Report, November 1944, 5–6, Green papers, carton 13.

46 For details of British proposals for mediation and the withdrawal of foreign forces from Spain see DSR 852.00/4280, 852.00/4294; *FRUS,* 1936, vol. 2, 578–83, 587–97, 615–25, 1937, vol. 1, 216. Roosevelt also received information at this time suggesting doubts in Berlin about the likely success of continued German intervention in Spain. William E. Dodd to Roosevelt, 7 December 1936, *FDR and FA,* vol. 3, 527. For Germany and the Cuse shipment see Claude G. Bowers to Cordell Hull, 31 December 1936, DSR 852.00/4258; *FRUS,* 1936, vol. 2, 624.

47 Material for the Morgan-Green Report, November 1944, Green papers, carton 13, 6.

48 Material for the Morgan-Green Report, November 1944, Green papers, carton 13, 4.

49 Howson, *Arms for Spain,* 178.

50 Rosenman, ed., *The Public Papers and Addresses of Franklin D. Roosevelt,* 620–22; Offner, *American Appeasement,* 157.

51 Traina, *American Diplomacy and the Spanish Civil War,* 84–92.

52 Rosenman, ed., *The Public Papers and Addresses of Franklin D. Roosevelt,* 634.

53 U.S. Congressional Record, 75th Congress, 1st session, 1936, vol. 81, part 1, 76–93; Traina, *American Diplomacy and the Spanish Civil War,* 95.

54 *Washington Post,* 8 January 1937.

55 Rosenman, ed., *The Public Papers and Addresses of Franklin D. Roosevelt,* 185; Divine, *The Reluctant Belligerent,* 36–41; Cole, *Roosevelt and the Isolationists,* 230–34.

56 Traina, *American Diplomacy and the Spanish Civil War,* 109–10. As Traina suggests, influential congressmen may have feared that an antifascist FDR would later take a stand on Spain.

57 Rosenman, ed., *The Public Papers and Addresses of Franklin D. Roosevelt,* 185.

58 For example, Albert Fried argued: "it was well known that [Roosevelt] reluctantly went along with the January 1937 Joint Congressional Resolution." Fried, *FDR and His Enemies,* 148.

59 Claude G. Bowers to Roosevelt, 26 August 1936, Claude G. Bowers to Cordell Hull, 23 September 1936, *FDR and FA,* vol. 3, 395–400, 435–39; Claude G. Bowers to Cordell Hull, 30 December 1936, Roosevelt papers, PSF, box 50.

60 Roosevelt, ed., *F.D.R: His Personal Letters,* 614.

61 Norman Thomas to Roosevelt, 31 August 1936, 29 December 1936, Roosevelt to Norman Thomas, 25 January 1937, *FDR and FA,* vol. 3, 408–9, 565–66, 592–93; Divine, *The Reluctant Belligerent,* chapter 2.

62 Little, *Malevolent Neutrality,* 265; Carroll, *The Odyssey of the Abraham Lincoln Brigade,* 60. Examples of American officials emphasizing leftist violence can be seen in *FRUS,* 1936, vol. 2, 459, 461, 679–80, 723–24.

63 In April 1937 Joseph Green visited Henry Stimson and suggested that there were over seventy thousand Italians in Spain, that the Republic was only moderately left-wing, and that it retained the support of the great majority of the people. "Green's knowledge of the situation made him strongly anxious to have the rebels defeated." Stimson diary, 15 April 1937.

64 William Phillips journal, 4 August 1936; *FRUS,* 1936, vol. 2, 447, 450–51, 455, 467, 575. Washington was aware that British pressure on the French not to intervene in Spain was based to a large extent on the fear that a general war might result.

Chapter 5: American Men, American Oil, American Arms

1 Jackson, *The Spanish Republic and the Civil War*, chapters 16–24; Carr, *Modern Spain*, 142–46; Preston, *Franco*, 177–80, 212, 241–42; Whealey, *Hitler and Spain*, 60; Alpert, *A New International History of the Spanish Civil War*, 140; Brendon, *The Dark Valley*, 332–33.

2 Koch, *The Breaking Point*, 89–90.

3 Brendon, *The Dark Valley*, 332; Preston, *Franco*, 243–47, 281–96; Alpert, *A New International History of the Spanish Civil War*, 141; Jackson, *The Spanish Republic and the Civil War*, chapter 22.

4 Conkin, *The New Deal*, 90.

5 Burns, *Roosevelt*, 291–340; Morgan, *FDR*, 485; Ickes, *The Secret Diary of Harold L. Ickes*, vol. 2, 340.

6 Hull, *The Memoirs of Cordell Hull*, vol. 1, 479.

7 In August 1937 surveys of American opinion toward the Sino-Japanese war showed that only 1 percent of respondents sympathized with Japan, but also that 55 percent sympathized with neither side. Gallup, *The Gallup Poll*, survey 94. See also Almond, *The American People and Foreign Policy*; Rosenau, *Public Opinion and Foreign Policy*; Cantril and Strunk, *Public Opinion*, 807–8.

8 Valaik, "Catholics, Neutrality, and the Spanish Embargo," 74.

9 Divine, *The Reluctant Belligerent*, 34; Benson, *Writers in Arms*; Christenson, *Reel Politics*, 56–58.

10 Taylor, *The United States and the Spanish Civil War*, 121.

11 Kenwood, ed., *The Spanish Civil War*, 287; Martin, *American Liberalism and World Politics*.

12 "The Spanish Civil War," Ernest Cuneo papers, box 51, 4–8, 18–21.

13 Carr, *The Spanish Tragedy*, 232; Falcoff and Pike, *The Spanish Civil War*, 3; Gornick, *The Romance of American Communism*; Guttmann, *Wound in the Heart*, 151–2.

14 Harris, *The United States and the Italo-Ethiopian Crisis*, 144; Falcoff and Pike, *The Spanish Civil War*, 22–24.

15 The pro-Nationalist American Committee for Spanish Relief, for example, raised $29,000 after spending $30,000 on fund-raising. Traina, *American Diplomacy and the Spanish Civil War*, 192.

16 Guttmann, *Wound in the Heart*, 28.

17 Hemingway, *For Whom the Bell Tolls*, 432; Sanders, "Ernest Hemingway's Spanish Civil War Experience"; Koch, *The Breaking Point*, 68–69. This reflected a
remarkable alteration in Hemingway's views compared to 1935, when he commented: "Of the hell broth that is brewing in Europe we have no need to drink."
Morgan, *FDR,* 438. See also Weintrub, *The Last Great Cause*; Guttmann, *Wound
in the Heart*, chapter 5.

18 Cook, *Eleanor Roosevelt*, 445, 504.

19 Moorehead, *Gellhorn*, 111.

20 Flynn, *Roosevelt and Romanism*, 41; Cole, *Senator Gerald P. Nye and American
Foreign Relations*, 223–34. According to Roosevelt, allowing arms sales to either
side in Spain would be "involving ourselves directly in that European strife
from which our people desire so deeply to remain aloof." Roosevelt to Norman
Thomas, 25 January 1937, *FDR and FA,* vol. 3, 592–93; Cole, *Roosevelt and the
Isolationists*, 224–26.

21 Norman Thomas to Roosevelt, 29 December 1936, *FDR and FA,* vol. 3, 565–66;
Guttmann, *Wound in the Heart*, chapter 5.

22 Guttmann, *Wound in the Heart*, 112, 161–62.

23 Swanberg, *Norman Thomas*, 210–13; Joseph Green to Mr. Savage, November
1944, Material for the Morgan-Green Report, Green papers, carton 13, 21.

24 Kanawada, *Franklin D. Roosevelt's Diplomacy and American Catholics, Italians,
and Jews*; Thomas, *The Spanish Civil War*, 46–47, 171–76; Flynn, *Roosevelt and
Romanism*, 34–40; Crosby, "Boston's Catholics and the Spanish Civil War"; Guttmann, *Wound in the Heart*, chapter 3.

25 Guttmann, *Wound in the Heart*, 29; Hamilton, *JFK,* 182–84.

26 Keene, *Fighting for Franco*, chapter 7.

27 John W. McCormack to Roosevelt, 10 June 1937, Sumner Welles to Marvin H.
McIntyre, 18 June 1937, *FDR and FA,* vol. 5, 355, 398–401. Roosevelt sought to
co-opt the opposition by using Catholic welfare groups to bring the children to
the United States, but he discovered that immigration laws prevented their arrival. Flynn, *Roosevelt and Romanism*, 39–41; Kanawada, *Franklin D. Roosevelt's
Diplomacy and American Catholics, Italians, and Jews*, 52–54; Traina, *American
Diplomacy and the Spanish Civil War*, 194–96; Crosby, "Boston's Catholics and
the Spanish Civil War," 85.

28 Guttmann, *Wound in the Heart*, 65.

29 Flynn, *Roosevelt and Romanism*, 52–55; Falcoff and Pike, *The Spanish Civil War*,
20–22; Guttmann, *Wound in the Heart*; Moffat diary, 23 January 1939.

30 Leuchtenburg, *Franklin D. Roosevelt and the New Deal*, 184.

31 Kanawada, *Franklin D. Roosevelt's Diplomacy and American Catholics, Italians,
and Jews*, 50–52; Kantowicz, "Cardinal Mundelein of Chicago and the Shaping
of Twentieth-Century American Catholicism," 65–68.

32 Nelson and Hendricks, eds., *Madrid 1937*, 45.

33 Rubin, *Spain's Cause Was Mine*, 3, 12.

34 Richard Polenberg, "The Ethical Responsibilities of the Scientist: The Case of J. Robert Oppenheimer," *The Achievement of American Liberalism*, ed. Chafe.

35 Collum, *African Americans in the Spanish Civil War*; Esenwein, *The Spanish Civil War*, 159.

36 Nelson and Hendricks, eds., *Madrid 1937*, 32.

37 Thomas, *The Spanish Civil War*, 377–80, 465, 637; Carroll, *The Odyssey of the Abraham Lincoln Brigade*; Edwards, *Airmen without Portfolio*.

38 Keene, *Fighting for Franco*, chapter 3.

39 Norman Thomas papers, microfilm copy, reel 79; Taylor, *The United States and the Spanish Civil War*, chapter 5.

40 Press Conference, 2 February 1937, Roosevelt to Marvin H. McIntyre, 26 February 1937, *FDR and FA,* vol. 4, 143, 266. Details of the State Department's dealings with the volunteers are in *FRUS,* 1937, vol. 1, 417, 528–34, 540, 547–48, 552, 555.

41 "The Spanish Civil War," Ernest Cuneo papers, box 51, 12–15.

42 Simon, ed., *As We Saw the Thirties*, 235.

43 Gardner Jackson to Marvin MacIntyre, 2 February 1937, Roosevelt papers, OF 422, box 1.

44 Press Conference, 7 June 1938, *FDR and FA,* vol. 10, 215–16.

45 William F. Gorman to Roosevelt, 9 June 1938, Roosevelt papers, OF 422-c, box 2.

46 For a memorandum on this topic recounting the main facts see Joseph C. Green to R. Walton Moore, 28 September 1937, memorandum, Moore papers, box 19, "Spanish Revolution." See also DSR 852.00/4750–54; Memorandum, 24 February 1937, Hull papers, microfilm copy, reel 32; Ickes, *The Secret Diary of Harold L. Ickes*, vol. 2, 93.

47 Morgan-Green Report, 116–17; Joseph C. Green to R. Walton Moore, 28 September 1937, Moore papers, box 19, "Spanish Revolution"; "The Spanish Civil War," Ernest Cuneo papers, box 51, 4–8, 18–21. "What the President desires is to avoid the impression that this Government is preventing humanitarian assistance being rendered, and therefore thinks that whenever an application to go to Spain is made, it should be ascertained from the Red Cross whether the medical men and nurses responsible for the expedition are reputable people who can be counted on to confine themselves and those who go with them to strictly humanitarian work, and that upon such an assurance being obtained, passports should be issued. [Roosevelt] does not believe that the Red Cross will be in a position to guarantee against irregularities, but it is believed that from its knowledge of the persons in charge of an expedition it will be able to give satisfactory information as to their character, experience and good faith, and thus protect our Government from any involvement that would violate its general policy." R. Walton Moore to Cordell Hull, 12 March 1937, Moore papers, box 19, "Spanish Revolution"; Cordell Hull memorandum, 24 February 1937, *FRUS,* 1937, vol. 1, 248; Traina, *American Diplomacy and the Spanish Civil War*, 190; Hull, *The Memoirs of Cordell Hull*, vol. 1, 505.

48 Iz Feinstein to Thomas G. Corcoran, undated, *FDR and FA,* vol. 4, 267.

49 Ickes, *The Secret Diary of Harold L. Ickes*, vol. 2, 210–11; Cordell Hull memorandum, 7 September 1937, FRUS, 1937, vol. 1, 386; Traina, *American Diplomacy and the Spanish Civil War*, 275.

50 Roosevelt and Brough, *A Rendezvous with Destiny*, 139; Howson, *Arms for Spain*, 73.

51 Alpert, *A New International History of the Spanish Civil War*, chapter 14; Preston, *The Spanish Civil War*, 116; "Spanish Loyalists Spent $14,500,000 for Materials Here during Last Year," *New York Times*, 5 January 1939. The undersecretary of the Spanish foreign ministry was probably exaggerating when he commented in 1945, "without American petroleum and American trucks and American credit, we could never have won the civil war." Beevor, *The Spanish Civil War*, 114–15, 282.

52 Fernando de los Rios to Roosevelt, 8 June 1937, *FDR and FA*, vol. 5, 346–47; Whealey, "How Franco Financed His War—Reconsidered," 147.

53 *Life*, 1 July 1940, 56–68.

54 Cashman, *America, Roosevelt and World War Two*, 70–72.

55 Alpert, *A New International History of the Spanish Civil War*, 100, 119; Aster, *Anthony Eden*, 16–35; Peters, *Anthony Eden at the Foreign Office*, 1–20; Buchanan, *Britain and the Spanish Civil War*, 54–55; Enrique Moradiellos, "The Allies and the Spanish Civil War," *Spain and the Great Powers in the Twentieth Century*, ed. Balfour and Preston, 117.

56 Reynolds, *The Creation of the Anglo-American Alliance*, chapter 1; Traina, *American Diplomacy and the Spanish Civil War*, 42; Buchanan, *The Spanish Civil War and the British Labour Movement*; Watkin, *Britain Divided*.

57 Cole, *Roosevelt and the Isolationists*, 228–32.

58 FRUS, 1936, vol. 2, 450–51, 455, 473, 535, 586–87, 600–605, 1937, vol. 1, 215–16, all detail the increasingly brazen nature of aid to Franco. Roosevelt was aware of this large-scale intervention, telling Ickes in February 1937 that forty thousand Italian troops were fighting for Franco. Ickes, *The Secret Diary of Harold L. Ickes*, vol. 2, 73, 103. On the perspectives of Hull and the British see Hull, *The Memoirs of Cordell Hull*, vol. 1, 510–12; Cordell Hull to Robert W. Bingham, 27 March 1937, Robert W. Bingham to Cordell Hull, 31 March 1937, FRUS, 1937, vol. 1, 268–72.

59 The Basque government originally claimed that sixteen hundred people were killed in the attack, but recent estimates suggest a figure of two to three hundred. Beevor, *The Battle for Spain*, 232.

60 Southworth, *Guernica! Guernica!*, 89, 109–36; Cordell Hull to Jerry O'Connell, 7 May 1937, FRUS, 1937, vol. 1, 294–95; Jerry O'Connell to Cordell Hull, 2 June 1937, DSR 852.00/5873; Taylor, *The United States and the Spanish Civil War*, 88–90.

61 Norman Thomas to Roosevelt, 9 June 1937, *FDR and FA*, vol. 5, 349–50; Cole, *Roosevelt and the Isolationists*, 229.

62 Dallek, *Franklin D. Roosevelt and American Foreign Policy*, 142; Swanberg, *Norman Thomas*, 218; Kanawada, *Franklin D. Roosevelt's Diplomacy and American Catholics, Italians, and Jews*, 52.

63 Roosevelt to Cordell Hull, 29 June 1937, *FDR and FA,* vol. 5, 431.

64 Cordell Hull to Jerry O'Connell, 7 May 1937, FRUS, 1937, vol. 1, 294–95; Taylor, *The United States and the Spanish Civil War,* 90; Memorandum, 28 June 1937, Green papers, carton 13; DSR 852.00/6336.

65 Cordell Hull to Robert W. Bingham, 30 June 1937, Cordell Hull to William Phillips, 30 June 1937, William Phillips to Cordell Hull, 1 July 1937, Robert W. Bingham to Cordell Hull, 6 July 1937, FRUS, 1937, vol. 1, 344, 345–46, 353; FO 954/27, Public Records Office; Hull, *The Memoirs of Cordell Hull,* vol. 1, 510–13.

66 Norman Thomas to Roosevelt, 26 August 1937, Roosevelt to Norman Thomas, 6 September 1937, *FDR and FA,* vol. 6, 380–81, 447.

67 Ickes, *The Secret Diary of Harold L. Ickes,* vol. 2, 210–11.

68 Roosevelt to Sumner Welles, 3 July 1937, *FDR and FA,* vol. 6, 32.

69 John Dos Passos, *The Theme Is Freedom* (New York: Dodd, Mead, 1956).

70 Greer, *What Roosevelt Thought,* 177; Morgan-Green Report, 213–26.

71 Borg, "Notes on Roosevelt's Quarantine Speech"; Wilz, *From Isolation to War,* 62–63.

72 Dallek, *Franklin D. Roosevelt and American Foreign Policy,* 159; Sumner Welles memorandum, 18 October 1937, FRUS, 1937, vol. 1, 425–26; Martha Gellhorn to Eleanor Roosevelt, 1938, Eleanor Roosevelt papers, box 1459.

73 Roosevelt, *This I Remember,* 132. Similarly, Watkins argued that FDR failed to aid the Loyalists in 1937 "because he did not want to jeopardize his efforts to enlarge the Supreme Court." Watkins, *Righteous Pilgrim,* 667.

74 Robert Divine writes, for example, that Roosevelt "did not dare endanger the large Catholic vote that was vital to the Democratic political machine." Divine, *The Illusion of Neutrality,* 227.

Chapter 6: Roosevelt's Perceptions, 1938–1939

1 Roosevelt to Claude Bowers, 26 January 1939, *FDR and FA,* vol. 13, 186.

2 Dallek, *Franklin D. Roosevelt and American Foreign Policy,* 145–57, 192–96; Doenecke, "Beyond Polemics," 222–26.

3 Davis, *FDR: Into the Storm,* 313.

4 Robert H. Whealey, "Foreign Intervention in the Spanish Civil War," *The Republic and the Civil War in Spain,* ed. Carr, 226. On 27 July 1938 Eden explained to Henry L. Stimson why he had resigned: "namely the issue over the Italian agreement which he thought was bad strategy and unnecessarily played into Mussolini's hands. [Eden] showed me a striking postalcard which was being circulated through the French mail showing the effect of German and Italian intervention in the Spanish war upon the future [strategic] fortunes of Great Britain and France." Stimson diary, microfilm copy, 27 July 1938. See also Rose, "The Resignation of Anthony Eden," 924–25; McKercher, *Transition of Power,* 251; Gardner, *Spheres of Influence,* 8–26; Joseph P. Kennedy to Cordell Hull, 15 April 1938, *FDR and FA,* vol. 9, 411–16; Parker, *Chamberlain and Appeasement.*

5   Traina, *American Diplomacy and the Spanish Civil War*, 122–23.

6   Reynolds, *The Creation of the Anglo-American Alliance*, 17.

7   Gardner, *Spheres of Influence*, 6, 15.

8   Cole, *Charles A. Lindbergh and the Battle against American Intervention in World War Two*, 37 n. 16; Farnham, *Roosevelt and the Munich Crisis*, 74.

9   Roosevelt, *Complete Presidential Press Conferences of Franklin D. Roosevelt*; Press conference, 21 April 1938, *FDR and FA*, vol. 9, 449–53; Harper, *American Visions of Europe*, 55; Roosevelt to John Cudahy, 9 March 1938, *FDR and FA*, vol. 9, 87; Langer and Gleason, *Challenge to Isolation*, 26–28; Ickes, *The Secret Diary of Harold L. Ickes*, vol. 2, 322–23.

10   Radosh, Habeck, and Sevostianov, eds., *Spain Betrayed*, 428–29.

11   Cole, *Roosevelt and the Isolationists*, 278; Farnham, *Roosevelt and the Munich Crisis*, 76; Dallek, *Franklin D. Roosevelt and American Foreign Policy*, 155–56; Gardner, *Spheres of Influence*, 4–7. Neville Chamberlain saw little utility in the type of international conference favored by President Roosevelt, suggesting that it would "excite the derision of Germany and Italy." MacLeod, *Neville Chamberlain*, 212–13.

12   Blum, *From the Morgenthau Diaries*, vol. 1, 501; Ickes, *The Secret Diary of Harold L. Ickes*, vol. 2, 275, 324–25, 344–47, 368–69, 372–77, 385, 391–99, 406, 414, 419–20, 427–28, 575; Dallek, *Franklin D. Roosevelt and American Foreign Policy*, 158; Farnham, *Roosevelt and the Munich Crisis*, 98.

13   McKercher, *Transition of Power*, 274; Haight, "Roosevelt as Friend of France," 90; Haight, *American Aid to France*, 10–12; Dallek, *Franklin D. Roosevelt and American Foreign Policy*, 164–66; Cole, *Roosevelt and the Isolationists*, 300–302; Lash, *Roosevelt and Churchill*, 25–28.

14   Divine, *The Reluctant Belligerent*, chapter 3; Alpert, *A New International History of the Spanish Civil War*, 167; Taylor, *Munich*; Weinberg, "Munich after Fifty Years," 165–78.

15   Davis, *FDR: Into the Storm*, 345.

16   Reynolds, *From Munich to Pearl Harbor*, 40; Farnham, *Roosevelt and the Munich Crisis*, 138–39; Ickes, *The Secret Diary of Harold L. Ickes*, vol. 2, 484.

17   Farnham, *Roosevelt and the Munich Crisis*, 150–60; Watt, *How War Came*, 130–31; Dallek, *Franklin D. Roosevelt and American Foreign Policy*, 172; Cole, *Roosevelt and the Isolationists*, 285. Hitler told the German economics expert Hjalmar von Schacht that treaties were to be respected only as long as they were useful, adding: "Mr. Chamberlain is such a nice old man and I have signed so many photographs and books, that I thought I would give him my signature as a pleasant souvenir." Gardner, *Spheres of Influence*, 46.

18   Ickes, *The Secret Diary of Harold L. Ickes*, vol. 2, 609; Casey, *Cautious Crusade*, 9; Haight, *American Aid to France*, 98; Cole, *Roosevelt and the Isolationists*, 304–6; Dallek, *Franklin D. Roosevelt and American Foreign Policy*, 167–68. For the perceived threat to the United States see Farley, *Jim Farley's Story*, 158; Reynolds, *The Creation of the Anglo-American Alliance*, 40–41; Farnham, *Roosevelt and the*

Munich Crisis, 187; Divine, *The Reluctant Belligerent*, 59; Reynolds, *From Munich to Pearl Harbor*, 50–51.

19 Drummond, *The Passing of American Neutrality*, 75; Dallek, *Franklin D. Roosevelt and American Foreign Policy*, 183–84, 220–21, 228.

20 MacDonald, "Deterrent Diplomacy," 301.

21 Farnham, *Roosevelt and the Munich Crisis*, 148; Josephus Daniels diary, 14 January 1939.

22 Farnham, *Roosevelt and the Munich Crisis*, 142, 148, 151, 183.

23 Roosevelt to Josephus Daniels, 14 November 1938, Josephus Daniels papers, microfilm copy.

24 Kanawada, *Franklin D. Roosevelt's Diplomacy and American Catholics, Italians, and Jews*, 54.

25 Sumner Welles to Roosevelt, 7 December 1938, 9 January 1939, *FDR and FA*, vol. 12, 270, vol. 13, 78.

26 Friedman, *Nazis and Good Neighbors*, 9.

27 Haglund, *Latin America and the Transformation of American Strategic Thought*, 6; Dallek, *Franklin D. Roosevelt and American Foreign Policy*, 175; Craven and Cate, eds., *The Army Air Forces in World War II*, vol. 1, 117–21; Frye, *Nazi Germany and the American Hemisphere*, 173–75, 186–92; Gellman, *Good Neighbor Diplomacy*, 105–16; MacDonald, "Deterrent Diplomacy," 305.

28 Haglund, *Latin America and the Transformation of American Strategic Thought*, 58–63.

29 Roosevelt, *Complete Presidential Press Conferences of Franklin D. Roosevelt*, entry for 20 April 1938. In the spring of 1938 the State Department also showed concern about the impact of a victory by Franco on Latin American security. In a memorandum in March, the department expressed fears that a Nationalist triumph would help Berlin and Rome acquire "a permanent foothold" in the western hemisphere, which could expand their influence "like a disease." Traina, *American Diplomacy and the Spanish Civil War*, 155–56, 277–78.

30 Claude G. Bowers to Roosevelt, 9 May 1938, *FDR and FA*, vol. 10, 24; Claude G. Bowers to Cordell Hull, 6 December 1938, DSR 852.00/8699.

31 Gellman, *Secret Affairs*, 150.

32 Haglund, *Latin America and the Transformation of American Strategic Thought*, 88.

33 Claude G. Bowers to Roosevelt, 24 October 1938, *FDR and FA*, vol. 11, 427–30.

34 Oswaldo Aranha to Sumner Welles, 8 November 1938, *FDR and FA*, vol. 12, 101.

35 Haglund, *Latin America and the Transformation of American Strategic Thought*, 99.

36 Press Conference, 15 November 1938, *FDR and FA*, vol. 12, 84–88.

37 For details of Roosevelt's willingness to aid Latin American security see *FDR and FA*, vol. 12, 97–119, 264, 290–92, 318–22.

38 Sumner Welles to Roosevelt, 15 December 1938, *FDR and FA*, vol. 12, 318–22.

39 Ickes, *The Secret Diary of Harold L. Ickes*, vol. 2, entry for 18 December 1938.

40 Sumner Welles to Cordell Hull, 16 December 1938, Cordell Hull to Sumner Welles, 19 December 1938, Cordell Hull papers, microfilm copy, reel 17.
41 Speech by Roosevelt, 4 January 1939, *FDR and FA,* vol. 13, 1–25.
42 Hull, *The Memoirs of Cordell Hull,* vol. 1, 602.
43 Josephus Daniels diary, 14 January 1939.
44 "Conference with the Senate Military Affairs Committee," 31 January 1939, *FDR and FA,* vol. 13, document 1565.
45 Doenecke and Stoler, *Debating Franklin D. Roosevelt's Foreign Policies,* 42.
46 Neglecting the impact of the Spanish Civil War, D. C. Watt explained Roosevelt's perceptions as having erroneously been "drawn from the over-heated imaginations of some South American socialist journalists." Watt, *Succeeding John Bull,* 79. The fear that Nazi agents could foment internal discord and deliver nations through propaganda and subversion reached a state of paranoia in the United States, especially in 1940. Roosevelt in May 1940 highlighted the threat to the western hemisphere posed by Nazi long-range aircraft and "the treacherous use of the 'fifth column,'" a phrase which originated in the Spanish Civil War. Steele, *Propaganda in an Open Society,* 71–72; Gellman, *Good Neighbor Diplomacy,* 115; Friedman, *Nazis and Good Neighbors,* 2, 42, 129.
47 These figures exaggerate slightly. Paul Preston, "Italy and Spain in Civil War and World War, 1936–1943," *Spain and the Great Powers in the Twentieth Century,* ed. Balfour and Preston, 173–76; Whealey, *Hitler and Spain,* 131–36; Alpert, *A New International History of the Spanish Civil War,* 92–94; Preston, *Franco,* 306.
48 Claude G. Bowers to Roosevelt, 20 February 1938, *FDR and FA,* vol. 8, 345.
49 Franklin D. Roosevelt Official File, microfilm copy, Library of Congress, part 3, Departmental Correspondence, reel 6, "Navy Department Jan–Feb 1938."
50 Roosevelt to Claude G. Bowers, 7 March 1938, *FDR and FA,* vol. 9, 65–66.
51 Press conference, 21 April 1938, *FDR and FA,* vol. 9, 449–53; press conference, 3 June 1938, *FRUS,* 1938, vol. 1, 204.
52 Bessie, ed., *Alvah Bessie's Spanish Civil War Notebooks,* 16.
53 Preston, *Franco,* 302–6; Jackson, *The Spanish Republic and the Civil War,* chapter 26.
54 Moffat diary, 12, 14 March 1938; Dallek, *Franklin D. Roosevelt and American Foreign Policy,* 160.
55 Thomas, *The Spanish Civil War,* chapters 67–69.
56 Claude G. Bowers to Roosevelt, 18 August 1938, Roosevelt to Claude G. Bowers, 31 August 1938, *FDR and FA,* vol. 11, 74–82, 122.
57 Ickes, *The Secret Diary of Harold L. Ickes,* vol. 2, 569.
58 Burns, *Roosevelt,* 423.
59 Roosevelt to Claude G. Bowers, 7 March 1938, *FDR and FA,* vol. 9, 65; Leutze, *Bargaining for Supremacy,* 26.
60 Thomas, *The Spanish Civil War,* 871; Joseph P. Kennedy to Cordell Hull, 15 April 1938, *FDR and FA,* vol. 9, 411–16; *FRUS,* 1938, vol. 1, 188–92.
61 Roosevelt to Cordell Hull, 29 June 1937, *FDR and FA,* vol. 5, 431.

62 Roosevelt to Claude G. Bowers, 31 August 1938, *FDR and FA,* vol. 11, 122.

63 Ickes, *The Secret Diary of Harold L. Ickes,* vol. 2, 571.

Chapter 7: Covert Aid

1 FO 115:3415, Public Records Office.

2 Press conference, 21 April 1938, *FDR and FA,* vol. 9, 449–53.

3 Eleanor Roosevelt to Martha Gellhorn, 26 January 1939, Eleanor Roosevelt papers, box 688. The Gallup organization asked the following biased question: "Are you in favor of direct retaliatory measures against Franco's piracy?"

4 Gallup poll, 18–23 December 1938, obtained through www.lexisnexis.com.

5 Orwell, *Homage to Catalonia,* 221.

6 Eleanor Roosevelt to Martha Gellhorn, 26 January 1939, Eleanor Roosevelt papers, box 688.

7 V. A. L. Mallet to Halifax, 17 January 1939, FO 115:3418, Public Records Office.

8 Guttmann, *Wound in the Heart,* 29; Gallup poll, 4–9 February 1939, obtained through www.lexisnexis.com. See also Cantril and Strunk, *Public Opinion,* 807–8; Hero, *American Religious Groups View Foreign Policy,* 22, 280; Gallup, *The Gallup Poll,* 90, 92, 132, 138, 159.

9 Quoted in an unpublished study by Young, "Public Attitudes towards American Foreign Policy in the Spanish Civil War," 1, 32, 94–95, located in "Material for the Morgan-Green Report," Green papers, carton 13.

10 Sanders, "Ernest Hemingway's Spanish Civil War Experience," 139.

11 Cook, *Eleanor Roosevelt,* 444–45, 452–54, 456, 503–8.

12 For details of the experience of the volunteers in 1938 see Carroll, *The Odyssey of the Abraham Lincoln Brigade,* 171–88.

13 Valaik, "Catholics, Neutrality, and the Spanish Embargo," 77; Flynn, *Roosevelt and Romanism,* 33–39.

14 Flynn, *Roosevelt and Romanism,* 50; Ickes, *The Secret Diary of Harold L. Ickes,* vol. 2, 604; Schwarz, *The Speculator,* 348.

15 Kanawada, *Franklin D. Roosevelt's Diplomacy and American Catholics, Italians, and Jews,* 59; Breckinridge Long diary, 27 March, 1 April 1938.

16 Breckinridge Long diary, 27 March, 1 April, 10 April 1938; Dallek, *Franklin D. Roosevelt and American Foreign Policy,* 159; Kanawada, *Franklin D. Roosevelt's Diplomacy and American Catholics, Italians, and Jews,* 58–59; Traina, *American Diplomacy and the Spanish Civil War,* 130; Marvin H. McIntyre to Roosevelt, 27 April 1938, Roosevelt papers, OF 422-C. Surprisingly, General Franco's constant denunciations of Freemason conspiracies contain a kernel of truth. At a Masonic dinner Tom Connally urged Nye to introduce a resolution to lift the Spanish embargo, although he declined to join Nye's campaign. Cole, *Roosevelt and the Isolationists,* 235–36.

17 Moffat diary, 4, 5, 9 May 1938.

18 Roosevelt, *This I Remember,* 132; Kanawada, *Franklin D. Roosevelt's Diplomacy*

    and American Catholics, Italians, and Jews, 54. For a discussion of FDR's efforts to educate public opinion see Farnham, *Roosevelt and the Munich Crisis*, 88.

19   Breckinridge Long diary, 19 March, 1 April 1938.

20   Powell, *Mexico and the Spanish Civil War*, 68; Dallek, *Franklin D. Roosevelt and American Foreign Policy*, 160; Lerner, *Ideas for the Ice Age*, 227.

21   Roosevelt, *Complete Presidential Press Conferences of Franklin D. Roosevelt*, entries for 20–23 April; Press conference, 21 April 1938, *FDR and FA,* vol. 9, 449–53; Breckinridge Long diary, 30 April 1938; Kanawada, *Franklin D. Roosevelt's Diplomacy and American Catholics, Italians, and Jews*, 57.

22   Bowers diary, 30 April 1938.

23   Joseph P. Kennedy to Cordell Hull, 9 May 1938, *FRUS,* 1938, vol. 1, 188–92.

24   For details of Messersmith's views see *FDR and FA,* vol. 11, 272; *FRUS,* 1937, vol. 1, 140–45, 1938, vol. 1, 17–24; Traina, *American Diplomacy and the Spanish Civil War*, 123–24; MacDonald, "Deterrent Diplomacy," 299; Farnham, *Roosevelt and the Munich Crisis*, 74, 99; McKercher, *Transition of Power*, 264.

25   Berle, *Navigating the Rapids*, 169.

26   Farnham, *Roosevelt and the Munich Crisis*, 99; Morgan, *FDR,* 505; MacDonald, "Deterrent Diplomacy," 300; Haglund, *Latin America and the Transformation of American Strategic Thought*, 86–87.

27   Memorandum, 11 May 1938, "1938 Unidentified," Herbert Feis papers, box 126; Farnham, *Roosevelt and the Munich Crisis*, 99.

28   Taylor, *The United States and the Spanish Civil War*, 185.

29   Moffat diary, 2–4 May 1938.

30   R. Walton Moore to Cordell Hull, 5, 6 May 1938, Moore papers, box 19, "Spanish Revolution."

31   Moffat diary, 6 May 1938. For a transcript of Hull's press conference see the *New York Times*, 7 May 1938.

32   Breckinridge Long diary, 8 May 1938.

33   Claude G. Bowers to Cordell Hull, 25 February, 10 June 1938, Hull papers, carton 42; DSR 852.00/8133. FDR used a similar "gangster" analogy in Roosevelt to John Cudahy, 9 March 1938, *FDR and FA,* vol. 9, 87. In December 1938 Bowers restated his argument that the American embargo led to the "wholesale slaughter" of Spanish Loyalist civilians. Claude G. Bowers to Cordell Hull, 7 December 1938, DSR 852.00/8700.

34   Bowers diary, 1 December 1938.

35   Roosevelt to Claude G. Bowers, 7 March 1938, *FDR and FA,* vol. 9, 66.

36   Farnham, *Roosevelt and the Munich Crisis*, 94.

37   Joseph P. Kennedy to Cordell Hull, 15 April 1938, *FDR and FA,* vol. 9, 415; Cole, *Roosevelt and the Isolationists*, 285; MacDonald, "Deterrent Diplomacy," 301; Craig and Gilbert, *The Diplomats*, 649–81.

38   Breckinridge Long diary, 30 April, 8 May 1938. In July, Long wrote to Bowers claiming that the original resolution which he drafted would have succeeded. Breckinridge Long to Claude G. Bowers, 10 July 1938, Bowers papers II.

39 Kanawada, *Franklin D. Roosevelt's Diplomacy and American Catholics, Italians, and Jews*, 64; Thomas, *The Spanish Civil War* (3rd edn), 825.

40 Kanawada, *Franklin D. Roosevelt's Diplomacy and American Catholics, Italians, and Jews*, 61.

41 Ickes, *The Secret Diary of Harold L. Ickes*, 7 May 1938. Robert Bendiner also raised the possibility that the 5 May story was deliberately planted by the administration to inflame Catholic opposition. Bendiner, *The Riddle of the State Department*, 61.

42 Kanawada, *Franklin D. Roosevelt's Diplomacy and American Catholics, Italians, and Jews*, 64; Ickes, *The Secret Diary of Harold L. Ickes*, 7 May 1938.

43 Arthur Krock to James Ragland, 25 February 1957, Krock papers, box 51.

44 "Material for the Morgan-Green Report," Green papers, carton 13.

45 Ickes, *The Secret Diary of Harold L. Ickes*, 1 May, 18 December 1938.

46 James Ragland and Arthur Krock correspondence, 19 July, 8 August 1962, Krock papers, box 51.

47 Krock told Holman Hamilton in 1965 that at Hull's request he had written an editorial in the *New York Times* on 20 March 1938, "to prepare the way for a move to repeal the Neutrality Act." Sehlinger and Hamilton, *Spokesman for Democracy*, 197. The evidence suggests that Hull supported wider revision of the neutrality laws rather than action specifically on the Spanish embargo.

48 Moffat diary, 10 May 1938.

49 Ickes, *The Secret Diary of Harold L. Ickes*, vol. 2, 389–90.

50 Richard S. Allen, "G. Hall Roosevelt and the '100 Plane Deal,'" unpublished paper, 1979, located in the vertical file on G. Hall Roosevelt at the Franklin D. Roosevelt Library, 9; Thomas, *The Spanish Civil War*, 826.

51 Eleanor Roosevelt Oral History Project, Franklin D. Roosevelt Library, "Martha Gellhorn," box 2, 19–20.

52 Traina, *American Diplomacy and the Spanish Civil War*, 273–74.

53 Kanawada, *Franklin D. Roosevelt's Diplomacy and American Catholics, Italians, and Jews*, 61, 67.

54 Flynn, *Roosevelt and Romanism*, 44; Divine, *The Illusion of Neutrality*, 222; Memorandum, 10 May 1938, Louis Fischer papers, box 16.

55 Jay Allen to Claude G. Bowers, received 23 April 1938, Bowers papers III; Sehlinger and Hamilton, *Spokesman for Democracy*, 197–98, 301.

56 Breckinridge Long diary, 11 May 1938.

57 Cordell Hull to Roosevelt, 10 May 1938, *FDR and FA*, vol. 10, 70–75; Moffat diary, 13 May 1938. The draft memorandum opposing the resolution has Roosevelt's scrawled consent, "O.K. FDR."

58 Freidel, *Franklin D. Roosevelt*, 271–72; Davis, *FDR: Into the Storm*, 252–53; Traina, *American Diplomacy and the Spanish Civil War*, 279; Cook, *Eleanor Roosevelt*, 505–7; Howson, *Arms for Spain*, 176.

59 Traina, *American Diplomacy and the Spanish Civil War*, chapter 4; Joint Resolution of Congress, 8 January 1937.

60 Bessie, ed., *Alvah Bessie's Spanish Civil War Notebooks*, 25; Wyden, *The Passionate War*, 465.

61 Memorandum, 23 February 1938, Sumner Welles papers, box 166; "Navy Department Jan–Feb 1938," Franklin D. Roosevelt Official File, microfilm copy, Library of Congress, Part 3: Departmental Correspondence, reel 6.

62 Radosh, Habeck, and Sevostianov, eds., *Spain Betrayed*, 424–29. Other documents in the book detail Soviet and Loyalist connivance to transship American aircraft to Spain via Russia.

63 Traina, *American Diplomacy and the Spanish Civil War*, 160–69; Howson, *Arms for Spain*, 173–77, 236.

64 Radosh, Habeck, and Sevostianov, eds., *Spain Betrayed*, 428–29.

65 Eleanor Roosevelt to Martha Gellhorn, 23 May 1938, Eleanor Roosevelt papers, box 668.

66 William C. Bullitt to Cordell Hull, 9 May 1938, FRUS, 1938, vol. 1, 192–93. Between December 1937 and August 1938 only 152 Soviet planes were sent to Spain. Howson, *Arms for Spain*, 239–43.

67 Traina, *American Diplomacy and the Spanish Civil War*, 79–80, 168, 280; Thomas, *The Spanish Civil War*, 825–26; "Spanish Loyalists Spent $14,500,000 for Materials Here during Last Year," *New York Times*, 5 January 1939; Memorandum for the President, 11 April 1942, Roosevelt papers, OF 491.

68 Memorandum, 19 May 1938, Green papers, carton 13; Brownell and Billings, *So Close to Greatness*, 217–18; Allen, "G. Hall Roosevelt and the '100 Plane Deal,'" 3; Memorandum, 13 June 1938, Green papers, carton 13.

69 This section is based on Blum, *From the Morgenthau Diaries*, 506–8.

70 Memoranda, 20 January, 25 January 1938, Welles papers, box 166; General counsel to Harry Hopkins, 20 June 1939, Harry Hopkins papers, container 119.

71 For details of the court case see Everest, *Morgenthau, the New Deal and Silver*, 125–31; Morgenthau diary, 2 June, 6 June 1938.

72 Blum, *From the Morgenthau Diaries*, 506–8.

73 Morgenthau diary, 2 June 1938; Everest, *Morgenthau, the New Deal and Silver*, 125–31.

74 William C. Bullitt to Cordell Hull, 21 June 1938, Sumner Welles to William C. Bullitt, 21 June 1938, FRUS, 1938, vol. 1, 351–52.

75 Morgan-Green report, 73–74; memoranda, 24 December 1936, 4, 5 January 1937, Green papers, carton 13; Howson, *Arms for Spain*, 164–77; Howson, *Aircraft of the Spanish Civil War*, 52; Allen, "G. Hall Roosevelt and the '100 Plane Deal,'" 3; Traina, *American Diplomacy and the Spanish Civil War*, 79–80, 168, 280; Freidel, *Franklin D. Roosevelt*, 271.

76 This presumably refers to Harold Elstner Talbot (1888–1957) of Dayton, Ohio, who was involved with the Dayton Wright Company and the Chrysler Corporation and was chairman of the board of North American Aviation in 1931–32. He later became Secretary of the Air Force (1953–55) under Eisenhower.

77 There is no record of a meeting on this day in the files at the Roosevelt Library,

although such a sensitive meeting would not necessarily appear in State Department records.

78 Details of these British proposals can be found in Herschel V. Johnson to Cordell Hull, 9 June 1938, DSR 852.00/8125.

79 *FRUS,* 1938, vol. 1, 352.

80 William C. Bullitt to Roosevelt, 21 June 1938, *FDR and FA,* vol. 10, 300–303.

81 Tom Corcoran was a Loyalist sympathizer and close political advisor of FDR. Ickes, *The Secret Diary of Harold L. Ickes,* vol. 2, 12 May 1938.

82 Ickes, *The Secret Diary of Harold L. Ickes,* vol. 2, 424.

83 Cook, *Eleanor Roosevelt,* 507–8.

84 G. Hall Roosevelt to Roosevelt, 23 July 1938, Roosevelt papers, PPF 285. The misspelling of "plane" implies that whoever recorded the message was unaware of its meaning.

85 Memorandum, 13 October 1938, Green papers, carton 13. There is no documentary substantiation that any second visit in fact occurred.

86 Joseph C. Green to John Morgan, 2 March 1944, Morgan-Green Report, 143, Green papers, carton 13.

87 Roosevelt papers, PPF 285; Traina, *American Diplomacy and the Spanish Civil War,* 270; Allen, "G. Hall Roosevelt and the '100 Plane Deal,'" "Addenda," 3; Ickes, *The Secret Diary of Harold L. Ickes,* vol. 2, 1 January 1939; Missy LeHand to Miles Sherover, 21 April 1939, Roosevelt papers, OF 249, OF 4901.

88 Morgan, *FDR,* 39; Marks, *Wind over Sand,* 1; Heinrichs, *Threshold of War,* vii.

89 Reynolds, *The Creation of the Anglo-American Alliance,* 36, 49. For details of how Churchill in turn exaggerated the imminence of American intervention in the Second World War in 1940 see Jenkins, *Churchill,* 612–13.

90 Radosh, Habeck, and Sevostianov, eds., *Spain Betrayed,* 428–29.

91 Beasley, Shulman, and Beasley, eds., *The Eleanor Roosevelt Encyclopedia,* 458–59; *New York Times,* 26 September 1941. Hall, for example, became chairman of the Grand Rallye Ligne Internationale des Aviateurs of the United States. Allen, "G. Hall Roosevelt and the '100 Plane Deal,'" 1.

92 Morgan, *FDR,* 446.

93 Beasley, Shulman, and Beasley, eds., *The Eleanor Roosevelt Encyclopedia,* 459. G. Hall Roosevelt in *Odyssey of an American Family* includes a deeply admiring chapter on FDR.

94 Jay Allen to James Roosevelt, 28 March 1938, James Roosevelt papers, box 62; Moffat Diary, 31 March 1938.

95 Moffat diary, 24 March 1938, 3 January 1939; Adolf Berle to R. Walton Moore, 19 May 1938, Adolf Berle papers; Kanawada, *Franklin D. Roosevelt's Diplomacy and American Catholics, Italians, and Jews,* 55–56.

96 Andrew, *For the President's Eyes Only,* 75–122; George and George, *Presidential Personality and Performance,* 204–5; Heinrichs, *Threshold of War*; Kimball, *The Juggler.* See also Michael Fullilove's Oxford University D. Phil. thesis (2003) on Roosevelt's use of unofficial envoys.

97 Haight, *American Aid to France*, 3–10; Farnham, *Roosevelt and the Munich Crisis*, 73–75; Murphy, *Diplomat among Warriors*, 32–35, 69; Brownell and Billings, *So Close to Greatness*, 256–60.

98 Howson, *Aircraft of the Spanish Civil War*, 305; Howson, *Arms for Spain*, 239; Payne, *The Spanish Civil War, the Soviet Union and Communism*, 155.

99 Hull, *The Memoirs of Cordell Hull*, vol. 1, 481.

100 Ickes, *The Secret Diary of Harold L. Ickes*, vol. 2, 585–86; Louis Fischer to Claude Bowers, 6 February 1939, Louis Fischer papers, box 16; Davis, *FDR: The War President*, 745.

Chapter 8: Mediation, Relief, Repealing the Arms Embargo

1 Flynn, *Roosevelt and Romanism*, 41.

2 For details of mediation proposals in 1936 see *FRUS, 1936*, vol. 2, 489, 492, 495, 498, 587, 590, 596–97, 606.

3 William Phillips journal, 17 August 1936; Ellis Briggs memorandum, 7 July 1938, William C. Bullitt to Cordell Hull, 7 July 1938, *FRUS, 1938*, vol. 1, 225, 227; Sumner Welles to Roosevelt, 30 June 1937, Memorandum for the Under Secretary of State, 3 July 1937, Roosevelt papers, OF 422, box 1; Moffat diary, 26 January 1938. On Latin American mediation proposals see also *FRUS, 1936* vol. 2, 488, 517, 579, 1937, vol. 1, 318–24, 1938, vol. 1, 225; José Camprubi to Roosevelt, 2 November 1937, Roosevelt to Stephen T. Early, 6 November 1937, Stephen T. Early to José Camprubi, 6 November 1937, *FDR and FA*, vol. 7, 165, 178–79; Taylor, *The United States and the Spanish Civil War*, 62–63; Thomas, *The Spanish Civil War*, 334; Jablon, *Crossroads of Decision*, 122–27.

4 Roosevelt to Claude G. Bowers, 31 August 1938, *FDR and FA*, vol. 11, 122.

5 Memorandum, 1 November 1938, Berle papers.

6 In New York Berle met Monsignor York, a supporter of Franco who appeared favorable to American mediation and agreed to discuss it with Bishop Molloy. Nothing is known to have come out of these discussions. Memorandum, 7 November 1938, Berle papers. Secretary of State Cordell Hull does not appear to have been significantly involved in the planning for the mediation scheme. Hull's letter to Judge John McDuffie on 3 November 1938 rejected the possibility of American mediation in Spain. DSR 852.00/8601.

7 There are some parallels between this Pan-American mediation initiative and an earlier plan dated 13 July 1937. This report, stamped "strictly confidential," was written by Raymond Buell, president of the Foreign Policy Association. It described the embargo as unjust but argued that lifting it would represent a "severe moral judgment" against Germany and Italy, and leave the United States with the responsibility of restricting outside intervention in Spain. This dilemma could be escaped only by Pan-American mediation, which would strengthen ties in the western hemisphere and prevent fascist penetration of Latin America. Because Spain had divided isolationist opinion, mediation "should command greater support on behalf of the American pub-

lic than any other cooperative proposal in the political field." Pan-American mediation in Spain could also provide a model to employ in future civil conflicts in Latin American. The memorandum was read by Hull, Welles, Moffat, Moore, and Hornbeck, but no action followed. "Spain 1937," Norman H. Davis papers, box 53; Traina, *American Diplomacy and the Spanish Civil War*, 277. When José Camprubi met Roosevelt to discuss Spain in January 1937, Camprubi also outlined a possible scheme for Pan-American mediation. José Camprubi to Roosevelt, 7, 30 January, 2 November 1937, *FDR and FA*, vol. 4, 10, 129–30, vol. 7, 165.

8 Memorandum and attached draft telegram, 10 November 1938, Berle papers.

9 "Proposed Telegram from the Lima Conference to the Spanish Government and to General Franco," undated, Berle papers, box 62.

10 Memorandum for the President, 19 November 1938, Berle papers.

11 Claude G. Bowers to Roosevelt, 18 August 1938, *FDR and FA*, vol. 11, 75. For evidence that Spanish Republican leaders had sought a mediated solution from 1936 see Jackson, *The Spanish Republic and the Civil War*, 441–44, 459.

12 Bowers diary, 12 October 1938; Claude G. Bowers to Cordell Hull, 13 October 1938, *FRUS*, 1938, vol. 1, 246. Franco privately made clear that he would reject any form of negotiated peace. Preston, *Franco*, 314, 316; Thomas, *The Spanish Civil War*, 867.

13 Thomas, *The Spanish Civil War*, 556–57; Whealey, "Foreign Intervention," *The Republic and the Civil War in Spain*, ed. Carr, 227. If war had broken out in September 1938, the British, French, and Russians would most likely have allied with Spanish Loyalists fighting against German and Italian troops in Spain. This was a war that the Spanish Republic might well have won. Roosevelt in September 1938 thought that a wider European conflict would lead to the defeat of the Nationalists, because the French "would promptly liquidate Franco in Spain." Ickes, *The Secret Diary of Harold L. Ickes*, vol. 2, 481.

14 Adolf A. Berle to Roosevelt, 19 November 1938, *FDR and FA*, vol. 12, 135–36.

15 FO 115:3417, Public Records Office. Thomson added that "in positive achievements the Conference may be ranked as a failure—negatively it may claim to be a success; for at least it took no backward step."

16 Roosevelt and Brough, *A Rendezvous with Destiny*, 191. The Vatican did make a very tentative attempt to mediate in Spain in May 1937 but was rebuffed by Franco. Preston, *Franco*, 277.

17 Sumner Welles to Cordell Hull, 1 December, 15 December 1938, Cordell Hull papers, microfilm, reel 17.

18 Moffat diary, 15 December 1938; *FRUS*, 1938, vol. 1, 258–60; DSR 852.00/8688, 852.00/8704.

19 Details of the Cuban request for mediation are in *FRUS* 1937, vol. 1, 466–67.

20 Hull, *Memoirs*, vol. 1, chapter 42; Dallek, *Franklin D. Roosevelt and American Foreign Policy*, 177.

21 Cordell Hull to Sumner Welles, 17 December 1938, Cordell Hull papers, microfilm, reel 17; "Cuban draft on Spain," undated, Berle papers, box 62.

22 "Lima Conference," Cordell Hull papers, microfilm, reel 79; Cordell Hull to Sumner Welles, 19 December 1938, Cordell Hull papers, microfilm, reel 17.

23 "Lima Conference," *Herald Tribune*, 21 December 1938, Gardner Jackson papers, container 44.

24 Memorandum, 10 January 1939, Berle papers.

25 "Lima Conference," *Herald Tribune*, 21 December 1938, Gardner Jackson papers, container 44.

26 FO 115:3416, Public Records Office.

27 Memorandum, 22 July 1938, Sumner Welles papers.

28 Details of the humanitarian aid plans are in *FRUS*, 1938, vol. 1, 364, 367, 368–69; Traina, *American Diplomacy and the Spanish Civil War*, 196–97; Moffat diary, 30–31 July, 4–24 August, 6 September 1938; Claude G. Bowers to Cordell Hull, 8 July 1938, Bowers papers II. On 20 September 1938 the British ambassador in Washington described American relief efforts as "partly explained by the embarrassing size of the 1938 wheat crop." FO 115:3416, file 415, Public Records Office.

29 Moffat diary, 16 September 1938.

30 Details of these appeals can be found in the Roosevelt papers, OF 422; Thomas Dreiser to Roosevelt, 1 September 1938, Claude G. Bowers to Roosevelt, 17 November 1938, Roosevelt to Claude G. Bowers, 6 December 1938, Thomas Dreiser to Roosevelt, 5 January 1939, *FDR and FA*, vol. 11, 142, vol. 12, 89–94, 265–66, vol. 13, 44; *FRUS*, 1938, vol. 1, 364–81.

31 "A special commission will be set up composed of a few men in the higher brackets to whom the President will write." Moffat diary, 12 December 1938.

32 G. S. Bishop to Ernst Toller, 6 October 1938, Roosevelt papers, OF 422, box 1.

33 Marvin H. McIntyre to Norman H. Davis, 21 December 1938, *FDR and FA*, vol. 12, 342–45; Moffat diary, 21 December 1938.

34 Moffat diary, 16 September, 19–20 November 1938; Traina, *American Diplomacy and the Spanish Civil War*, 201; Claude G. Bowers to Cordell Hull, 1 October 1938, *FDR and FA*, vol. 11, 278–84.

35 Ickes, *The Secret Diary of Harold L. Ickes*, 7 January 1939.

36 Moffat diary, 13 January 1939; Traina, *American Diplomacy and the Spanish Civil War*, 200.

37 Norman H. Davis to Roosevelt, 2 February 1939, *FDR and FA*, vol. 13, 231–33; Moffat diary, 17 January 1939.

38 On 7 November Roosevelt and Berle discussed mediation in the Spanish Civil War. Commenting on this meeting on 19 November, Berle noted that if Franco refused the president's mediation plan, it would "clear the way for changing our position in the matter of the Spanish embargo," implying that this possibility had been discussed twelve days earlier. Adolf A. Berle to Roosevelt, 19 November 1938, *FDR and FA*, vol. 12, 135–36.

39 Moffat diary, 19, 20 November 1938.

40 Harold L. Ickes to Roosevelt, 23 November 1938, Roosevelt to Harold L. Ickes, 25 November 1938, *FDR and FA*, vol. 12, 161–62, 182–83. Ickes later told Bow-

ers that he thought the embargo was "one of the most shameful chapters in American history." Harold L. Ickes to Claude G. Bowers, 11 January 1939, Bowers papers II.

41 Burns, *Roosevelt*, 340, 359–69. For the link between Maury Maverick's defeat and his support for the Spanish Loyalists see Weiss, "Maury Maverick and the Liberal Bloc," 892.

42 Homer Cummings diary, microfilm copy, 18 December 1938; Burns, *Roosevelt*, 340, 359–69.

43 Roosevelt to Harold L. Ickes, 25 November 1938, *FDR and FA,* vol. 12, 182–83.

44 Memoranda, 25 November, 3 December 1938, Green papers, carton 13; Sumner Welles to Roosevelt, 25, 30 November, 1938, Sumner Welles papers, box 150; Memorandum, 11 April 1938, Green papers, carton 13.

45 Cordell Hull to Raymond Leslie Buell, 21 March 1938, Memorandum, 31 March 1938, Cordell Hull to Roosevelt, 18 November 1938, Sumner Welles to Roosevelt, 30 November 1938, *FDR and FA,* vol. 9, 204–5, 281–87, vol. 12, 120–21, 226–29; Dallek, *Franklin D. Roosevelt and American Foreign Policy,* 178; FO 115:3412, Public Records Office.

46 Roosevelt to Homer S. Cummings, 28 November 1938, *FDR and FA,* vol. 12, 196.

47 Golden W. Bell to Homer S. Cummings, 5 December 1938, *FDR and FA,* vol. 12, 243–52.

48 Traina, *American Diplomacy and the Spanish Civil War,* 215.

49 Homer Cummings diary, microfilm copy, 18 December 1938; Homer S. Cummings to Roosevelt, 19 December 1938, *FDR and FA,* vol. 12, 340, Ickes, *The Secret Diary of Harold L. Ickes,* vol. 2, 566.

50 Sumner Welles to Roosevelt, 25 November 1938, Roosevelt to Sumner Welles, 21 December 1938, Memorandum for Sumner Welles, 24 January 1939, Memorandum for the Attorney-General, 6 February 1939. Roosevelt papers, PSF: Spain, box 50, OF 422, box 1, file 1.

51 Ickes, *The Secret Diary of Harold L. Ickes,* vol. 2, 18 December 1938.

52 Ickes, *The Secret Diary of Harold L. Ickes,* vol. 2, 528; Dallek, *Franklin D. Roosevelt and American Foreign Policy,* 179; Cole, "Senator Key Pittman and American Neutrality Policies, 1933–1940."

53 Sumner Welles to Roosevelt, 17 December 1938, *FDR and FA,* vol. 12, 338–39; Moffat diary, 16 December 1938; Thomas, *The Spanish Civil War,* 569–73.

54 Speech by Roosevelt, 4 January 1939, *FDR and FA,* vol. 13, 1–25.

55 Sumner Welles to Samuel Rosenman, 27 June 1941, "Spain," Samuel I. Rosenman papers, container 41.

56 Moffat diary, 4, 9 January 1939.

57 Bowers diary, 24 January 1939; Claude G. Bowers to Louis Fischer, 18 February 1939, Louis Fischer papers, box 16; Sehlinger and Hamilton, *Spokesman for Democracy,* 198.

58 Warren F. Kimball, "The United States," *The Origins of World War Two,* ed. Boyce and Maiolo, 142.

59 Claude G. Bowers to Cordell Hull, 14 January 1939, Bowers papers II.

60 "Comments on Roosevelt: Franco Press in Spain Doubts Speech Referred to War There," *New York Times*, 7 January 1939; Claude G. Bowers to Cordell Hull, 7 January 1939, DSR 852.00/8817; Claude G. Bowers to Roosevelt, 20 February 1938, 7 January 1939, 16 February 1939, Bowers papers II; *FDR and FA,* vol. 8, 340–45, vol. 13, 328–33; Preston, *Franco,* 313.

61 Moffat diary, 19 January 1939.

62 Roosevelt to Claude G. Bowers, 26 January 1939, *FDR and FA,* vol. 13, 186.

63 Morgan-Green Report, 153.

64 Young, "Public Attitudes towards American Foreign Policy in the Spanish Civil War," 1, 32, 94–95, located in "Material for the Morgan-Green Report," Green papers, carton 13.

65 Moffat diary, 9, 19 January 1939; Traina, *American Diplomacy and the Spanish Civil War,* 210–16; Kanawada, *Franklin D. Roosevelt's Diplomacy and American Catholics, Italians, and Jews,* 62, 69–70; Hooker, ed., *The Moffat Papers,* 227; Divine, *The Illusion of Neutrality,* 236–38; Flynn, *Roosevelt and Romanism,* 47–50; Valaik, "Catholics, Neutrality, and the Spanish Embargo," 79–81; "K. of C. Board Urges Keeping of Embargo," *New York Times,* 16 January 1939.

66 Moffat diary, 19, 23 January 1939.

67 Eleanor Roosevelt to Martha Gellhorn, 26 January 1939, Eleanor Roosevelt papers, box 688.

68 Moffat diary, 21–23 January 1939; Hooker, *The Moffat Papers,* 227–28; Breckinridge Long diary, 25 January 1939.

69 Cole, *Roosevelt and the Isolationists,* 303.

70 Roosevelt to Josephus Daniels, 9 November 1936, Daniels papers.

71 Traina, *American Diplomacy and the Spanish Civil War,* 212–13.

72 Moffat diary, 11 January 1939; Michael Francis Doyle to Colonel McIntyre, 15 January 1939, Roosevelt Papers, OF 422-c, box 2.

73 Traina, *American Diplomacy and the Spanish Civil War,* 204.

74 Cole, *Roosevelt and the Isolationists,* 307.

75 Moffat diary, 16 January 1939.

76 Dallek, *Franklin D. Roosevelt and American Foreign Policy,* 180; Ickes, *The Secret Diary of Harold L. Ickes,* vol. 2, 561, 574–75.

77 Breckinridge Long diary, 25 January, 31 January 1939.

78 Stimson diary, microfilm copy, reel 6, 2–3.

79 *New York Times,* 24 January, 26 January 1939.

80 Moffat diary, 20 January 1939.

81 Moffat diary, 23 January 1939; Dallek, *Franklin D. Roosevelt and American Foreign Policy,* 180.

82 Ickes, *The Secret Diary of Harold L. Ickes,* vol. 2, 569.

83 Preston, *Franco,* 312.

84 Cordell Hull to Roosevelt, undated 1939, Roosevelt papers, PSF: Spain, box 50; Roosevelt to Cordell Hull, 23 February 1939, *FDR and FA,* vol. 13, 357; Moffat diary 27 February 1939; Ickes, *The Secret Diary of Harold L. Ickes,* vol. 2, 608–9.

85 Bowers diary, 11 March 1939; Moffat diary, 29 March, 30 March, 31 March 1939.

86 "Makes Stir Abroad: Britain and France Hail Message as Italy and Reich Denounce It," *New York Times*, 5 January 1939.

87 Moffat diary, 9 January 1939; Sumner Welles to Marvin H. McIntyre, 30 January 1939, Roosevelt papers, OF 422, box 1, file 1.

88 Ickes, *The Secret Diary of Harold L. Ickes*, vol. 2, 566.

89 Sumner Welles to Roosevelt, 15 November 1938, Sumner Welles papers, box 150.

Chapter 9: The Aftermath

1 Stein, *Beyond Death and Exile*; Carr, *The Spanish Tragedy*, 238–39; Graham, *The Spanish Civil War*, 120; Beevor, *The Battle for Spain*, 417.

2 I am grateful to Paul Preston for providing the latest figures on Nationalist killings (150,000–200,000) from his unpublished manuscript. For discussion see Thomas, *The Spanish Civil War*, 923–27; Carr, *The Spanish Tragedy*, 257–58; Jackson, *The Spanish Republic and the Civil War*, chapter 27. "His rule would be that of an all-powerful military colonial ruler. The enemy, the defeated Republicans, would be savagely crushed. The 'families' of the nationalist coalition would be manipulated like friendly tribes, bribed, enmeshed in competition among themselves, involved in corruption and repression in such a way as to make them suspicious of one another but unable to do without the supreme arbiter." Preston, *Franco*, 327.

3 Hull, *The Memoirs of Cordell Hull*, vol. 1, chapter 36.

4 Esenwein and Shubert, *Spain at War*, 206.

5 Edwards, *The British Government and the Spanish Civil War*, 213; Carley, *1939*, 144.

6 Whealey, *Hitler and Spain*, 136–37; Stone, "The European Great Powers and the Spanish Civil War," 217–19; Preston, "Italy and Spain in Civil War and World War, 1936–1943," *Spain and the Great Powers in the Twentieth Century*, ed. Balfour and Preston, 173–74.

7 Martin, *American Liberalism and World Politics*, 515–16.

8 Falcoff and Pike, *The Spanish Civil War*, 22.

9 The British chargé in Washington quoted Representative Hamilton Fish, who opposed the lifting of the Spanish embargo: "If the President or anyone else tries to get us into a foreign war it is our duty to see to it that he does not succeed." FO 115:3418, file 230, Public Records Office.

10 Valaik, "Catholics, Neutrality and the Spanish Embargo," 76; Flynn, *Roosevelt and Romanism*, 54.

11 Duram, *Norman Thomas*, 30; Fleischman, *Norman Thomas*, 327.

12 Schrecker, *Many Are the Crimes*, 96, 105; Carroll, *The Odyssey of the Abraham Lincoln Brigade*, 244–75.

13 Kanawada, *Franklin D. Roosevelt's Diplomacy and American Catholics, Italians, and Jews*, 60.

14 Press Conference, 5 June 1940, Roosevelt, *Complete Presidential Press Conferences of Franklin D. Roosevelt*.

15   Rosenman, *The Public Papers and Addresses of Franklin D. Roosevelt*, 191–93.

16   Sumner Welles to Samuel Rosenman, 27 June 1941, "Spain," Samuel I. Rosenman papers, container 41.

17   Roosevelt and Brough, *A Rendezvous with Destiny*, 139.

18   On 4 January 1939 the president declared: "The instinct of self-preservation should warn us that we ought not to let that happen anymore." On 27 January FDR stated: "we would never do such a thing again." Speech by Roosevelt, 4 January 1939, *FDR and FA*, vol. 13, 1–25; Ickes, *The Secret Diary of Harold L. Ickes*, vol. 2, 569.

19   Tusell, "Franco and Franklin D. Roosevelt," *FDR and His Contemporaries*, ed. Van Minnen and Sears, 177.

20   Davis, *FDR: Into the Storm*, 399; Roosevelt and Brough, *A Rendezvous with Destiny*, 222.

21   Ickes, *The Secret Diary of Harold L. Ickes*, vol. 3, 217. Arthur M. Schlesinger found that the "guilt generated by the abandonment of the republic lingered for a long time." Schlesinger Jr., *A Life in the Twentieth Century*, 210.

22   Columbia University Oral History Project, interview with Claude G. Bowers, 1954, 125–26; Claude G. Bowers to Arthur Schlesinger, 12, 14 April 1951, Bowers papers III.

23   Traina, *American Diplomacy and the Spanish Civil War*, 230–32.

24   Bowers, *My Mission to Spain*.

25   Sehlinger and Hamilton, *Spokesman for Democracy*, 201.

26   Sehlinger and Hamilton, *Spokesman for Democracy*, 200.

27   Swanberg, *Norman Thomas*, 218.

28   Sehlinger and Hamilton, *Spokesman for Democracy*, 200.

29   Truman, *Memoirs*, 190.

30   Cook, *Eleanor Roosevelt*, 507; Davis, *FDR: The War President*, 645.

31   Rosenman, ed., *The Public Papers and Addresses of Franklin D. Roosevelt*, 1939, 512–22.

32   "The Spanish Civil War," unpublished paper, Ernest Cuneo Papers, container 115, 27–28.

33   In August 1943 Roosevelt wrote to Ambassador Carlton Hayes, criticizing the anti-American sentiment in the Spanish press—orchestrated, he believed, by the Spanish government. Roosevelt to Carlton J. H. Hayes, 14 August 1943, Roosevelt papers, PSF, box 50, "Spain 1940–45." For concerns over Latin America see FRUS, 1940, vol. 2, 839–41, 845–50. For Roosevelt's wish to avoid oil transshipments from Spain to Germany see Ickes, *The Secret Diary of Harold L. Ickes*, vol. 3, 271–72. For Cordell Hull's views see FRUS, 1941, vol. 2, 914.

34   Denis Smyth, "Franco and the Allies in the Second World War," *Spain and the Great Powers in the Twentieth Century*, ed. Balfour and Preston, 189, 209; Preston, *Franco*, 355.

35   Roosevelt papers, PSF, box 69, details Alexander W. Weddell's correspondence with the president. See also Halstead, "Historians in Politics"; Carlton J. H.

Hayes to Roosevelt, 3 May 1943, 17 April 1944, Roosevelt papers, PSF, box 50, "Spain 1940–45." Hull noted that "those segments of our own population who had passionately embraced the Loyalist cause during the Civil War continually urged us to break off diplomatic relations with Spain or to take other actions that assuredly would have brought Spain into the war on the Axis side." Hull, *The Memoirs of Cordell Hull*, vol. 2, 1187; Halstead, "Historians in Politics," 393.

36 Paul Preston, "Franco's Foreign Policy 1939–1953," and Norman J. W. Goda, "Germany's Conception of Spain's Strategic Importance," both in *Spain in an International Context*, ed. Leitz and Dunthorn.

37 Tusell, "Franco and Franklin D. Roosevelt," *FDR and His Contemporaries*, ed. Van Minnen and Sears, 177; Preston, *Franco*, chapter 14; Preston, "Franco and Hitler." Relations between the United States and Spain are described in *FRUS*, 1940, vol. 2, 810, 820–26; Preston, *Franco*, 360–61.

38 Carr, *The Spanish Tragedy*, 230.

39 Christian Leitz, "Nazi Germany and Francoist Spain, 1936–1945," *Spain and the Great Powers in the Twentieth Century*, ed. Balfour and Preston, 127. Franco declared Mussolini "the greatest political figure in the world. Whereas Hitler is a mystic, a diviner and very close to the mentality of the Slavs, Mussolini in contrast is human, clear in his ideas, never far from reality, in a word, 'a true Latin genius.'" *Spain and the Great Powers in the Twentieth Century*, ed. Balfour and Preston, 175.

40 Memorandum, 16 December 1940, Roosevelt papers, PSF, box 50, "Spain 1940–45"; PSF, Safe File, "State Department 1939–1940," "State Department June–Dec 1940," microfilm copy, Library of Congress, reel 8, reel 20; Feis, *The Spanish Story*, 61; Hull, *The Memoirs of Cordell Hull*, vol. 1, 876.

41 Thomas Lamont to Roosevelt, 8 February 1941, Roosevelt papers, microfilm copy, Library of Congress, reel 20; Preston, *Franco*, 375–76.

42 "Our Spanish Policy," undated, Cordell Hull papers, microfilm copy, reel 49; Hull, *The Memoirs of Cordell Hull*, vol. 2, 1188–92, 1326; Stafford, *Roosevelt and Churchill*, 88–110.

43 Smyth, *Diplomacy and Strategy of Survival*; Denis Smyth, "Franco and the Allies in the Second World War," *Spain and the Great Powers in the Twentieth Century*, ed. Balfour and Preston, 194–203; Preston, *Franco*, 442; Davis, *FDR: The War President*, 582–84. The Allies developed the "Backbone" plan to occupy Spain if Franco allowed German troops to cross the Pyrenees. Schmitz, *Thank God They're on Our Side*, 158.

44 Preston, *Franco*, 506; Hull, *The Memoirs of Cordell Hull*, vol. 2, 1329; Edwards, *Anglo-American Relations and the Franco Question*, 5. American liberals pressuring for a break in relations with Franco Spain tended to blame a reactionary State Department for policy decisions. Warren, *Noble Abstractions*, 54–55.

45 Edwards, *Anglo-American Relations and the Franco Question*, 9–10, 47; Hull, *The Memoirs of Cordell Hull*, vol. 2, 1331–33; Kimball, ed., *Churchill and Roosevelt*, vol. 3, 78. Liberals also opposed the Allied willingness to deal with the Vichy

leader Admiral Jean-François Darlan after the North African landings in 1942. At a press conference, Roosevelt quoted the Balkan proverb, "My children, you are permitted in time of great danger to walk with the Devil until you have crossed the bridge." Casey, *Cautious Crusade*, 112–18.

46 Carlton Hayes, "Memorandum on the Spanish Situation with Special Reference to Relations between Spain and the United States," February 1945, Roosevelt papers, PSF, box 50, "Spain 1940–45"; Warren, *Noble Abstractions*, 54.

47 Roosevelt to Carlton J. H. Hayes, 14 March 1945, "Spain 1940–45," Roosevelt papers, PSF, box 50.

48 Roosevelt to Norman Amour, 10 March 1945, Roosevelt papers, PSF, box 50, "Spain, 1940–45." For details of Armour's conversations with Franco about this message see *FRUS*, 1945, vol. 5, 668–80.

49 Stein, *Beyond Death and Exile*, chapter 11; Gallo, *Spain under Franco*, 147–49.

50 *FRUS: The Conference of Berlin (Potsdam)*, vol. 2, 1171–76, 1509–10; Stein, *Beyond Death and Exile*, 183–86; Florentino Portero, "Spain, Britain and the Cold War," *Spain and the Great Powers in the Twentieth Century*, ed. Balfour and Preston, 211–18.

51 Joseph Grew to the Secretary of State, 31 July [?1945], Cordell Hull papers, microfilm version, reel 49.

52 Edwards, *Anglo-American Relations and the Franco Question*, 42–44; Preston, *Franco*, 530; Stein, *Beyond Death and Exile*, 189–90.

53 The Potsdam negotiations can be found in *FRUS: The Conference of Berlin (Potsdam)*, vol. 2, 1171–76, 1509–10.

54 Schmitz, *Thank God They're on Our Side*, 162; Florentino Portero, "Spain, Britain and the Cold War," *Spain and the Great Powers in the Twentieth Century*, ed. Balfour and Preston, 219–20; Stein, *Beyond Death and Exile*, 189.

55 Florentino Portero, "Spain, Britain and the Cold War," *Spain and the Great Powers in the Twentieth Century*, ed. Balfour and Preston, 216–26; Preston, *Franco*, 541–42.

56 Schmitz, *Thank God They're on Our Side*, 164–68; Florentino Portero, "Spain, Britain and the Cold War," *Spain and the Great Powers in the Twentieth Century*, ed. Balfour and Preston, 220–26; Boris Liedtke, "Spain and the USA, 1945–1975," *Spain and the Great Powers in the Twentieth Century*, ed. Balfour and Preston, 229–43.

57 Adler, *The Isolationist Impulse*, 181; Hayes, *The United States and Spain*.

58 Hoover, *Masters of Deceit*, 71–72.

Chapter 10: From a Vicarious Sacrifice to a Grave Mistake

1 Howson, *Arms for Spain*, 248.

2 Martha Gellhorn to Eleanor Roosevelt, 1938, Eleanor Roosevelt papers, box 1459.

3 Ickes, *The Secret Diary of Harold L. Ickes*, vol. 2, 569.

4 Flynn, *Roosevelt and Romanism*, 44–55.

5   Ickes, *The Secret Diary of Harold L. Ickes*, vol. 2, 569; Press conference, 5 June 1940, Roosevelt, *Complete Presidential Press Conferences of Franklin D. Roosevelt*.

6   For an overview of Roosevelt's capacity as an educator see Chris Van Aller, "FDR's Foreign Policy Persona," *Franklin D. Roosevelt and the Formation of the Modern World*, ed. Howard and Pederson.

7   Davis, *FDR: Into the Storm*, 388.

8   Watt, *Succeeding John Bull*, 83.

9   Ward, *Before the Trumpet*, 6.

10   Traina, *American Diplomacy and the Spanish Civil War*, 228.

11   Thomas, *The Spanish Civil War*, 825.

12   Dallek, *Franklin D. Roosevelt and American Foreign Policy*, 160. For details of Nye's views see Cole, *Senator Gerald P. Nye and American Foreign Relations*.

13   Martin, *American Liberalism and World Politics*, 230.

14   Kanawada, *Franklin D. Roosevelt's Diplomacy and American Catholics, Italians, and Jews*, 70.

15   This concurs with Thomas Graham's opinion that "public opinion influences presidential decisions primarily about tactics, timing, and political communications strategy, rather than determining the ultimate goals of an administration's foreign policy." Graham, "Public Opinion and U.S. Foreign Policy Making," 201.

16   Thomas, *The Spanish Civil War*, 826.

17   Ickes, *The Secret Diary of Harold L. Ickes*, vol. 3, 217.

18   Rosenman, *The Public Papers and Addresses of Franklin D. Roosevelt*, 191–93.

19   Roosevelt, *This I Remember*, 132.

20   Bowers diary, 11 March 1939; Sehlinger and Hamilton, *Spokesman for Democracy*, 199; Douglas Little, "Claude Bowers and His Mission to Spain: The Diplomacy of a Jeffersonian Democrat," *U.S. Diplomats in Europe*, ed. Jones, 130, 135.

21   Jablon, *Crossroads of Decision*, 119.

22   Moffat diary, 19, 20 November 1938.

23   Memorandum, 11 May 1938, Herbert Feis papers, box 126, "1938 Unidentified."

24   Kanawada, *Franklin D. Roosevelt's Diplomacy and American Catholics, Italians, and Jews*, 64.

25   Ickes, *The Secret Diary of Harold L. Ickes*, vol. 2, 569.

26   Little, *Malevolent Neutrality*.

27   Ickes, *The Secret Diary of Harold L. Ickes*, vol. 2, 16 July 1938.

28   Farnham, *Roosevelt and the Munich Crisis*, 91; Dallek, *Franklin D. Roosevelt and American Foreign Policy*, 172–75; Haight, *American Aid to France*, 24–25.

Bibliography

A Note on Sources

The major archival sources for a study of Roosevelt and the Spanish Civil War can be found in the Franklin D. Roosevelt papers in the Roosevelt library, Hyde Park, New York. The Official File (OF), the President's Personal File (PPF), and the President's Secretary's File (PSF) all contain important material. A large number of these documents have been reproduced in the series *Franklin D. Roosevelt and Foreign Affairs*, which covers the period 1933–39. Edgar B. Nixon edited volumes 1–3, encompassing 1933–36. Confusingly, the documents covering 1937–39 were later published in two separate series, which are identical except for being arranged in a different number of volumes. It is the Clearwater version that is used in this book.

The State Department records in the National Archives contain thousands of documents related to the Spanish Civil War from the standpoint of the State Department and U.S. foreign ambassadors and officials. Many of the key documents are published in the series *Foreign Relations of the United States* (FRUS). The State Department files are invaluable for comprehending official positions and the day-to-day operation of Spanish policy. They can be quite limited as a guide to the behind-the-scenes debates and particularly Roosevelt's perceptions of Spain. They also contain surprisingly little relevant material on the development of several of the initiatives to aid the Spanish Republic in 1938. First, the president was wary of setting out his true beliefs in official documents. Second, Roosevelt sometimes bypassed the State Department in policy making. Third, official documents often suggest a unified and resolved administration position, masking the uncertainty of individuals and the divisions between factions and personalities. Fourth, memoranda occasionally excluded potentially embarrassing material, as with the covert aid episode. These documents can be supplemented by the Cordell Hull papers and memoirs, the Sumner Welles papers, the R. Walton Moore papers, the Claude G. Bowers papers, and the Herbert Feis papers.

There are two very useful collections at Princeton University. The Joseph Green papers detail efforts to enforce the moral and legal embargo at a time when Green was head of the Office of Arms and Munitions Control. Of particular importance is the Morgan-Green report, written by John Morgan and Joseph Green in 1944–45. This is an internal State Department analysis of Spanish Civil War policy, with a focus on the control of arms exports. Note also the revealing correspondence between Morgan and Green and between Green and Savage concerning the preparation of the report, much of which is not included in the final version. The Arthur Krock papers also include a number of useful items. Attention should be drawn to the correspondence between Krock and Professor James Ragland about Spanish policy between 1957 and 1964. There is also some relevant material in the "Spanish correspondence" box of the Louis Fischer papers.

A number of diaries are invaluable for comprehending the beliefs of policy makers, including Roosevelt. Harold Ickes's diary is a crucial source covering the whole period. The William Phillips journal (Harvard University) is useful for understanding the origins of the moral embargo in 1936. The J. Pierrepont Moffat diary (also at Harvard University) is a major source for 1938–39, including a great deal of information on the private negotiations between the president and the State Department over Spanish policy. The Breckinridge Long diary is very useful, especially for the events surrounding the Nye Resolution in May 1938, when Long acted as a lobbyist for the Loyalists. There is also relevant information in the Henry Morgenthau diary on the purchase of Spanish silver, and a few references in the Homer S. Cummings diary on Roosevelt and the Spanish embargo in December 1938. The Henry L. Stimson diary can be used for the views of Joseph Green, Anthony Eden, and Joseph Kennedy on the Spanish Civil War, as well as for the events surrounding Stimson's letter to the *New York Times* in January 1939, in which he declared his opposition to the embargo. Claude G. Bowers's diary provides considerable detail on his life as the ambassador to Spain, although he was somewhat out of the loop in terms of decision making in Washington.

Other archival sources are revealing about particular aspects of the Spanish Civil War. The Adolf Berle papers are vital for understanding Roosevelt's mediation plan of 1938. The Cordell Hull papers and the Gardner Jackson papers are also useful on this issue. The Josephus Daniels papers are disappointing, given that Daniels was ambassador to Mexico. There is some information on the Mexican reaction to the Spanish Civil War, but very little on efforts to transship American arms to Spain via Mexico. The Norman Thomas papers and the Ernest Cuneo papers are helpful on the issue of American volunteers for the international brigades. The Eleanor Roosevelt papers, especially the correspondence with Martha Gellhorn, include some new insights into FDR's views of the Spanish conflict. The Samuel I. Rosenman papers discuss details of the drafting in 1943 of Roosevelt's assessment of Spanish policy for the series *Public Papers and Addresses*. The William C. Bullitt papers were not available, although there is substantial coverage of Bullitt's role in the Spanish Civil War in the other sources.

International sources used include material from the Public Records Office in London and the Russian archives, in the form of the documents printed in the recent collection by Radosh and Sevostianov, *Spain Betrayed: The Soviet Union in the Spanish Civil War*. Additional primary sources include opinion poll data and newspapers from the period, especially the *New York Times* and the *Washington Post*.

These primary sources have been supplemented by several hundred secondary sources, with a rich literature separately available on Roosevelt and the Spanish Civil War, although little specifically on the interaction between the two. Over thirty years after it was written, Richard P. Traina's *American Diplomacy and the Spanish Civil War* remains by far the most reliable existing guide on American policy toward Spain in 1936–39, although my book provides a substantially new interpretation of events. Traina's focus is on the State Department and international factors, and there has been comparatively little attention paid to Roosevelt's beliefs about the war. Furthermore, I use a range of sources which were either unavailable to Traina or unused, including documents on the covert aid episode in the Roosevelt papers and on the mediation scheme in the Berle papers, together with the Bowers papers, the Green papers, the Welles papers (which have only recently become available), the Krock papers, the Long papers, the international sources, and nearly four decades of additional research on this period by historians to whom I am greatly indebted.

Primary Sources

MANUSCRIPTS AND ARCHIVES

Franklin D. Roosevelt Library, Hyde Park, N.Y.
    Adolf A. Berle Jr. papers
    Ernest Cuneo papers
    Charles Fahy papers
    Harry L. Hopkins papers
    Harold Ickes diary
    Gardner Jackson papers
    R. Walton Moore papers
    Henry Morgenthau Jr. papers
    Eleanor Roosevelt papers
    Eleanor Roosevelt Oral History Project
    Franklin D. Roosevelt papers
        President's Personal File (PPF)
        President's Secretary's File (PSF)
        Map Room File
        Official File (OF)
        Vertical File
    James Roosevelt papers
    Samuel I. Rosenman papers
    Harold D. Smith papers

Henry L. Stimson diary
Sumner Welles papers
Microfilm
 Homer S. Cummings diary
 Josephus Daniels papers
National Archives, Washington
 RG 59: General Records of the Department of State Decimal File
Houghton Library, Harvard University
 Jay Pierrepont Moffat diary
 William Phillips papers
 Cordell Hull papers (microfilm copy)
 Columbia University Oral History Project
Seeley G. Mudd Manuscript Library, Princeton University
 Joseph C. Green papers
 Louis Fischer papers
 Arthur Krock papers
Library of Congress, Washington
 Norman H. Davis papers
 Herbert Feis papers
 Harold Ickes papers
 Breckinridge Long papers
  Microfilm
   Franklin D. Roosevelt papers, Official File
    Norman Thomas papers
Lilly Library, Indiana University
 Claude G. Bowers papers
British Public Records Office, London
 FO 115: Foreign Office: Embassy, United States of America: General Correspondence
 FO 954: Private Papers of Sir Anthony Eden

PUBLISHED DOCUMENTS

Butler, Rohan, and Sir E. L. Woodward, eds. *Documents on British Foreign Policy, 1919–1939*, 2nd Series, vol. xvii, Western Pact Negotiations; Outbreak of Spanish Civil War, June 1936–January 1937. London: HMSO, 1946–85.
Documents on German Foreign Policy, series D, vol. iii. London: HMSO, 1949.
Nixon, Edgar B., ed. *Franklin D. Roosevelt and Foreign Affairs*, vols.1–3. Cambridge: Belknap Press of Harvard University Press, 1969.
Roosevelt, Franklin D. *Complete Presidential Press Conferences of Franklin D. Roosevelt*. New York: De Capo, 1972.
Rosenman, Samuel I., ed. *The Public Papers and Addresses of Franklin D. Roosevelt*. New York: Russell and Russell, 1938–50.

Schewe, Donald B. *Franklin D. Roosevelt and Foreign Affairs, January 1937–August 1939*, vols. 4–14. New York: Clearwater, 1979–83.

U.S. Department of State. *Foreign Relations of the United States: Diplomatic Papers*, 1933, vol. 1; 1936, vol. 2; 1937, vol. 1; 1938, vol. 1; 1939, vol. 2. Washington: U.S. Government Printing Office, various.

PUBLISHED MEMOIRS, DIARIES, AND CORRESPONDENCE

Berle, Adolf A. *Navigating the Rapids, 1918–1971: From the Papers of Adolf A. Berle*. New York: Harcourt Brace Jovanovich, 1973.

Blum, John Morton. *From the Morgenthau Diaries*. Boston: Houghton Mifflin, 1959–67.

Bowers, Claude G. *My Mission to Spain: Watching the Rehearsal for World War II*. London: Victor Gollancz, 1954.

Bullitt, Orville H., ed. *For the President, Personal and Secret: Correspondence between Franklin D. Roosevelt and William C. Bullitt*. London: Andre Deutsch, 1973.

Connally, Tom. *My Name Is Tom Connally*. New York: Thomas Y. Crowell, 1954.

Cooper, Duff. *Old Men Forget: An Autobiography of Duff Cooper*. London: Hart Davis, 1953.

Farley, Jim. *Jim Farley's Story*. New York: Whittlesey House, 1948.

Hooker, Nancy H., ed. *The Moffat Papers: Selections from the Diplomatic Papers of Jay Pierrepont Moffat, 1919–1943*. Cambridge: Harvard University Press, 1956.

Hull, Cordell. *The Memoirs of Cordell Hull*, vol. 1. London: Hodder and Stoughton, 1948.

Ickes, Harold L. *The Secret Diary of Harold L. Ickes*, vols. 1–3. New York: Simon and Schuster, 1954.

Kimball, Warren, ed. *Churchill and Roosevelt: The Complete Correspondence*. Princeton: Princeton University Press, 1984.

Phillips, William. *Ventures in Diplomacy*. London: J. Murray, 1955.

Roosevelt, Eleanor. *This I Remember*. London: Hutchinson, 1950.

Roosevelt, Elliott, ed. *F.D.R.: His Personal Letters*. New York: Duell, Sloan, and Pierce, 1950.

Roosevelt, Elliott, and James Brough. *A Rendezvous with Destiny: The Roosevelts of the White House*. London: W. H. Allen, 1977.

Roosevelt, James. *Affectionately, FDR: A Son's Story of a Courageous Man*. New York: Harcourt, Brace and Company, 1960.

Roosevelt, James, and Bill Libby. *My Parents: A Differing View*. London: W. H. Allen, 1977.

Roosevelt, James, and Sidney Shalett. *Affectionately, FDR: A Son's Story of a Lonely Man*. New York: Harcourt, Brace and Company, 1959.

Truman, Harry S. *Memoirs*. New York: Signet, 1965.

Welles, Sumner. *The Time for Decision*. London: Hamish Hamilton, 1944.

———. *Seven Decisions That Shaped History*. New York: Harper and Brothers, 1950.

Secondary Sources

Adamthwaite, Anthony. *France and the Coming of the Second World War*. London: Frank Cass, 1977.

Adler, Selig. *The Isolationist Impulse: Its Twentieth Century Reaction*. New York: Abelard-Schuman, 1961.

Almond, Gabriel. *The American People and Foreign Policy*. Westport: Greenwood, 1960.

Almond, Gabriel, and Stephen Genco. "Clouds, Clocks and the Study of Politics," *World Politics* 29, no. 4 (1977).

Alpert, Michael. *A New International History of the Spanish Civil War*. London: Macmillan, 1994.

Andrew, Christopher. *For the President's Eyes Only: Secret Intelligence and the American President from Washington to Bush*. London: Harper Collins, 1995.

Aster, Sidney. *Anthony Eden*. London: Weidenfeld and Nicolson, 1976.

Baer, George W. *The Coming of the Italian-Ethiopian War*. Cambridge: Harvard University Press, 1967.

Balfour, Sebastian, and Paul Preston, eds. *Spain and the Great Powers in the Twentieth Century*. London: Routledge, 1999.

Baram, P. J. "Undermining the British: Department of State Policies in Egypt and the Suez Canal before and during World War Two," *Historian* 40, no. 4 (1978).

Barnett, Corelli. *The Collapse of British Power*. Gloucester: Alan Sutton, 1987.

Barron, Gloria. *Leadership in Crisis: FDR and the Path to Intervention*. Port Washington, N.Y.: Kennikat, 1973.

Beasley, Maurine H., Holly C. Shulman, and Henry R. Beasley, eds. *The Eleanor Roosevelt Encyclopedia*. New York: Greenwood, 2001.

Beevor, Antony. *The Spanish Civil War*. London: Orbis, 1982.

———. *The Battle for Spain: The Spanish Civil War, 1936–1939*. New York: Penguin, 2006.

Bendiner, Robert. *The Riddle of the State Department*. New York: Ferris Printing, 1942.

Bennett, Edward M. *Franklin D. Roosevelt and the Search for Security: American-Soviet Relations, 1933–1939*. Wilmington, Del.: Scholarly Resources, 1985.

Benson, Frederick R. *Writers in Arms: The Literary Impact of the Spanish Civil War*. New York: New York University Press, 1967.

Bessie, Dan, ed. *Alvah Bessie's Spanish Civil War Notebooks*. Lexington: University Press of Kentucky, 2002.

Black, Conrad. *Franklin Delano Roosevelt: Champion of Freedom*. New York: Public Affairs, 2003.

Blumenthal, Henry. *Illusion and Reality in Franco-American Diplomacy, 1914–1945*. Baton Rouge: Louisiana State University Press, 1986.

Bolloten, Burnett. *The Spanish Civil War: Revolution and Counterrevolution*. London: Harvester Wheatsheaf, 1991.

Bolt, Ernest C., Jr. *Ballots before Bullets: The War Referendum Approach to Peace in America, 1914-1941*. Charlottesville: University Press of Virginia, 1977.

Borg, Dorothy. "Notes on Roosevelt's Quarantine Speech," *Political Science Quarterly* 72, no. 3 (1957).

Boyce, Robert, and Joseph A. Maiolo, eds. *The Origins of World War Two: The Debate Continues*. New York: Palgrave Macmillan, 2003.

Brendon, Piers. *The Dark Valley: A Panorama of the 1930s*. London: Jonathan Cape, 2000.

Brown, Michael E., Sean M. Lynn-Jones, and Steven E. Miller, eds. *Debating the Democratic Peace*. Cambridge: MIT Press, 1996.

Brown, Seyom. "Idealism, Realpolitik or Domestic Politics: A Clinton Era Retrospective on FDR's Foreign Policies," *The New Deal and the Triumph of Liberalism*, ed. Sidney M. Milkis and Jerome M. Mileur. Boston: University of Massachusetts Press, 2002.

Brownell, Will, and Richard N. Billings. *So Close to Greatness: A Biography of William C. Bullitt*. New York: Macmillan, 1998.

Buchanan, Tom. *The Spanish Civil War and the British Labour Movement*. Cambridge: Cambridge University Press, 1991.

———. *Britain and the Spanish Civil War*. Cambridge: Cambridge University Press, 1997.

Buffet, Cyril, and Beatrice Heuser, eds. *Haunted by History: Myths in International Relations*. Providence: Berghahn, 1998.

Burns, James MacGregor. *Roosevelt: The Lion and the Fox*. London: Secker and Warburg, 1956.

———. *The Three Roosevelts: The Leaders Who Transformed America*. London: Atlantic, 2001.

Buzan, Barry. "The Level of Analysis Problem in International Relations Reconsidered," *International Relations Theory Today*, ed. Ken Booth and Steve Smith. Cambridge: Polity, 1995.

Cantril, Hadley, and Mildred Strunk. *Public Opinion, 1935-46*. Westport: Greenwood, 1951.

Carley, Michael Jabara. *1939: The Alliance That Never Was and the Coming of World War II*. Chicago: Ivan R. Dee, 1999.

Carr, Raymond. *The Spanish Tragedy: The Civil War in Perspective*. London: Weidenfeld and Nicolson, 1977.

———. *Modern Spain, 1875-1980*. Oxford: Oxford University Press, 1980.

———, ed. *The Republic and the Civil War in Spain*. London: Macmillan, 1971.

Carroll, Peter. *The Odyssey of the Abraham Lincoln Brigade: Americans in the Spanish Civil War*. Stanford: Stanford University Press, 1994.

Casey, Steven. *Cautious Crusade: Franklin D. Roosevelt, American Public Opinion and the War against Nazi Germany*. Oxford: Oxford University Press, 2001.

Cashman, Sean Dennis. *America, Roosevelt and World War Two*. New York: New York University Press, 1989.

Chafe, William H., ed. *The Achievement of American Liberalism: The New Deal and Its Legacies.* New York: Columbia University Press, 2003.

Chomsky, Noam. *American Power and the New Mandarins.* London: Chatto and Windus, 1969.

Christenson, Terry. *Reel Politics: American Political Movies from Birth of a Nation to Platoon.* Oxford: Blackwell, 1987.

Cole, Wayne S. "Senator Key Pittman and American Neutrality Policies, 1933–1940," *Mississippi Valley Historical Review* 46, no. 4 (1960).

———. *Senator Gerald P. Nye and American Foreign Relations.* Minneapolis: University of Minnesota Press, 1962.

———. *Charles A. Lindbergh and the Battle against American Intervention in World War Two.* New York: Harcourt Brace Jovanovich, 1970.

———. *Roosevelt and the Isolationists, 1932–45.* Lincoln: University of Nebraska Press, 1983.

———. "Feature Review," *Diplomatic History* 23, no. 1 (1999).

Collum, Danny Duncan. *African Americans in the Spanish Civil War: "This Ain't Ethiopia, But It'll Do."* New York: G. K. Hall, 1992.

Colton, Joel. *Léon Blum: Humanist in Politics.* New York: Alfred A. Knopf, 1966.

Conkin, Paul K. *The New Deal.* Arlington Heights, Ill.: Harlan Davidson, 1975.

Cook, Blanche Wiesen. *Eleanor Roosevelt,* vol. 2, *1933–1938.* New York: Viking, 1999.

Cortada, James W. *Two Nations over Time: Spain and the United States, 1776–1977.* Westport: Greenwood, 1978.

———. *A City in War: American Views on Barcelona and the Spanish Civil War, 1936–39.* Wilmington, Del.: Scholarly Resources, 1985.

Coverdale, John F. *Italian Intervention in the Spanish Civil War.* Princeton: Princeton University Press, 1975.

Craig, Gordon A., and Felix Gilbert. *The Diplomats, 1919–1939.* Princeton: Princeton University Press, 1953.

Craven, Wesley Frank, and James L. Cate, eds. *The Army Air Forces in World War II.* Chicago: University of Chicago Press, 1948–55.

Crosby, Donald F. "Boston's Catholics and the Spanish Civil War, 1936–1939," *New England Quarterly* 44, no. 1 (1971).

Crowley, James B. *Japan's Quest for Autonomy: National Security and Foreign Policy, 1930–38.* Princeton: Princeton University Press, 1966.

Dallek, Robert. *Franklin D. Roosevelt and American Foreign Policy, 1932–1945.* New York: Oxford University Press, 1979.

———. *The American Style of Foreign Policy: Cultural Politics and Foreign Affairs.* Oxford: Oxford University Press, 1983.

———. *Hail to the Chief: The Making and Unmaking of American Presidents.* New York: Oxford University Press, 2001.

Davis, Kenneth S. *FDR: Into the Storm, 1937–1940: A History.* New York: Random House, 1993.

———. *FDR: The War President, 1940–1943: A History.* New York: Random House, 2000.

Dickinson, Mathew. *Bitter Harvest: FDR, Presidential Power and the Growth of the Presidential Branch*. Cambridge: Cambridge University Press, 1997.

Divine, Robert A. *The Illusion of Neutrality*. Chicago: University of Chicago Press, 1962.

———. *The Reluctant Belligerent: American Entry into World War Two*. New York: John Wiley and Sons, 1965.

———. *Roosevelt and World War II*. Baltimore: Johns Hopkins University Press, 1969.

Dobson, Alan P. *U.S. Economic Statecraft for Survival, 1933–1991: Of Sanctions, Embargoes and Economic Warfare*. London: Routledge, 2002.

Doenecke, Justus D. "Non-interventionism of the Left: The Keep America Out of War Congress, 1938–1941," *Journal of Contemporary History* 12, no. 2 (1977).

———. "Beyond Polemics: An Historiographical Re-appraisal of American Entry into World War II," *History Teacher* 12, no. 2 (1979).

———. "U.S. Policy and the European War, 1939–1941," *Diplomatic History* 19, no. 4 (1995).

———. *Storm on the Horizon: The Challenge to American Intervention, 1939–1941*. Lanham, Md.: Rowman and Littlefield, 2000.

Doenecke, Justus D., and Mark A. Stoler. *Debating Franklin D. Roosevelt's Foreign Policies, 1933–1945*. New York: Rowman and Littlefield, 2005.

Dreifort, John E. *Yvon Delbos at the Quai d'Orsay: French Foreign Policy during the Popular Front, 1936–1938*. Lawrence: University Press of Kansas, 1973.

Drummond, Donald F. *The Passing of American Neutrality, 1937–1941*. Ann Arbor: University of Michigan Press, 1955.

Duram, James C. *Norman Thomas*. New York: Twayne, 1974.

Eckstein, Harry. "Case Study and Theory in Political Science," *Handbook of Political Science*, ed. Fred I. Greenstein and Nelson W. Polsby, vol. 7, *Strategies of Inquiry*. Reading, Mass.: Addison-Wesley, 1975.

Edwards, Jill. *The British Government and the Spanish Civil War*. London: Macmillan, 1979.

———. *Anglo-American Relations and the Franco Question, 1945–55*. Oxford: Clarendon, 1999.

Edwards, John Carver. *Airmen without Portfolio: US Mercenaries in Civil War Spain*. London: Praeger, 1997.

Esch, P. A. M. van der. *Prelude to War: The International Repercussions of the Spanish Civil War (1936–1939)*. The Hague: Martinus Nijhoff, 1951.

Esenwein, George R. *The Spanish Civil War: A Modern Tragedy*. New York: Routledge, 2005.

Esenwein, George R., and Adrian Shubert. *Spain at War: The Spanish Civil War in Context, 1931–1939*. London: Longman, 1995.

Everest, Allan Seymour. *Morgenthau, the New Deal and Silver: A Story of Pressure Politics*. New York: King's Crown, 1950.

Falcoff, Mark, and Fredrick D. Pike. *The Spanish Civil War, 1936–9: American Hemispheric Perspectives*. Lincoln: University of Nebraska Press, 1982.

Farnham, Barbara Rearden. *Roosevelt and the Munich Crisis: A Study of Political Decision-Making*. Princeton: Princeton University Press, 1997.

Farnsworth, Beatrice. *William C. Bullitt and the Soviet Union*. Bloomington: Indiana University Press, 1967.

Farrell, Nicholas. *Mussolini: A New Life*. London: Weidenfeld and Nicolson, 2003.

Feis, Herbert. *The Spanish Story: Franco and the Nations at War*. New York: Alfred A. Knopf, 1948.

Fleischman, Harry. *Norman Thomas: A Biography: 1884-1968*. New York: W. W. Norton, 1969.

Flynn, George Q. *Roosevelt and Romanism: Catholics and American Diplomacy, 1937-45*. Westport: Greenwood, 1976.

Foot, Rosemary. *The Wrong War: American Policy and the Dimensions of the Korean Conflict, 1950-1953*. Ithaca: Cornell University Press, 1985.

Freedman, Lawrence. "Logic, Politics and Foreign Policy Processes: A Critique of the Bureaucratic Politics Model," *International Affairs* 52, no. 3 (1976).

Freidel, Frank. *Franklin D. Roosevelt: A Rendezvous with Destiny*. Boston: Little, Brown, 1990.

Fried, Albert. *FDR and His Enemies*. New York: St. Martin's, 1999.

Friedman, Max Paul. *Nazis and Good Neighbors: The United States Campaign against the Germans of Latin America in World War II*. Cambridge: Cambridge University Press, 2003.

Frye, Alton. *Nazi Germany and the American Hemisphere, 1933-1941*. New Haven: Yale University Press, 1967.

Furet, François. *The Passing of an Illusion: The Idea of Communism in the Twentieth Century*. Chicago: University of Chicago Press, 1999.

Gaddis, John Lewis. *The United States and the Origins of the Cold War*. New York: Columbia University Press, 1972.

———. *Strategies of Containment*. Oxford: Oxford University Press, 1982.

Gallo, Max. *Spain under Franco: A History*. New York: E. P. Dutton, 1974.

Gallup, George H. *The Gallup Poll: Public Opinion, 1935-1971*. New York: Random House, 1972.

Gardner, Lloyd C. *Economic Aspects of New Deal Diplomacy*. Madison: University of Wisconsin Press, 1964.

———. *Spheres of Influence: The Partition of Europe, from Munich to Yalta*. London: John Murray, 1993.

Gellman, Irwin F. *Good Neighbor Diplomacy: United States Policies in Latin America, 1933-1945*. Baltimore: Johns Hopkins University Press, 1979.

———. *Secret Affairs: Franklin D. Roosevelt, Cordell Hull and Sumner Welles*. Baltimore: Johns Hopkins University Press, 1995.

George, Alexander L. "Case Studies and Theory Development: The Method of Structured Focused Comparison," *Diplomacy: New Approaches*, ed. Paul Gordon Lauren. London: Macmillan, 1979.

———. *Presidential Decisionmaking in Foreign Policy: The Effective Use of Information and Advice*. Boulder: Westview, 1980.

George, Alexander L., and Juliette L. George. "The Causal Nexus between Cognitive Beliefs and Decision-making Behaviour: The 'Operational Code' Belief System," *Psychological Models in International Politics*, ed. Lawrence Falkowski. Boulder: Westview, 1979.

———. *Presidential Personality and Performance*. Boulder: Westview, 1998.

Glantz, Mary E. *FDR and the Soviet Union: The President's Battles over Foreign Policy*. Lawrence: University Press of Kansas, 2005.

Gordenker, Leon. "The Legacy of Franklin D. Roosevelt's Internationalism," *FDR and His Contemporaries: Foreign Perceptions of an American President*, ed. Cornelis A. van Minnen and John F. Sears. New York: St. Martin's, 1992.

Gornick, Vivian. *The Romance of American Communism*. New York: Basic, 1977.

Graham, Heather. *The Spanish Republic at War, 1936–1939*. Cambridge: Cambridge University Press, 2002.

———. *The Spanish Civil War: A Very Short Introduction*. Oxford: Oxford University Press, 2005.

Graham, Otis L., and Meghan Robinson Wander. *Franklin D. Roosevelt: His Life and Times: An Encyclopedic View*. New York: Da Capo, 1985.

Graham, Thomas. "Public Opinion and U.S. Foreign Policy Making," *The New Politics of American Foreign Policy*, ed. David A. Deese. New York: St. Martin's, 1994.

Greer, Thomas H. *What Roosevelt Thought: The Social and Political Ideas of Franklin D. Roosevelt*. East Lansing: Michigan State University Press, 1958.

Guttmann, Allen. *Wound in the Heart: America and the Spanish Civil War*. New York: Free Press of Glencoe, 1962.

———, ed. *American Neutrality and the Spanish Civil War*. Boston: D. C. Heath, 1963.

Haglund, David G. *Latin America and the Transformation of American Strategic Thought, 1936–1940*. Albuquerque: University of New Mexico Press, 1984.

Haight, John McVickar. "Roosevelt as Friend of France," *Causes and Consequences of World War II*, ed. Robert A. Divine. Chicago: Quadrangle, 1969.

———. *American Aid to France, 1938–40*. New York: Atheneum, 1970.

———. "Franklin D. Roosevelt and a Naval Quarantine of Japan," *Pacific Historical Review* 40, no. 2 (1971).

Haines, Gerald K., and J. Samuel Walker, eds. *American Foreign Relations: A Historiographical Review*. Westport: Greenwood, 1981.

Halperin, Morton, and Graham Allison. "Bureaucratic Politics," *Theory and Policy in International Relations*, ed. Raymond Tanter and Richard Ullman. Princeton: Princeton University Press, 1972.

Halstead, Charles R. "Historians in Politics: Carlton J. H. Hayes as American Ambassador to Spain, 1942–1945," *Journal of Contemporary History* 15, no. 4 (1980).

Hamilton, Nigel. *JFK: Reckless Youth*. New York: Random House, 1992.

Harper, John Lamberton. *American Visions of Europe: Franklin D. Roosevelt, George F. Kennan, and Dean G. Acheson*. Cambridge: Cambridge University Press, 1994.

Harris, Brice. *The United States and the Italo-Ethiopian Crisis*. Stanford: Stanford University Press, 1964.

Harrison, Richard. "A Presidential Demarche: Franklin D. Roosevelt's Personal Diplomacy and Great Britain, 1936–37," *Diplomatic History* 5, no. 3 (1981).

———. "Testing the Water: A Secret Probe towards Anglo-American Cooperation in 1936," *International History Review* 7, no. 2 (1985).

Haslam, Jonathan. *The USSR and the Struggle for Collective Security in Europe, 1933–39*. London: Macmillan, 1984.

Hayes, Carlton J. H. *The United States and Spain*. New York: Sheed and Ward, 1951.

Heinrichs, Waldo. *Threshold of War: Franklin D. Roosevelt and American Entry into World War II*. Oxford: Oxford University Press, 1988.

———. *Diplomacy and Force: America's Road to War, 1931–1941*. Chicago: Imprint Publications, 1996.

Herman, Margaret. "When Leader Personality Will Affect Foreign Policy: Some Propositions," *In Search of Global Patterns*, ed. James Rosenau. New York: Free Press, 1976.

Herman, Margaret, and Joe D. Hagan. "International Decision Making: Leadership Matters," *Foreign Policy* 110 (1998).

Hero, Alfred O. *American Religious Groups View Foreign Policy: Trends in Rank and File Opinion, 1937–69*. Durham: Duke University Press, 1973.

Herzstein, Robert E. *Roosevelt and Hitler: A Prelude to War*. New York: Paragon House, 1989.

Hillgruber, Andreas. *Germany and the Two World Wars*. Cambridge: Harvard University Press, 1981.

Hoffmann, Stanley. "The Case for Leadership," *Foreign Policy* 81 (1990–91).

Hollis, Martin, and Steve Smith. *Explaining and Understanding International Relations*. Oxford: Clarendon, 1990.

Holsti, Ole R. "Cognitive Dynamics and Images of the Enemy," *Image and Reality in World Politics*, ed. John Farrell and Asa Smith. New York: Columbia University Press, 1968.

———. "Foreign Policy Decision Makers Viewed Psychologically: Cognitive Process Approaches," *In Search of Global Patterns*, ed. James Rosenau. New York: Free Press, 1976.

———. "Foreign Policy Formation Viewed Cognitively," *Structure of Decision: The Cognitive Maps of Political Elites*, ed. Robert Axelrod. Princeton: Princeton University Press, 1976.

Hoover, J. Edgar. *Masters of Deceit: The Story of Communism in America*. London: Dent, 1958.

Howard, Thomas C., and William D. Pederson, eds. *Franklin D. Roosevelt and the Formation of the Modern World*. London: M. E. Sharpe, 2003.

Howson, Gerald. *Aircraft of the Spanish Civil War, 1936–39*. London: Putnam Aeronautical, 1990.

———. *Arms for Spain: The Untold Story of the Spanish Civil War*. London: John Murray, 1998.

Ivens, Joris. *The Camera and I*. Berlin: Seven Seas, 1969.

Jablon, Howard. "Franklin D. Roosevelt and the Spanish Civil War," *Social Studies* 56 (1965).

———. *Crossroads of Decision: The State Department and Foreign Policy, 1933–37.* Lexington: University Press of Kentucky, 1983.

Jackson, Gabriel. *The Spanish Republic and the Civil War, 1931–39.* Princeton: Princeton University Press, 1965.

Janeway, Eliot. *The Struggle for Survival.* New Haven: Yale University Press, 1951.

Jenkins, Roy. *Churchill.* London: Pan, 2002.

Jervis, Robert. *Perception and Misperception in International Politics.* Princeton: Princeton University Press, 1976.

Jonas, Manfred. *Isolationism in America, 1935–1941.* Chicago: Imprint Publications, 1990.

Jones, Kenneth Paul, ed. *U.S. Diplomats in Europe, 1919–1941.* Santa Barbara: ABC-Clio, 1981.

Kanawada, Leo V. *Franklin D. Roosevelt's Diplomacy and American Catholics, Italians, and Jews.* Ann Arbor: UMI Research Press, 1982.

Kantowicz, Edward R. "Cardinal Mundelein of Chicago and the Shaping of Twentieth-Century American Catholicism," *Journal of American History* 68, no. 1 (1981).

Kazin, Alfred. "The Wound That Will Not Heal: Writers and the Spanish Civil War," *New Republic*, 25 August 1986.

Keene, Judith. *Fighting for Franco: International Volunteers in Nationalist Spain during the Spanish Civil War, 1936–39.* New York: Leicester University Press, 2001.

Kenwood, Alun, ed. *The Spanish Civil War: A Cultural and Historical Reader.* Providence: Berg, 1993.

Khong, Yuen Foong. *Analogies at War: Korea, Munich, Dien Bien Phu, and the Vietnam Decisions of 1965.* Princeton: Princeton University Press, 1992.

Kimball, Warren. *The Juggler: Franklin Roosevelt as Wartime Statesman.* Princeton: Princeton University Press, 1991.

———, ed. *America Unbound: World War II and the Making of a Superpower.* New York: St. Martin's, 1992.

Kinsella, William. *Leadership in Isolation: FDR and the Origins of the Second World War.* Boston: G. K. Hall, 1978.

Koch, Stephen. *The Breaking Point: Hemingway, Dos Passos, and the Murder of José Robles.* New York: Counterpoint, 2005.

Kolko, Gabriel. *The Politics of War: Allied Diplomacy and the World Crisis of 1943–1945.* London: Weidenfeld and Nicolson, 1969.

Knox, MacGregor. *Mussolini Unleashed, 1939–1941: Politics and Strategy in Fascist Italy's Last War.* Cambridge: Cambridge University Press, 1986.

Langer, William L., and S. Everett Gleason. *Challenge to Isolation, 1937–1940.* London: Royal Institute of International Affairs, 1952.

Large, David Clay. *Between Two Fires: Europe's Path in the 1930s.* New York: W. W. Norton, 1990.

Larson, Deborah Welch. *Origins of Containment: A Psychological Explanation*. Princeton: Princeton University Press, 1985.

Lash, Joseph P. *Eleanor and Franklin*. New York: W. W. Norton, 1971.

———. *Roosevelt and Churchill, 1939–1941: The Partnership That Saved the West*. New York: W. W. Norton, 1976.

Leitz, Christian, and David J. Dunthorn, eds. *Spain in an International Context, 1936–1959*. New York: Berghahn, 1999.

Lerner, Max. *Ideas for the Ice Age: Studies in a Revolutionary Era*. New York: Viking, 1941.

Leuchtenberg, William. *Franklin D. Roosevelt and the New Deal, 1932–1940*. New York: Harper and Row, 1963.

Leutze, James R. *Bargaining for Supremacy: Anglo-American Naval Collaboration, 1937–1941*. Chapel Hill: University of North Carolina Press, 1977.

Liddell Hart, Basil. *The Memoirs of Captain Liddell Hart*. London: Cassell, 1965.

Little, Douglas. "Antibolshevism and American Foreign Policy, 1919–1939: The Diplomacy of Self-Delusion," *American Quarterly* 35, no. 4 (1983).

———. *Malevolent Neutrality: The United States, Great Britain and the Origins of the Spanish Civil War*. Ithaca: Cornell University Press, 1985.

Loewenheim, Francis L., and Herbert Feis. *The Historian and the Diplomat: The Role of History and Historians in American Foreign Policy*. New York: Harper and Row, 1967.

Louis, William Roger. *Imperialism at Bay: The United States and the Decolonization of the British Empire, 1941–1945*. Oxford: Clarendon, 1977.

Lovell, John P. *The Challenge of American Foreign Policy*. New York: Macmillan, 1985.

MacDonald, Callum. *The United States, Britain and Appeasement, 1936–1939*. New York: St. Martin's, 1981.

———. "Deterrent Diplomacy: Roosevelt and the Containment of Germany, 1938–1940," *Paths to War: New Essays on the Origins of the Second World War*, ed. Robert Boyce and Esmonde M. Robertson. London: Macmillan, 1989.

Mack Smith, Denis. *Mussolini*. London: Paladin, 1983.

Maclean, J. "Belief Systems and Ideology in International Relations: A Critical Approach," *Belief Systems and International Relations*, ed. Richard Little and Steve Smith. Oxford: B. Blackwell, 1988.

MacLeod, Iain. *Neville Chamberlain*. London: F. Muller, 1961.

Maddox, Robert James. *William E. Borah and American Foreign Policy*. Baton Rouge: Louisiana State University Press, 1969.

Marks, Frederick M. *Wind over Sand: The Diplomacy of Franklin Roosevelt*. Athens: University of Georgia Press, 1988.

Martel, Gordon, ed. *The Origins of the Second World War Reconsidered: A. J. P. Taylor and the Historians*. New York: Routledge, 1999.

Martin, James Joseph. *American Liberalism and World Politics, 1931–1941: Liberalism's Press and Spokesmen on the Road Back to War between Mukden and Pearl Harbor*. New York: Devin-Adair, 1964.

Mathews, Herbert L. *Half of Spain Died: A Reappraisal of the Spanish Civil War*. New York: Scribner, 1973.

May, Ernest R. *"Lessons" of the Past: The Use and Misuse of History in American Foreign Policy*. New York: Oxford University Press, 1975.

McKercher, B. J. C. *Transition of Power: Britain's Loss of Global Pre-eminence to the United States, 1930–1945*. Cambridge: Cambridge University Press, 1999.

Millis, Walter. *Road to War: America 1914–1917*. New York: Houghton Mifflin, 1935.

Miscamble, Wilson D. "Catholics and American Foreign Policy from McKinley to McCarthy: A Historiographical Survey," *Diplomatic History* 4, no. 3 (1980).

Moorehead, Caroline. *Gellhorn: A Twentieth Century Life*. New York: Henry Holt, 2003.

Morgan, Ted. *FDR: A Biography*. London: Grafton, 1986.

Murphy, Robert D. *Diplomat among Warriors*. New York: Doubleday, 1964.

Nelson, Cary, ed. *The Wound and the Dream: Sixty Years of American Poems about the Spanish Civil War*. Urbana: University of Illinois Press, 2002.

Nelson, Cary, and Jefferson Hendricks, eds. *Madrid 1937: Letters of the Abraham Lincoln Brigade from the Spanish Civil War*. New York: Routledge, 1996.

Neustadt, Richard E. *Presidential Power and the Modern Presidents: The Politics of Leadership from Roosevelt to Reagan*. New York: Macmillan, 1990.

Nisbet, Robert. *Roosevelt and Stalin: The Failed Courtship*. London: Simon and Schuster, 1989.

Offner, Arnold A. *American Appeasement: United States Foreign Policy and Germany, 1933–38*. New York: W.W. Norton, 1969.

———. *America and the Origins of World War II*. Boston: Houghton Mifflin, 1971.

———. *The Origins of World War II*. New York: Praeger, 1975.

Orwell, George. *The Penguin Complete Longer Non-fiction of George Orwell*. Harmondsworth: Penguin, 1983.

Padelford, Norman J. *International Law and Diplomacy in the Spanish Civil Strife*. New York: Macmillan, 1939.

Parker, R. A. C. *Chamberlain and Appeasement: British Policy and the Coming of the Second World War*. Basingstoke: Macmillan, 1993.

Parrish, Michael E. *Anxious Decades: America in Prosperity and Depression, 1920–1941*. London: W. W. Norton, 1992.

Payne, Stanley G. *The Spanish Revolution*. New York: W. W. Norton, 1970.

———. *The Spanish Civil War, the Soviet Union and Communism*. New Haven: Yale University Press, 2004.

Peters, A. R. *Anthony Eden at the Foreign Office, 1931–1938*. Aldershot: Gower, 1986.

Pike, David Wingeate. *Conjecture, Propaganda, and Deceit and the Spanish Civil War: The International Crisis over Spain, 1936–1939, as Seen in the French Press*. Stanford: California Institute of International Studies, 1968.

Pike, Frederick B. *FDR's Good Neighbor Policy: Sixty Years of Generally Gentle Chaos*. Austin: University of Texas Press, 1995.

Powell, Thomas G. *Mexico and the Spanish Civil War*. Albuquerque: University of New Mexico Press, 1981.

Pratt, Julius. *Cordell Hull, 1933–1944*, vols. 1–2. New York: Cooper Square, 1964.

Preston, Paul. *The Coming of the Spanish Civil War: Reform, Reaction and Revolution in the Second Republic, 1931–1936*. London: Macmillan, 1978.

———. *The Spanish Civil War, 1936–39*. London: Weidenfeld and Nicolson, 1986.

———. "Franco and Hitler: The Myth of Hendaye 1940," *Contemporary European History* 1 (1992).

———. *Franco: A Biography*. London: Harper Collins, 1993.

———. *The Spanish Civil War: Dreams and Nightmares*. London: Imperial War Museum, 2001.

Preston, Paul, and Ann L. Mackenzie, eds. *The Republic Besieged: Civil War in Spain, 1936–1939*. Edinburgh: Edinburgh University Press, 1996.

Puzzo, Dante A. *Spain and the Great Powers, 1936–1941*. New York: Arno, 1962.

Radosh, Ronald, Mary R. Habeck, and Grigory Sevostianov, eds. *Spain Betrayed: The Soviet Union in the Spanish Civil War*. London: Yale University Press, 2001.

Ragland, James. *Yearbook*. Philadelphia: American Philosophical Society, 1960, 1962.

Range, Willard. *Franklin D. Roosevelt's World Order*. Athens: University of Georgia Press, 1959.

Rauch, Basil. *Roosevelt: From Munich to Pearl Harbor: A Study in the Creation of a Foreign Policy*. New York: Creative Age, 1950.

Reynolds, David. *The Creation of the Anglo-American Alliance, 1937–41: A Study in Competitive Cooperation*. London: Europa, 1981.

———. *From Munich to Pearl Harbor: Roosevelt's America and the Origins of the Second World War*. Chicago: Ivan R. Dee, 2001.

Roberts, Geoffrey. *Unholy Alliance: Stalin's Pact with Hitler*. Bloomington: Indiana University Press, 1989.

Robertson, Esmonde M. *Mussolini as Empire Builder: Europe and Africa, 1932–1936*. London: Macmillan, 1977.

Roosevelt, G. Hall. *Odyssey of an American Family: An Account of the Roosevelts and Their Kin as Travelers, from 1613 to 1938*. London: Harper and Brothers, 1939.

Rose, Norman. "The Resignation of Anthony Eden," *Historical Journal* 25, no. 4 (1982).

Rosenau, James N. *Public Opinion and Foreign Policy: An Operational Formulation*. New York: Random House, 1961.

———. *Domestic Sources of Foreign Policy*. New York: Free Press, 1967.

Rossi, Mario. *Roosevelt and the French*. Westport: Praeger, 1993.

Rubin, Hank. *Spain's Cause Was Mine: A Memoir of an American Medic in the Spanish Civil War*. Carbondale: Southern Illinois University Press, 1997.

Russett, Bruce, and Harvey Starr. *World Politics: The Menu for Choice*. New York: W. H. Freeman, 1992.

Sanders, David. "Ernest Hemingway's Spanish Civil War Experience," *American Quarterly* 12, issue 2, part 1 (1960).

Schlesinger, Arthur M., Jr. *The Age of Roosevelt*, vols.1–3. Boston: Houghton Mifflin, 1957–60.

————. *A Life in the Twentieth Century: Innocent Beginnings, 1917–1950*. New York: Houghton Mifflin, 2000.

Schmidt, Gustav. *The Politics and Economics of Appeasement: British Foreign Policy in the 1930s*. Leamington Spa: Berg, 1984.

Schmitz, David F. *The United States and Fascist Italy, 1922–1940*. Chapel Hill: University of North Carolina Press, 1988.

————. *Thank God They're on Our Side: The United States and Right-Wing Dictatorships, 1921–1965*. Chapel Hill: University of North Carolina Press, 1999.

Schrecker, Ellen. *Many Are the Crimes: McCarthyism in America*. Princeton: Princeton University Press, 1998.

Schwarz, Jordan A. *The Speculator: Bernard M. Baruch in Washington, 1917–1965*. Chapel Hill: University of North Carolina Press, 1981.

Sehlinger, Peter J., and Holman Hamilton. *Spokesman for Democracy: Claude G. Bowers, 1878–1958*. Indianapolis: Indiana Historical Society, 2000.

Sherwood, Robert. *Roosevelt and Hopkins: An Intimate History*. New York: Harper, 1948.

Shlaim, Avi. "Truman's Belief System: Russia and the Berlin Blockade," *Belief Systems and International Relations*, ed. Richard Little and Steve Smith. Oxford: B. Blackwell, 1988.

Sidey, Hugh. "An International Natural Resource," *Time*, 4 February 1974.

Simon, Herbert. *Models of Man, Social and Rational: Mathematical Essays on Rational Human Behavior in a Social Setting*. New York: Wiley, 1957.

————. "Human Nature in Politics," *American Political Science Review* 79, no. 2 (1985).

Simon, Rita James, ed. *As We Saw the Thirties: Essays on Social and Political Movements of a Decade*. Urbana: University of Illinois Press, 1967.

Singer, David. "The Levels of Analysis Problem in International Relations," *World Politics* 14, no. 1 (1961).

Skowronek, Stephen. *The Politics Presidents Make: Leadership from John Adams to Bill Clinton*. Cambridge: Harvard University Press, 1998.

Small, Melvin. *Johnson, Nixon, and the Doves*. New Brunswick: Rutgers University Press, 1988.

————. *Democracy and Diplomacy: The Impact of Domestic Politics on U.S. Foreign Policy, 1789–1994*. Baltimore: John Hopkins University Press, 1994.

Smith, Steve. "Foreign Policy Analysis: British and American Orientations and Methodologies," *Political Studies* 31, no. 4 (1983).

————. "Belief Systems and the Study of International Relations," *Belief Systems and International Relations*, ed. Richard Little and Steve Smith. Oxford: B. Blackwell, 1988.

Smith, Tony. *America's Mission: The United States and the Worldwide Struggle for Democracy in the Twentieth Century*. Princeton: Princeton University Press, 1994.

Smyth, Denis. *Diplomacy and Strategy of Survival: British Policy and Franco's Spain, 1940–41*. Cambridge: Cambridge University Press, 1986.

Snyder, Richard, H. W. Bruck, and Burton Sapin. *Foreign Policy Decision-Making*. New York: Free Press of Glencoe, 1962.

Southworth, Herbert Rutledge. *Guernica! Guernica! A Study of Journalism, Diplomacy, Propaganda, and History*. Berkeley: University of California Press, 1977.

Sperber, Murray A., ed. *And I Remember Spain: A Spanish Civil War Anthology*. New York: Macmillan, 1974.

Stafford, David. *Roosevelt and Churchill: Men of Secrets*. London: Abacus, 2000.

Steele, Richard W. *Propaganda in an Open Society: The Roosevelt Administration and the Media, 1933–1941*. London: Greenwood, 1985.

Stein, Louis. *Beyond Death and Exile: The Spanish Republicans in France, 1939–1955*. Cambridge: Harvard University Press, 1979.

Stone, Glyn. "The European Great Powers and the Spanish Civil War, 1936–1939," *Paths to War: New Essays on the Origins of the Second World War*, ed. Robert Boyce and Esmonde M. Robertson. London: Macmillan, 1989.

———. "Britain, France and the Spanish Problem, 1936–39," *Decisions and Diplomacy: Essays in Twentieth Century International History*, ed. Dick Richardson and Glyn Stone. London: Routledge, 1995.

Swanberg, W. A. *Norman Thomas: The Last Idealist*. New York: Scribner, 1976.

Taylor, A. J. P. *The Origins of the Second World War*. London: Hamish Hamilton, 1965.

Taylor, Foster Jay. *The United States and the Spanish Civil War*. New York: Bookman, 1956.

Taylor, Telford. *Munich: The Price of Peace*. Garden City, N.Y.: Doubleday, 1979.

Thomas, Hugh. *The Spanish Civil War*. London: Eyre and Spottiswoode, 1961; 3d edn, rev. and enlarged, London: Penguin, 1977.

Thomas, Martin. *Britain, France and Appeasement: Anglo-French Relations in the Popular Front Era*. Oxford: Berg, 1997.

Thorne, Christopher G. *Allies of a Kind: The United States, Britain and the War against Japan, 1941–1945*. London: Hamish Hamilton, 1978.

———. *Border Crossings: Studies in International History*. Oxford: Basil Blackwell, 1988.

Tierney, Dominic. "Franklin D. Roosevelt and Covert Aid to the Loyalists in the Spanish Civil War, 1936–1939," *Journal of Contemporary History* 39, no. 3 (2004).

———. "Irrelevant or Malevolent? UN Arms Embargoes and Civil Wars," *Review of International Studies* 31, no. 4 (2005).

Tocqueville, Alexis de. *Recollections*, ed. J. P. Mayer and A. P. Kerr. London: Macdonald, 1970.

Traina, Richard. *American Diplomacy and the Spanish Civil War*. Bloomington: Indiana University International Studies, 1968.

Tugwell, Rexford. *The Democratic Roosevelt*. New York: Doubleday, 1957.

Tusell, Javier. "Franco and Franklin D. Roosevelt," *FDR and His Contemporaries: Foreign Perceptions of an American President*, ed. Cornelis A. van Minnen and John F. Sears. New York: St. Martin's, 1992.

Utley, Jonathan G. *Going to War with Japan, 1937–1941*. Knoxville: University of Tennessee Press, 1985.

Valaik, J. David. "Catholics, Neutrality, and the Spanish Embargo, 1937–1939," *Journal of American History* 54, no. 1 (1967).

Van Minnen, Cornelis A., and John F. Sears, eds. *FDR and His Contemporaries: Foreign Perceptions of an American President*. New York: St. Martin's, 1992.

Veatch, Richard. "The League of Nations and the Spanish Civil War, 1936–9," *European History Quarterly* 20, no. 2 (1990).

Vogler, John. "Perspectives on the Foreign Policy System: Psychological Approaches," *Understanding Foreign Policy*, ed. Michael Clarke and Brian White. Aldershot: E. Elgar, 1989.

Walker, Stephen G. "The Evolution of Operational Code Analysis," *Political Psychology* 11, no. 2 (1990).

Wallace, William. *Foreign Policy and the Political Process*. London: Macmillan, 1971.

Waltz, Kenneth. *Foreign Policy and Democratic Politics*. Boston: Little, Brown, 1967.

———. *Theory of International Politics*. London: McGraw-Hill, 1979.

Ward, Geoffrey C. *Before the Trumpet: Young Franklin Roosevelt, 1882–1905*. New York: Harper and Row, 1985.

Warner, Geoffrey. "France and Non-Intervention in Spain, July–August 1936," *International Affairs* 38, no. 2 (1962).

Warren, Frank A. *Noble Abstractions: American Liberal Intellectuals and World War II*. Columbus: Ohio State University Press, 1999.

Watkin, K. W. *Britain Divided: The Effects of the Spanish Civil War on British Public Opinion*. London: T. Nelson, 1963.

Watkins, T. H. *Righteous Pilgrim: The Life and Times of Harold L. Ickes, 1874–1952*. New York: Henry Holt, 1990.

Watt, Donald Cameron. *Succeeding John Bull: America in Britain's Place, 1900–1975: A Study of the Anglo-American Relationship and World Politics in the Context of British and American Foreign-Policy-Making in the Twentieth Century*. Cambridge: Cambridge University Press, 1984.

———. *How War Came: The Immediate Origins of the Second World War, 1938–1939*. London: Heinemann, 1989.

Weber, Eugen. *The Hollow Years*. London: W. W. Norton, 1994.

Weinberg, Gerhard L. *The Foreign Policy of Hitler's Germany: Diplomatic Revolution in Europe, 1933–1936*. Chicago: University of Chicago Press, 1970.

———. *The Foreign Policy of Hitler's Germany: Starting World War II, 1937–1939*. Chicago: University of Chicago Press, 1980.

———. "Munich after Fifty Years," *Foreign Affairs* 67, no. 1 (fall 1988).

Weintrub, Stanley. *The Last Great Cause: The Intellectuals and the Spanish Civil War*. London: W. H. Allen, 1968.

Weiss, Stuart L. "Maury Maverick and the Liberal Bloc," *Journal of American History* 57, no. 4 (1971).

Welles, Benjamin. *Sumner Welles: FDR's Global Strategist: A Biography*. Basingstoke: Macmillan, 1997.

Whealey, Robert H. "How Franco Financed His War—Reconsidered," *Journal of Contemporary History* 12, no. 1 (1977).

————. *Hitler and Spain: The Nazi Role in the Spanish Civil War*. Lexington: University Press of Kentucky, 1989.

White, Michael. "Analysing Foreign Policy," *Understanding Foreign Policy*, ed. Michael Clarke and Brian White. Aldershot: E. Elgar, 1989.

Wilz, John Edward. *From Isolation to War, 1931–1941*. London: Routledge, 1969.

Wood, Bryce. *The Making of the Good Neighbor Policy*. New York: Columbia University Press, 1961.

Woods, Ngaire, ed. *Explaining International Relations since 1945*. Oxford: Oxford University Press, 1996.

Wyden, Peter. *The Passionate War: The Narrative History of the Spanish Civil War, 1936–39*. New York: Simon and Schuster, 1983.

Young, Robert J. *In Command of France: French Foreign Policy and Military Planning, 1933–1940*. Cambridge: Harvard University Press, 1978.

Index

Abraham Lincoln Battalion, 64, 147
Acheson, Dean, 147
African Americans, 65
Airpower: American, 79–80, 102, 104–8, 129; German, 20, 76–77, 79, 83–85; Italian, 21, 84–85; Nationalist, 5; Soviet, 21. *See also* covert aid; military aid
Alfonso XIII, King, 16
Alicante victory fiesta, 55
Allen, Bob, 123
Allen, Jay, 95, 99, 101
Anderson, Jane, 62–63
Anti-Comintern Pact, 15
Appeasement: by Chamberlain, 69, 76–79, 115; dangers of, 95–96; FDR's views of, 29–30, 31, 77; of Mussolini, 29. *See also* Munich conference
Argentina, 22, 120
Armour, Norman, 144
Arms embargo, 54, 132–33; American public opinion and, 59, 89–90, 127–28, 136; Borah's views of, 10; Bowers's views of, 53, 97, 101, 127; British views of, 69, 95, 137; Bullitt's opposition to, 98; cabinet members' opposition to, 92; Catholic views of, 5, 7, 70, 89–91, 99–101, 113, 128–30; circumvention of, 102–3; congressional activity concerning, 51–52, 92–93, 95, 100–102, 125–26, 128; enforcement against European fascists of, 69–73, 91, 150, 155; enforcement against Italy of, 27, 30; FDR's regrets

over, 9, 86–87, 93–94, 99, 124, 131, 138–39, 151; FDR's support of, 45, 53, 98; Hull's support of, 96, 97; idealists vs. realists and, 40, 41–42; Kennedy's support of, 98; Loyalist defeat hastened by, 5; Mexican opposition to, 94–95; nonmilitary trade restrictions and, 52; Nye's support of, 61; pro-Loyalist support of, 89, 91; repeal of, 93–95, 101, 124–25, 130–31, 154; start of, 4; validity of, 72–73. *See also* covert aid; isolationism; military aid; nonintervention
Asturias, 16–17, 56
Atrocities, 33, 48
Attlee, Clement, 146
Austria, 76

Badajoz, 48
Baldwin, Stanley, 19, 69
Barcelona, 17, 41, 126
Baruch, Bernard, 92
Basque region, 56, 70, 80
Basque refugees, 63
Belchite, 57
Bell, Golden W., 125
Bensmann, Nick, 68–69
Berle, Adolf, 96, 104, 113, 117–18, 159, 188 n. 38
Bernard, John T., 52
Bertandias, Victor, 104
Bessie, Alvah, 85
Biddle, Francis, 80
Bingham, Robert, 70, 71

Dominic Tierney is an assistant professor in the Department of Political Science at Swarthmore College.

Library of Congress Cataloging-in-Publication Data
Tierney, Dominic, 1977–
FDR and the Spanish Civil War : neutrality and commitment in the struggle that divided America / Dominic Tierney.
p. cm.— (American encounters / global interactions)
Includes bibliographical references and index.
ISBN 978-0-8223-4055-3 (cloth : alk. paper)
ISBN 978-0-8223-4076-8 (pbk. : alk. paper)
1. United States—Foreign relations—Spain. 2. Spain—Foreign relations—United States. 3. Roosevelt, Franklin D. (Franklin Delano), 1882–1945—Political and social views. 4. Spain—History—Civil War, 1936–1939—Diplomatic history. 5. United States—Foreign relations—1933–1945. 6. United States—Foreign relations—1933–1945—Decision making. 7. Intervention (International law)—History—20th century. I. Title. II. Title: Franklin Delano Roosevelt and the Spanish Civil War.
E183.8.S7T54 2007
973.917—dc22
2007003432